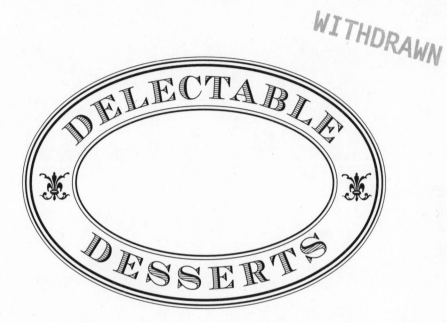

DELECTABLE DESSERTS

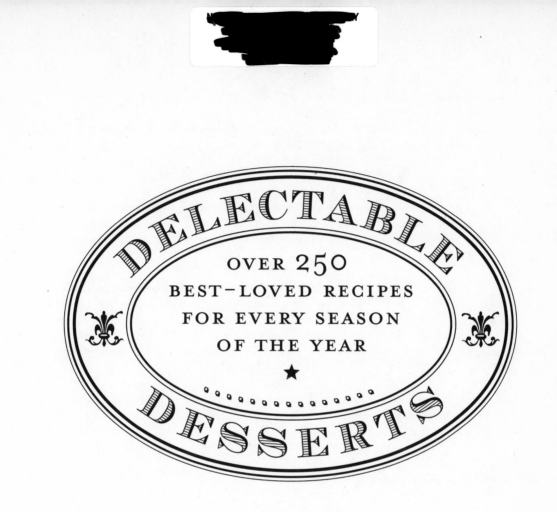

DELECTABLE DESSERTS

OVER 250
BEST-LOVED RECIPES
FOR EVERY SEASON
OF THE YEAR

★

WENDY LOUISE AND **MARYANN KOOPMANN**

SOURCEBOOKS, INC.®
NAPERVILLE, ILLINOIS

Copyright © 2009 by Wendy Louise
Cover and internal design © 2009 by Sourcebooks, Inc.
Cover design by Pamela Harvey
Cover photos © sandoclr/iStockphoto.com; Lanalanglois/Dreamstime.com; Andrea Skjold/iStockphoto.com; Justine Gecewicz/iStockphoto.com

Published by Sourcebooks, Inc.
P.O. Box 4410, Naperville, Illinois 60567-4410
(630) 961-3900
Fax: (630) 961-2168
www.sourcebooks.com

Library of Congress Cataloging-in-Publication Data

Louise, Wendy.
 Delectable desserts : over 250 best-loved recipes for every season of the year / by Wendy Louise with MaryAnn Koopmann.
   p. cm.
Includes index.
1. Desserts. I. Koopmann, MaryAnn. II. Title.
TX773.L68 2009
641.8'6—dc22

                              2008027161

       Printed and bound in the United States of America.
          CHG 10 9 8 7 6 5 4 3 2 1

A Dedication from Wendy Louise

For

Caleb and Eddie

Two guys who are just as important in heaven as they were here on earth

To my coauthor MaryAnn, for sharing her recipes and expertise

And lastly, to Marie Antoinette, for uttering that all-too-infamous phrase,

"Let them eat cake..."

A Dedication with Hugs from MaryAnn Koopmann

For

My dear husband Glenn H. Koopmann, who is always there to help, encourage, and support me in everything I do in life. I would be lost without you. I love you!

Also to my son and daughter, Glenn W. Koopmann and Angie Eisen, for believing in me and giving me a chance to bake new desserts for them through the years. I couldn't ask for more loving children and I am so blessed with my family.

A special thank-you to my grandchildren Breanne Eisen, Alicia Eisen, and Maxwell Koopmann, who bring me such happiness in life.

Lastly, to my friend Brook Noel, who has inspired and believed in me. I couldn't have done it without you! You are a very special person in my life and I will be forever grateful to you.

Contents

Acknowledgments

A very special thank-you goes out to our editor Sara Appino, and to all the people at Sourcebooks who have made this book possible. Thank you!

Introduction

Dessert, that exquisite delicacy that punctuates the end of a meal or repast...I daresay there's nary a person who doesn't like dessert—be it a simple bowl of fresh berries with cream or a sinful chocolate-mint brownie.

Desserts have saved many a dinner, soothed our souls, lifted our spirits, and earned our praises since childhood. From birthday cake to pumpkin pie, holiday cookies to ice cream sundaes, desserts have always been a favorite part of our dining experience. So come be a kid again. Within these pages, we know you'll find something to delight your palate and put that finishing touch on your meal.

One of my favorite memories from childhood is opening the refrigerator door to find that my mother had made chocolate or butterscotch pudding, chilling in special little dessert dishes, for dessert that night. Mom always topped the cooked pudding with real whipped cream just before serving. It is that kind of ambience that MaryAnn and I hope to bring to you with our selection of favorite recipes—some fancy, some very fancy, some seasonal, and some as simple as a cup of pudding. Our dessert selections can be enjoyed for everyday or special occasions, all throughout the year.

Wendy Louise

with MaryAnn Koopmann

Getting Started

Both MaryAnn and I agree that a good meal deserves a good dessert. Just as we plan our meals, so should we plan our desserts. Since desserts are the grand finale, we want them to be integrated with the meal and punctuate it perfectly. Here are some tips for making sure your dessert is nothing less than a fabulous exclamation point!

Always read and understand your recipe thoroughly. Make the dessert ahead, if possible, so you are not rushed at the time of serving.

Use the finest ingredients you can find, such as good quality chocolate and fruits in season. Have everything gathered within arm's reach before you begin cooking your recipe. Also use the best equipment possible, such as a pastry blender, a wire whisk, and a heavy saucepan.

Design your dessert according to your meal and the occasion. If you're serving a heavy meal, follow with a light and refreshing dessert. If you're serving a lighter meal, follow it guilt-free with a more substantial dessert. If it's a holiday or a theme meal, select a dessert that enhances your specific occasion.

Accompany your dessert with an appropriate beverage. Everything from an ice-cold glass of milk to an after-dinner coffee can further complement your sweet confection.

Think of your dessert as a special treat. Serve it in small, sensible portions, not overwhelming, "gut-buster" servings that overpower even the heartiest diner.

Presentation is just as important as the dessert itself! For example, my grandmother had special little berry bowls and spoons and a pretty pitcher to pass the cream.

- Use charming dessert plates, long-stemmed glasses, dessert forks, and always fresh napkins—pull out all the stops to present your special dessert.

- Top off the dessert with an appropriate garnish: a sprig of mint, chocolate curls, a twist of lemon, a bit of orange zest, some toasted nuts, a drizzle of sauce. That special touch will make the dessert unforgettable.

- Remember that temperature plays a great part in maximizing flavors. Serve pies warmed slightly, chilled desserts chilled, frozen desserts just slightly thawed, à la mode ice cream soft and melty, and fruits and cheeses at room temperature.

- For fruit desserts, use fruits that are in season and at the peak of ripeness. Have your produce manager help you pick out the perfect pineapple, the ripest melon, or the perfect papaya. Apples are best in the fall; peaches, in the summer—take advantage of the seasons.

- Think about where and how you will be serving your dessert: cookies or a sheet cake for picnics, flambés at the table, homemade cookies in your child's lunchbox, a batch of brownies for the office, a pretty cake or platter of fruit as the centerpiece on a buffet table, a treasured recipe at Christmas, and a pie for a potluck. Whether it's for two or twenty, pick an appropriate dessert that you can confidently serve and that the recipients can comfortably eat.

- Follow food safety rules for storing, chilling, holding, and other safety concerns.

- Let guests know if you use a liqueur, and ask ahead about any possible food allergies.

A NOTE ABOUT RAW EGGS AND EGG SAFETY

Several of the final desserts in this book contain raw or slightly cooked eggs, which we note at the beginning of the recipe. The FDA suggests using pasteurized-in-the-shell eggs when the recipe calls for raw eggs. These are considered a safe way to prevent the possibility of salmonella and other bacterial contaminations, conditions that can cause serious illness, especially in the elderly, the very young, and those with compromised immune systems. Look for these eggs in the refrigerated section of most grocery stores. The carton will be labeled "pasteurized," and although these eggs do cost a little more, they enable us to enjoy desserts such as homemade ice cream, chilled mousse mixtures, meringue pies and tortes, soft custards, and, of course, that "taste-test dab" of raw cookie dough. Mixtures containing raw eggs should always be stored in the refrigerator and served chilled, and any leftovers should be returned promptly to the refrigerator.

Some Safety Tips When Cooking with Any Eggs, Raw or Cooked

- Choose USDA Grade A or AA eggs with clean, uncracked or unbroken shells. Open the carton and check the eggs before you purchase them. (The USDA grade mark on egg cartons means the plant processed the eggs following the USDA's sanitation and good manufacturing processes.)

- Use only eggs that have remained refrigerated. And keep them cool on the way home, refrigerating them as soon as you get home.

- Use the eggs within the recommended time limits on the carton: raw shell eggs within three to five weeks and leftover yolks and whites within four days. If the packaging gives a "use by" date, adhere to it.

- Wash utensils, equipment, and work areas with warm soapy water before and after contact with eggs.

- Wash your hands frequently with soap and hot water during food handling and preparation.

Sugar 101

You will need an assortment of sugars for the different recipes in this book. Following is a little primer for the most common types you will be using, but this is by no means a complete listing of sugars available for the contemporary cook. You will find most in the baking/sugar section of almost any market.

Granulated Sugar

Also called "sugar," "white sugar," or "table sugar," it is the most commonly used cane sugar we have in our homes. It can also be found in a variety of textures, from castor sugar to coarse-ground crystal sugar.

Superfine Sugar

This is a finer grind of granulated sugar that dissolves faster for smoother results. Professional bakers have even more grinds of sugar for their use, but for home use, superfine is just right. Superfine sugar may also be referred to as "berry sugar," "bar sugar," or "castor sugar."

Confectioners' Sugar

This is a powdery grind of sugar also known as "powdered sugar," and it is sometimes seen in older recipes as "xxx" sugar. Use this sugar to make frosting and to "dust" and decorate cooled baked goods in place of frosting. Tap through a sieve when dusting to get the perfect spread and texture. It is also great for sweetening and whipping heavy cream and, of course, for making smooth-creamy frostings.

Sanding Sugar

Used for sprinkling, this is the coarsely ground sugar we use to decorate sugar cookies. It often comes in bright, jewel-tone colors, such as blue, green, and red. Other names are "decorating sugar," "coarse sugar," "crystal sugar," and "crystallized sugar."

Sugar Cubes

These are made from granulated sugar that has been compressed into cute little cubes. Sugar cubes are fun to set out for coffees and teas, when you don't want to use the packets or loose sugar. You can also use these as a vehicle for flaming liqueurs.

Brown Sugar

Depending on their molasses content, brown sugars come light or dark: the darker the color, the deeper the flavor. This cane sugar should be tamped down when measured, rather than just scooped—you'll notice most recipes say something like "½ cup brown sugar, packed."

Natural, Turbinado, Demerara, and Muscavado Sugars

These are all less refined cane sugars (also referred to as raw sugars), having a coarse grind, golden color, and robust, rich, almost caramel flavor. Most often we use them as a table sugar to enhance our coffee and tea or to sprinkle on cereal, but they can also be used in cooking and baking.

How to Use This Book

Each recipe has been divided into three parts: the ingredients listed in the order needed, a set of directions, and a how-to-serve section. We also offer extra tips or suggestions, additional information, or sometimes a little story, which are applicable to the recipe in the form of comments or boxed information.

Be sure to read through each recipe before beginning, as there will often be information after a listed ingredient that will be useful during prep time (for example: ½ cup butter, *melted and cooled*). Sometimes the list itself will be broken into segments to assist you further.

The book has been divided into twelve chapters, each pertaining to a month of the year. We often associate certain desserts with seasons or special times of the year. With this in mind, we gathered our recipes by month, but don't let that stop you from using them throughout the year.

Each chapter conveniently begins with a quick list of the recipes contained within that chapter. At the back of the book is a complete recipe index, alphabetically listing all recipes by category, such as cakes, frostings, pies, and more. We hope this dessert book will not only become a favorite resource for you for many years to come, but also will inspire you to make every dessert a "sweet success."

One

January

"Winter is the time for comfort—it is the time for home."
—Edith Sitwell

Recipes

As January begins the year, so begins our book with comfy desserts—enticing us with warm, homey treats from our cozy kitchen to yours.

Cheryl's Baked Winter Pears

Baked Alaska

Mother's Old-Fashioned Bread Pudding

Apple Bread Pudding

Surprise Sour Cream Pudding

Applesauce Sponge Pudding

Lumberjack Apple Pandowdy

Patty's Cherry Dessert

Cranberry Pear Upside-Down Cake

Banana Chip Bars

Zabaglione (Soft Italian Wine Custard)

MaryAnn's Homemade Chocolate Pudding

Peggy's Prune Pie

Kay's Mandarin Orange Pie

Aunt Louise's Egg Custard Pie

French Bistro Pound Cake

Banana Cake

White Fudge Frosting

In-a-Pinch Icing

Chocolate Cream Cheese Brownies with Frosting

Walnut Fudge Brownies

Alicia's Cheesecake Bars

Rocky Road Fudge Bars

Mock Baby Ruth Bars

Chinese Almond Cookies

Cheryl's Baked Winter Pears

Serving suggestion: 1 pear (i.e., 2 halves) per person

Winter pears, peeled, halved, and cored

Unsalted butter, 1 pat for each pear half

Strawberry jam, 1 teaspoon per pear half

Brown sugar, 1 pinch per pear half

Macaroons, crumbled, optional

Sherry or water

Whipped cream, sour cream, ice cream, or crème fraîche for serving

I like to use Bosc pears in this sophisticated dessert, which can complement an intimate dinner for two or be a special finale for a dinner party for many. It is easy to make, whether for two or ten.

Preheat the oven to 350°F. Butter a large baking dish.

Arrange prepared winter pears in a single layer, core side up, in the prepared baking dish. Slice a tiny bit off the rounded side of each pear half to make a flat and stable base, if you wish.

Dot each pear half in the center with the butter, strawberry jam, and brown sugar. Add a dab of crumbled macaroon, if desired. Sprinkle the pear with a little sherry or water.

Bake on the center rack, just until tender when pierced with a fork; the baking time varies according to the size and type of pear. Be careful not to overcook the pears so they retain their shape.

To Serve

Place 2 pear halves on a dessert plate, garnish with additional crumbled macaroons, and drizzle with the cooking juices. Serve warm as is, or garnish with whipped cream, sour cream, an ice cream of your choice, or crème fraîche (page 158).

Baked Alaska
Serves 8, advance preparation needed

Start making this dessert a day ahead of time or the night before, so everything is very, very cold. A boxed cake mix works perfectly well. You will make the meringue, assemble all the pieces and parts, and bake the final dessert at the very last minute!

At least a day before you plan to serve, line a 1½-quart mixing bowl with waxed paper. This will be your mold. Soften the ice cream slightly, and pack evenly around the bottom and up the sides of the lined bowl. Pack the center with the sherbet. Place another piece of waxed paper over the filled bowl, and press flat. Chill in the freezer until ready to assemble. Cut out a 9-inch round of heavy brown paper, and place it on a baking sheet. Center your prebaked 8-inch cake layer on the brown paper; refrigerate overnight or up to 24 hours.

To Serve
Preheat the oven to 450°F.

Place the egg whites and cream of tartar in a mixing bowl, and beat until soft peaks form. Add the sugar slowly, beating until stiff glossy peaks form. Set the meringue aside. Working quickly, bring the cake layer out of the refrigerator and the molded ice cream out of the freezer. Peel the waxed paper off the bottom of the bowl, and invert and unmold the ice cream from the bowl, centering it onto the cake layer. Peel off the remaining waxed paper from the ice cream. Continuing to work quickly, spread the meringue evenly over the ice cream and cake layer to cover the dessert entirely. Swirl to make peaks in the meringue.

Bake for 4 to 5 minutes, or just until the meringue begins to turn golden brown. Transfer the cake to a chilled dessert platter; serve immediately. Slice as if you were serving a cake, revealing the colorful, layered interior of this showy dessert.

1 quart ice cream

1 pint sherbet

1 (8-inch) round yellow cake layer, baked and cooled

5 egg whites, at room temperature

½ teaspoon cream of tartar

¾ cup sugar

Mother's Old-Fashioned Bread Pudding

Serves 6 to 8

2 cups whole milk

¼ cup butter

4 cups day-old bread, cubed

½ cup sugar

¼ teaspoon salt

1 cup raisins

¾ teaspoon ground cinnamon

¼ teaspoon ground nutmeg

2 eggs, slightly beaten

Whipped cream, vanilla ice cream, or half-and-half for serving

This is a great way to use up leftover bread, from hot dog buns to French bread, to raisin bread, to whole wheat—each gives this dessert a great taste all its own. Put it in the oven just as you sit down for dinner and you'll have a straight-out-of-the-oven dessert to finish off your meal.

Preheat the oven to 350°F, and butter a 1½-quart casserole dish.

Place the bread cubes in a large mixing bowl. Heat the milk and remaining butter to scalding, and pour over the bread cubes. Mix in the sugar, salt, raisins, cinnamon, nutmeg, and eggs. Pour the mixture into the casserole, and let it stand for ten minutes, or until the bread is thoroughly saturated with the custard mixture.

Bake for 40 to 45 minutes, or until a knife inserted into the center comes out clean.

To Serve

Serve warm with whipped cream, vanilla ice cream, or as my mother used to do: scoop each warm-from-the-oven serving into a dish, and pass half-and-half to pour over.

Apple Bread Pudding
Serves 6

Pick your favorite jarred applesauce to flavor this pudding.

Preheat the oven to 350°F. Grease a casserole dish.

Heat the butter in a large skillet over medium heat, and sauté the bread cubes. Spread them over the bottom of the casserole dish. Pour the applesauce over the cubes. Sprinkle the lemon juice, brown sugar, cinnamon, and salt over the applesauce. Pour the maple syrup over the top of it all.

Bake for 30 to 35 minutes.

To Serve
Scoop pudding into fancy dessert dishes. Serve warm with cream.

3 tablespoons butter

2 cups hard bread cubes (the kind you use for stuffing)

2 cups applesauce

½ teaspoon lemon juice

½ cup brown sugar

1½ teaspoons ground cinnamon

⅓ cup maple syrup

Pinch of salt

Heavy cream for serving

Surprise Sour Cream Pudding

Serves 12

2 tablespoons butter

½ cup granulated sugar

1 teaspoon vanilla extract

1 egg, beaten

1½ cups all-purpose flour

2 teaspoons baking powder

⅛ teaspoon salt

1 cup whole milk

2 cups brown sugar

2 cups sour cream

Heavy cream for serving

Batter rises to the top so be sure to use a deep pan to prevent the pudding from overflowing into your oven.

Preheat the oven to 375°F. Butter a deep baking dish.

Cream the butter and sugar; add the vanilla and egg. Sift together the flour, baking powder, and salt. Add the dry ingredients alternately with the milk, beating thoroughly after each addition. Arrange in the baking dish. Sprinkle the top with the brown sugar, and spoon sour cream over all.

Bake for 30 to 40 minutes, or until the batter rises to the top and the cream and sugar form a caramel sauce. Invert into another deep dish for serving.

To Serve

Scoop into dessert dishes, and serve hot or cold with cream.

Applesauce Sponge Pudding
Serves 6

Delight your family with this old-fashioned dessert.

Preheat the oven to 350°F.

Combine the applesauce, honey, lemon juice, and half the salt in a saucepan, heat, and pour into a baking dish. Scald the milk in the top of a double boiler over simmering water. Meanwhile, add the remaining salt, 2 tablespoons of the sugar, and the cinnamon to the beaten egg yolks. Blend the egg mixture with the milk, and continue to cook over simmering water, stirring constantly, until the mixture coats a spoon.

Remove from the heat. Pour into the center of the applesauce layer in the baking dish. Do not mix.

Beat the egg whites with the remaining 4 tablespoons sugar until stiff. Spread over the pudding.

Bake for 12 to 15 minutes, or until the meringue is lightly browned.

To Serve
Scoop into dessert dishes. Sprinkle with cinnamon, and serve with cream.

> Surprised to find salt in a dessert? A touch of salt deepens flavor and can accent sweetness. Two of humans' favorite flavors happen to be salty and sweet; put them together and we're really happy.

2 cups applesauce

½ cup honey

1 teaspoon lemon juice

¼ teaspoon salt, divided

1 cup whole milk

2 egg yolks, beaten

6 tablespoons sugar, divided

1 teaspoon ground cinnamon plus extra for sprinkling

2 egg whites

Heavy cream for serving

Lumberjack Apple Pandowdy

Serves 8

For Fruit:

4 to 5 cups sliced tart apples

½ cup sugar

Dash salt

½ teaspoon ground cinnamon or
1 teaspoon grated orange zest

2 to 3 tablespoons butter

Half-and-half for serving

For Biscuit Dough:

2 cups all-purpose flour

3 teaspoons baking powder

½ teaspoon salt

4 tablespoons shortening

¾ cup cold whole milk

An old-fashioned Midwestern dessert favorite

Preheat the oven to 350°F and butter a 9 x 13-inch baking dish or a cast-iron pan.

Toss the apples in a large bowl together with the sugar, salt, cinnamon or orange zest. Turn the mixture into the prepared dish or pan. Spread evenly and dot with the remaining butter; set aside.

For the biscuit dough, mix together the flour, baking powder, and salt in a large bowl. Cut in the shortening with a pastry blender or a fork until no lumps larger than peas remain. Make a well in the center, pour in the milk, and stir quickly until a soft dough forms.

Turn out onto a floured surface, and knead 10 to 12 times. Roll or pat the dough to ½-inch thick. Lay the dough over the apples. Pierce randomly with a fork to make vent holes.

Bake for 30 to 35 minutes, or until the dough is puffed and browned and the apples are tender.

To Serve

Serve warm. Scoop into bowls and pass half-and-half to pour over the top.

When I was a little girl and we spent summers at the lake house, Dad would always hire a retired woodsman to help with the yard work, for meager but fair pay and a hearty lunch to boot. After the long winters there would always be much work to be done.

One summer he hired Frank Laundry to fell trees and saw wood. I used to love to follow Mr. Laundry around and listen to his stories about the old days and how Wisconsin used to be. Frank was a little guy, to me ancient, wiry without an ounce to spare, and no teeth, so he was a little difficult to understand, and I thought his name so funny too. But he loved to tell his stories and seemed appreciative of my captive ear.

I can still remember the woodsy smell of the freshly falling sawdust, the swishing sound of his one-man saw, and his weathered voice, barely audible, with yet another story. Those stories have to be well over a hundred years old as I write this book today, and I don't remember so much what he said or the details anymore; I just know that now it's my turn to remember how Wisconsin used to be. So, Frank, this old-fashioned recipe is for you—an oldie but goodie from another place and another time.

Patty's Cherry Dessert

Serves 8

Just assemble and bake for a fun dessert—great for the beginner cook or a busy mom for a midweek dessert.

Preheat the oven to 350°F and butter a 9 x 13-inch cake pan. Spread the cherry pie filling in the bottom of the pan. Sprinkle the cake mix (straight from the box) over the pie filling. Drizzle the melted butter over the topping. Bake for 45 minutes.

To Serve

Spoon into dessert bowls while warm and top with vanilla ice cream.

2 (21 ounce) cans cherry pie filling

1 (18 ounce) boxed yellow cake mix

1/3 cup melted butter

Cranberry Pear Upside-Down Cake

Serves 6 to 8

For Glazed Fruit Layer:

1 cup fresh or frozen cranberries, cooked 5 minutes and drained

1 (20 ounce) can pear halves, drained; juice reserved

2 tablespoons melted butter

½ cup brown sugar

For Cake Batter:

1½ cups all-purpose flour

2½ teaspoons baking powder

⅓ cup softened butter

¾ cup sugar

1 teaspoon vanilla

1 egg

⅓ cup reserved pear juice

This is a very pretty dessert and is a nice variation from the usual pineapple upside-down cake.

Preheat the oven to 350°F. Combine the fruits, melted butter, and sugar, and arrange attractively in the bottom of a casserole dish, an 8-inch square glass baking dish, or a cast-iron skillet. Set aside.

To make the cake batter, combine the flour and baking powder. In a separate bowl, cream together the softened butter and the sugar, then mix in the vanilla, egg, and pear juice. Add the dry ingredients and mix well. Spread the batter over the arranged fruit layer. Bake for 40 minutes.

Remove the cake from the oven and let cool for 5 minutes before inverting onto a serving plate.

To Serve

Serve warm or at room temperature. Garnish with whipped cream if desired

Banana Chip Bars
Makes 12

If your bananas turn brown before you get a chance to eat them fresh, they're perfect for this recipe!

Preheat the oven to 375°F. Grease and flour a 9 x 13-inch baking pan. Cream the butter, granulated sugar, and brown sugar until fluffy. Add the egg and vanilla; beat well. Stir in the bananas; set aside.

In a separate bowl, stir together the flour, baking powder, and salt. Add the dry ingredients to the creamed mixture and beat well. Stir in the chocolate chips. Spread in the prepared baking pan. Bake for 35 to 40 minutes. Let cool before cutting.

To Serve
Cut into bars. If desired, frost with a favorite frosting.

¾ cup butter, softened

⅔ cup granulated sugar

⅔ cup packed brown sugar

1 egg

1 teaspoon vanilla

1 cup bananas, mashed

2 cups all-purpose flour

2 teaspoons baking powder

½ teaspoon salt

1 cup semisweet chocolate chips

Zabaglione (Soft Italian Wine Custard)

Serves 4 to 6

6 egg yolks

½ cup sugar

½ cup marsala or madeira wine

Strawberries for serving

Biscotti for serving (optional)

This dessert is so delicious and delicate, but it does require a bit of timing and skill. It gets its wonderful flavor from the sweet wine that is used. If you don't have marsala or madeira on hand, you can substitute sweet sherry. Warm or cold, zabaglione is traditionally served with a crunchy biscotti on the side, and/or an accompaniment of fresh berries.

Beat or whisk the first three ingredients constantly in the top of a double boiler over simmering water until the mixture doubles in volume and is smooth and fluffy. The end result will be an ultrarich, creamy, custardy (but soft) sauce.

The whole cooking process shouldn't take more than 10 to 15 minutes. Do not overcook because the eggs may curdle.

To Serve Warm

Pour the mixture into long-stemmed glasses, and serve warm. This mixture is very delicate and must be served immediately, or it will separate. Top with berries, and accompany with biscotti, if you wish.

To Serve Cold

To serve cold, set the mixture over a bowl of ice, and continue whisking the mixture until well chilled. Transfer chilled mixture to dessert glasses or cups, and store in the refrigerator for no longer than 3 hours.

Many recipes in this book call for a double boiler. If you don't have one, here's what to do:

Fill a saucepan with one or two inches of water, and heat the water to simmering over medium heat on your stovetop. Fit a heat-proof bowl snugly on top of the saucepan, making sure the bottom of the bowl does not touch the hot water underneath. Gently cook, heat, or melt the needed ingredient in the bowl. This is a handy way to cook delicate ingredients that require indirect heat, such as when melting chocolate or making sauces.

MaryAnn's Homemade Chocolate Pudding

Serves 6

No box mix can give us the rich fudgelike taste of this homemade pudding—just like mom used to make.

Blend together the sweetened condensed milk, salt, and 1½ cups water in the top of a double boiler. Add the chocolate. Cook over simmering water, stirring until the chocolate melts. In a small bowl, stir the cornstarch into ½ cup water to dissolve. Add the cornstarch mixture gradually, while stirring rapidly, to the pudding mixture. Continue to cook the pudding, stirring constantly, until thickened. Stir in the vanilla. Scoop into individual serving bowls. Refrigerate until ready to serve.

To Serve

Put a dab of whipped cream on top of each pudding, and place bowls on fancy plates.

1½ cups sweetened condensed milk

⅛ teaspoon salt

3 ounces unsweetened chocolate

3 tablespoons cornstarch

1 teaspoon vanilla extract

Whipped cream for serving

Peggy's Prune Pie

Serves 6 to 8

3 eggs, beaten

1 cup sugar

4 tablespoons all-purpose flour

Pinch of salt

Dash ground cinnamon

1 cup whole milk

½ cup prune juice

1 teaspoon vanilla extract

1 cup diced cooked prunes

1 (9-inch) unbaked piecrust

Whipped cream for serving

A very unusual pie, this is an heirloom family recipe that will bring you many compliments.

Preheat the oven to 375°F.

Mix together the beaten eggs, sugar, flour, salt, and cinnamon. Stir in the milk, prune juice, vanilla, and diced prunes. Pour the filling into the piecrust.

Bake for 50 to 60 minutes, or until the filling is set and a knife inserted in the center comes out clean. Remove from the oven, and cool.

To Serve
Top servings with whipped cream.

Kay's Mandarin Orange Pie

Serves 8

A taste of the tropics comes together in this pie for a mid-winter treat. You must make and serve this on the same day.

Spread the mandarin orange sections over the bottom of the piecrust. Arrange the banana slices over the oranges. Combine the heavy cream, milk, pudding, and vanilla; whip at high speed until thick. Pour over the fruit in the piecrust. Sprinkle the pie with the coconut. Refrigerate at least 1 hour before serving.

To Serve

Cut into wedges, and serve chilled.

For a variation, try a store-bought graham cracker crust, baked and cooled according to package instructions, or one from page 174.

1 prebaked piecrust, cooled

1 (12-ounce) can mandarin orange segments, well drained

2 bananas, sliced

1 cup heavy cream

¾ cup whole milk

1 (3.9-ounce) box instant banana pudding

½ teaspoon vanilla extract

¼ cup flaked coconut

Aunt Louise's Egg Custard Pie

Serves 6

1 unbaked (8-inch) piecrust, for a single crust pie

2 eggs

¼ cup sugar

⅛ teaspoon salt

1 cup whole milk

½ cup half-and-half

½ teaspoon vanilla extract

¼ teaspoon ground nutmeg

Whipped cream for serving (optional)

Prebaking the crust for 10 minutes and adding the filling while hot helps to prevent a soggy bottom crust. Do not overcook the pie, as the custard filling will continue to set while cooling.

Adjust the oven rack to the lower-middle position, and preheat the oven to 450°F. Bake the piecrust for 10 minutes.

Meanwhile, whisk the eggs with the sugar and salt. Heat the milk and half-and-half in a saucepan until the mixture is steaming. Whisk the hot mixture into the egg mixture, adding in a slow, steady stream. Whisk in the vanilla. Leaving the piecrust on the oven rack, pour the custard mixture into the hot crust, and sprinkle with the nutmeg. Reduce the oven temperature to 300°F.

Bake the pie for 30 to 35 minutes, just until a knife inserted near the center comes out clean. Do not overcook. Cool the pie on a wire rack at room temperature for 2 hours, then refrigerate.

To Serve

Slice the pie, and top each serving with a dollop of whipped cream, if desired. Return any remaining pie to the refrigerator and eat by the following day.

A tip for baking more than one pie at the same time: Position the pans so there are at least 2 inches between each pie and the sides of the oven for proper heat circulation. Or if baking on different racks, stagger the pans so that one doesn't sit directly over or beneath the other.

French Bistro Pound Cake
Serves 6

Rich and elegant, this dessert approaches sinfulness. You will find that making this is like making French toast.

Beat the eggs and milk (or better yet, half-and-half) together to blend. Dip the pound cake slices in the egg mixture to coat. Heat the butter in a large skillet, and pan-fry the cake slices, turning once, until both sides are golden brown.

To Serve

Serve warm, topped with strawberry sauce or your favorite fruit preserves. Garnish with whipped cream, crème Chantilly, sour cream, or crème fraîche. Accompany with a full-bodied, after-dinner coffee or espresso.

2 eggs

4 tablespoons whole milk or half-and-half

6 (¾-inch-thick) slices of store-bought pound cake

2 tablespoons butter

For the Toppings:

Strawberry sauce, jam, or preserves; or fruit preserves of your choice, such as apricot or cherry, at room temperature

Sour cream, crème Chantilly (page 128), whipped cream, or crème fraîche (page 158)

Banana Cake
Serves 12

2½ cups all-purpose flour

1⅔ cups sugar

1¼ teaspoons baking powder

1¼ teaspoons baking soda

1 teaspoon salt

⅔ cup shortening

⅔ cup buttermilk

1¼ cups mashed bananas (about 4 bananas)

2 eggs

Buttermilk is the secret ingredient for this Koopmann-favorite cake.

Preheat the oven to 350°F. Grease and flour a 9 x 13-inch baking pan.

Sift the dry ingredients together. Add the shortening, ⅓ cup of the buttermilk, and the bananas. Beat for 2 minutes, using an electric mixer. Add the remaining buttermilk and the eggs. Beat 2 minutes longer. Pour the batter into the prepared pan.

Bake for 45 minutes. Cool the cake completely.

To Serve
When the cake is cool, frost with your favorite frosting or try one of ours; see the index for frostings. Cut into squares, and serve.

When I first started baking, around the age of ten, I was clueless about different ingredients and thought that when a recipe called for "soda" it meant the soda pop we drink! Thank goodness I asked my Mom about it before I began to pour soda pop into my recipe! It gave us a memory that is now priceless, and I look back on it after all these years and chuckle.

If you find yourself without buttermilk and you need it for a recipe, you can use one of the following substitutes:

1. In a 1-cup measure, pour 1 tablespoon of lemon juice or white vinegar. Fill to the 1-cup mark with whole milk. Let the mixture stand for 10 minutes to thicken.

2. Use 1 cup of whole milk mixed with 1¾ teaspoons cream of tartar.

3. Substitute 1 cup plain yogurt or sour cream, or ½ cup of either mixed with an equal amount of whole milk.

White Fudge Frosting

Frosts 1 cake

Melt the butter in the hot milk. Pour over the sugar, and stir. Add the vanilla and salt. Beat until smooth.

To Serve

Frost a cake of your choice. Cut cake into slices, and serve.

> The key is to beat the frosting until it is as smooth as silk before you frost your wonderful cake of choice. Never frost a cake until the cake is cool, no matter what! Waiting the extra half hour will make for a beautiful cake.

4 teaspoons butter

5 teaspoons hot whole milk, scalded

3 cups confectioners' sugar

1 teaspoon vanilla extract

½ teaspoon salt

In-a-Pinch Icing

Makes approximately 1 cup

1 tablespoon butter, softened

Pinch of salt

1 tablespoon whole milk or cream

¾ to 1 cup confectioners' sugar

½ teaspoon vanilla, orange, or almond extract (optional)

This is a good starter frosting for the beginner cook. Increase or decrease the amounts, using the same ratio of ingredients called for, to make as much or as little frosting as you need.

Mix by hand the softened butter, salt, milk or cream, and enough sifted confectioners' sugar (adding slowly) to make the consistency you like. Wait for your cake to cool, and frost.

This basic icing makes a great topping for any of your baked items. Add vanilla, orange, or almond extract, if you wish.

Chocolate Cream Cheese Brownies with Frosting

Makes 12 to 16

Nothing like a good old-fashioned brownie to bite into!

Preheat the oven to 350°F. Grease the bottom of a 9 x 13-inch pan.

To make the brownies, cream together the sugar, butter, and cream cheese in a mixing bowl until light and fluffy. Beat in the eggs and vanilla. In a separate bowl, combine the flour, cocoa, baking powder, and salt. Gradually add the dry ingredients to the creamed mixture, and mix until well blended. Stir in the nuts. Spread the batter evenly in the prepared pan.

Bake for 30 to 35 minutes. Cool completely before frosting. When the brownies have cooled, combine all the frosting ingredients and blend until smooth. Spread the frosting onto the cooled brownies.

To Serve

Cut into bars, and serve.

For the Brownies:

2 cups granulated sugar

1 cup butter

1 (3-ounce) package cream cheese, at room temperature

3 eggs

1 teaspoon vanilla extract

1 cup all-purpose flour

¾ cup unsweetened cocoa powder

¼ teaspoon baking powder

¼ teaspoon salt

1 cup walnuts, chopped

For the Frosting:

3 tablespoons butter

3 tablespoons unsweetened cocoa powder

¾ teaspoon vanilla extract

1½ cups confectioners' sugar

2 tablespoons whole milk

1 tablespoon light corn syrup

Walnut Fudge Brownies

Makes 16

½ cup sifted all-purpose flour

⅛ teaspoon baking powder

⅛ teaspoon salt

1 cup sugar

½ cup butter, melted

2 eggs

2 ounces unsweetened chocolate, melted

½ teaspoon vanilla extract

1 cup walnuts, coarsely chopped

A good brownie always makes a welcome dessert—nice to pack in a lunchbox, too!

Preheat the oven to 325°F. Lightly grease an 8 x 8 x 2-inch baking pan.

Sift together the flour, baking powder, and salt; set aside. Beat the sugar, butter, and eggs in a small bowl using an electric mixer at medium speed until the mixture is light and fluffy. Beat in the melted chocolate and vanilla. Turning the mixer on low, blend in the flour mixture. Fold in the chopped walnuts. Spread evenly into the prepared pan.

Bake for 30 minutes. Cool for 10 minutes before cutting.

To Serve

With a sharp knife, cut into squares, then let cool completely in pan.

This recipe can easily be doubled into a 9 x 13-inch pan: Double the ingredient quantities, and prepare according to above directions. Increase the baking time to 50 minutes.

Alicia's Cheesecake Bars

Makes 6 to 9

Milk does a body good. Cheesecake Bars do the taste buds good!

Preheat the oven to 350°F.

Combine the flour and brown sugar in a large bowl. Cut in the butter until the mixture forms coarse crumbs. Reserve 1 cup of the crumbs for the topping. Press the remainder into the bottom of an 8-inch-square pan.

Bake for 15 minutes. Meanwhile, mix the cream cheese and sugar. Add the egg, milk, lemon juice, and vanilla, and beat well. Spread this batter over the hot crust. Combine the walnuts, reserved crumb mixture, and rolled oats. Sprinkle over all.

Return to oven and continue to bake for 20 to 25 minutes more. Cool.

To Serve

When completely cool, cut into squares. Place on a plate, and serve with a glass of milk.

1 cup all-purpose flour

⅓ cup brown sugar

6 tablespoons butter, softened

1 (8-ounce) package cream cheese, softened

¼ cup granulated sugar

1 egg

2 tablespoons whole milk

2 tablespoons lemon juice

½ teaspoon vanilla extract

2 tablespoons chopped walnuts

2 tablespoons rolled oats

Rocky Road Fudge Bars

Makes 36

For the Batter:

½ cup butter

1 ounce unsweetened chocolate

1 cup sugar

1 cup all-purpose flour

1 cup chopped walnuts

1 teaspoon baking powder

1 teaspoon vanilla extract

2 eggs

For the First Filling Layer:

6 ounces cream cheese, softened

½ cup sugar

2 tablespoons all-purpose flour

¼ cup butter, softened

1 egg

½ teaspoon vanilla extract

¼ cup chopped walnuts

6 ounces semisweet chocolate chips

For the Second Filling Layer:

3 cups miniature marshmallows

For the Topping:

¼ cup butter

2 ounces cream cheese, softened

1 ounce unsweetened chocolate

¼ cup whole milk

3 cups confectioners' sugar

1 teaspoon vanilla extract

Don't let this recipe scare you because of all the ingredients and stages. Once you start putting it together you will see how easy and fast it really is to make. This one is a winner!

Preheat the oven to 350°F. Grease and flour a 9 x 13-inch baking pan.

To make the batter, melt the butter and chocolate in a large saucepan over low heat. Add the remaining batter ingredients. Mix well; spread in the prepared pan.

To make the filling, combine the cream cheese, sugar, flour, butter, egg, and vanilla. Blend until smooth and fluffy. Stir in the nuts. Spread over the chocolate mixture. Sprinkle with the chocolate chips.

Bake for 25 to 30 minutes, or until a toothpick inserted in the center comes out clean. Sprinkle with the marshmallows, and bake 2 minutes longer to soften and melt. Remove from the oven; set aside.

To make the topping, melt the butter, cream cheese, chocolate, and milk in a large saucepan over low heat. Stir in the confectioners' sugar and vanilla until smooth. Immediately pour over the marshmallow layer, and swirl together. Cool completely.

To Serve

Cut into squares, and serve on a pretty platter.

Mock Baby Ruth Bars
Serves 16

If you like the well-known candy bar by the same name, this cookie is for you.

Preheat the oven to 400°F. Grease a 9 x 13-inch baking pan.

Mix the rolled oats, brown sugar, and corn syrup; pour the melted butter over the mixture, and stir. Add the ¼ cup peanut butter and the vanilla. Mix well; spread into the prepared pan. Bake for 12 minutes.

Carefully melt the chocolate chips and butterscotch chips in the top of a double boiler over hot water. As soon as the chips are melted, remove the mixture from the heat and add the remaining ²/₃ cup peanut butter and the peanuts. Spread on top of the bars.

To Serve
Cool and cut into squares. Place the bars on a platter.

4 cups rolled oats

1 cup brown sugar

¼ cup light corn syrup

²/₃ cup butter, melted

¼ plus ²/₃ cup chunky peanut butter

1 teaspoon vanilla extract

1 cup chocolate chips

½ cup butterscotch chips

1 cup salted roasted peanuts

Chinese Almond Cookies

Makes 2 dozen

3 cups all-purpose flour

¼ cup sugar

3 medium eggs, slightly beaten

1 tablespoon almond extract

1 teaspoon baking soda

¼ teaspoon baking powder

1⅛ cups shortening

1 egg yolk, beaten

24 whole blanched almonds

Look for blanched almonds in the baking section of your favorite market. To be authentic, use lard instead of shortening.

Preheat the oven to 350°F.

Combine all but the last two ingredients in the order given, and knead together. Shape the dough into 24 small, uniform balls, and place on ungreased cookie sheets. Flatten each ball with the flat bottom of a glass dipped in water. Brush the tops of the flattened cookies with the beaten egg yolk, and push an almond into the center of each.

Bake for 15 minutes, or until golden brown.

To Serve

Cool before serving.

When baking cookies, always make sure to use cool baking sheets, and leave plenty of room between the cookies. This allows both room for expansion and consistent oven air circulation between the cookies. Make all the cookies uniform in size for uniform cooking. Preferably, bake one sheet at a time on the center rack, or if using two sheets, switch their positioning halfway through the cooking time. Always cool down the sheets before putting on a new batch of dough. Follow these simple rules, and you'll have perfect cookies every time.

Two

February

*"That you have such a February face,
so full of frost, of storm and cloudiness…"
—William Shakespeare*

Recipes

February brings romantic desserts and dreamy treats to chase those winter blues and blahs away.

Italian Love Cake

Chocolate Espresso Bistro Cake

Old-Fashioned Rice Pudding

Caleb's Favorite Cherries Jubilee

MaryAnn's Cherry Cheese Torte

Strawberries Romanoff

Fancy Coffee Mousse

Delightful Chocolate Coffee Mousse

Coffee Crème Torte

Mousse au Chocolat

Orange Dream Pie

Crêpes

- The Batter

- The Cooking

Easy Your-Choice Dessert Crêpes

Brandy Alexander Crêpes

Paul's Crêpes Suzettes

Puff Pastry for Cream Puffs

Éclairs

- Easy Éclair Filling

- Easy Éclair Topping

My Honey's Apple Cake

Butterscotch Nut Torte

Cherry Pretzel Torte

Breanne's Chocolate Chip Cheesecake

Milk Chocolate Pecan Bars

Easy Meringue Dessert Shells

No-Fail "Next Day" Meringue Shells for Any Dessert

- Filling for Strawberry Schaum Tortes

- Filling for Coffee Café Meringues

Gail's Chocolate Meringue Pie Divine

Pastel Fudge-Filled Meringues

Meringue Pistachio Fudge Drops

Italian Love Cake

Serves 12

1 (18-ounce) box chocolate or yellow cake mix

2 (8-ounce) packages cream cheese, softened

16 ounces ricotta cheese

4 eggs

¾ cup sugar

½ teaspoon vanilla extract

½ teaspoon almond extract

Want to win your man? Bake this Italian Love Cake and watch him ask for more.

Preheat the oven to 325°F. Grease and flour a 9 x 13-inch baking pan.

Mix the chocolate or yellow cake according to package directions. Pour the batter into the prepared pan. Mix the cream cheese, ricotta, eggs, sugar, vanilla, and almond extract until smooth. Spoon the cream cheese mixture over the cake batter, being careful not to let it touch the sides of the pan.

As the cake bakes, the cheese will sink, forming the bottom layer. Bake for 50 minutes, or until cake tests done.

To Serve

Cool. Cut into squares and serve on a fancy dessert plate.

Chocolate Espresso Bistro Cake
Serves 10 to 12

This cake is just like one in Paris.

Preheat the oven to 325°F.

Separate the eggs, reserving 3 of the yolks for another use; set aside. Dissolve the espresso powder in ¾ cup warm water; set aside. In a mixing bowl, sift together the flour, sugar, baking powder, and salt. Make a well in the center and add the vegetable oil, the 5 egg yolks, the dissolved espresso, and the vanilla. Using an electric mixer, beat for 5 minutes until blended and smooth. Fold in the chocolate to mix throughout the batter; set aside.

Using clean beaters in a second bowl, beat the 8 egg whites with the cream of tartar until stiff peaks form. Slowly fold the first mixture into the stiff egg whites to make a light batter. Spoon the batter into an ungreased 10-inch tube pan.

Bake for 60 minutes, or until the top of the cake springs back when touched. Invert the pan to cool the cake. When cool, run a knife carefully around the edge of the pan, and remove the cake to a serving plate.

To Serve
Dust the cooled cake completely with confectioners' sugar, shaken through a sieve. Cut into slices, and serve with a cup of your favorite coffee.

8 eggs, at room temperature

1 tablespoon plus 1 teaspoon instant espresso or instant coffee powder

2 cups all-purpose flour

1½ cups granulated sugar

1 tablespoon baking powder

1 teaspoon salt

½ cup vegetable oil

1 teaspoon vanilla extract

3 ounces bittersweet chocolate, grated

½ teaspoon cream of tartar

Confectioners' sugar for serving

Old-Fashioned Rice Pudding

Serves 6

½ cup long grain rice

¼ teaspoon salt

2 cups whole milk

2 eggs, beaten

⅓ cup sugar

1 teaspoon vanilla extract

¼ cup raisins, steamed and drained

Dash grated nutmeg or grated cinnamon

Heavy cream for serving

This is a recipe my Grandmother made years ago and one that I still enjoy today.

Preheat the oven to 350°F. Grease a 1½-quart ovenproof casserole.

Bring 1 cup water to a boil; stir in rice and salt. Cover, reduce the heat to low, and cook until all the water is absorbed, for about 20 minutes. Add the milk, increase the heat to medium, and cook at a gentle boil, stirring occasionally, until the mixture thickens slightly, about 5 minutes.

Combine the eggs, sugar, and vanilla in a bowl. Stir in the rice mixture gradually, and mix well. Pour into the prepared casserole. Stir in the raisins, and sprinkle the nutmeg or cinnamon over the top. Place the casserole in a shallow pan containing about 1 inch of hot water.

Bake, uncovered, in the water bath for 45 to 50 minutes, or until a knife inserted near the center comes out clean.

To Serve

Serve warm or chilled. Place the pudding in bowls, and pass cream on the side.

Caleb's Favorite Cherries Jubilee

Serves 4

Showy but easy, Cherries Jubilee can be made for any number of guests—just double or triple the sauce ingredients and have enough ice cream on hand for everybody.

Drain the cherries, reserving their juice, right into a small saucepan. Mix a little of the juice with the cornstarch until dissolved, then add the cornstarch mixture to the juice already in the pan. Cook over low heat, whisking continuously, until the juice becomes a thickened and silky sauce. Add the cherries. Ignite the brandy in a long-handled ladle, and gently pour it into the saucepan mixture. Use water instead of brandy, if you prefer. Heat until everything is warmed through and the flame has extinguished.

1 (16-ounce) can pitted dark sweet cherries with juice

¼ cup brandy or water

1 tablespoon cornstarch

Scoops of vanilla ice cream for serving

To Serve

Place scoops of vanilla ice cream in pretty dessert bowls or stemmed glasses. Top each with warm cherries and sauce. Serve immediately.

MaryAnn's Cherry Cheese Torte

Serves 16

2 cups graham cracker crumbs

1½ cups plus 2 tablespoons sugar

½ cup butter, melted

4 egg whites

3 (8-ounce) packages cream cheese, softened

1½ teaspoons vanilla extract

2 cups sour cream

1 (21-ounce) can cherry pie filling

The key to this recipe is to get the egg whites very stiff—the result will be a very creamy cheese torte.

Preheat the oven to 350°F.

Combine the graham cracker crumbs, ½ cup of the sugar, and the melted butter. Mix well. Press into a 9-inch springform pan, reserving ½ cup of the crumb mixture for later.

Beat the egg whites until very stiff. Blend in 1 cup of the remaining sugar, the cream cheese, and 1 teaspoon of the vanilla. Pour over the graham cracker crust.

Bake for 25 minutes. Meanwhile, mix together the sour cream, the remaining 2 tablespoons sugar, and the remaining ½ teaspoon vanilla. Spread the sour cream mixture over the top of the hot torte, and sprinkle with the reserved crumb mixture. Increase the oven temperature to 475°F, and bake for 5 minutes more. Chill for 2 hours before spreading the cherry pie filling on top.

To Serve

Place the torte on a serving platter, and unhinge and remove the sides of the springform pan. Cut into wedges. The cherry topping will drizzle down the sides of each serving.

Strawberries Romanoff

Serves 4 to 6

Served in your prettiest stemmed glasses, this makes the perfect dessert to end a romantic meal.

Halve or slice the strawberries, depending on their size; set aside. Mix together the sugar, orange juice, and liqueur, and pour over the strawberries. Toss to coat. Divide among 4 to 6 stemmed glasses, and refrigerate until serving time.

To Serve

Serve chilled with a topping of sweetened whipped cream. Garnish each serving with a bit of orange peel for decoration. Make sure you get just the colored peel, and none of the bitter white pith underneath; a potato peeler works perfectly for this. It's that little detail that makes your presentation perfect.

2 cups strawberries, cleaned, dried, hulled, and chilled

1/3 cup sugar

1/4 cup freshly squeezed orange juice, chilled

1/4 cup Cointreau or Grand Marnier

Sweetened whipped cream for serving

Orange peel curls for garnish

Fancy Coffee Mousse

Serves 8

Note: The finished recipe contains raw eggs.

2 (0.25-ounce) envelopes unflavored gelatin

6 eggs

1 cup sugar

⅛ teaspoon salt

2 tablespoons instant coffee granules

2 cups heavy cream

1 teaspoon vanilla extract

2 tablespoons crème de cacao

Shaved chocolate curls (see page 127) for garnish

This was the first "fancy" dessert I ever made, and it has remained a favorite of mine to this day—light and coffee-flavored, it is a winner.

Put the gelatin and ½ cup cold water in a small saucepan, and heat it over low heat until it dissolves. Set aside, and let cool until syrupy.

Beat the eggs till frothy. Gradually beat in the sugar, salt, and instant coffee. Continue beating at medium speed until very thick, about 5 to 7 minutes; set aside. Beat the heavy cream and vanilla until stiff; set aside.

Gently fold together the egg mixture, crème de cacao, gelatin syrup, and three-quarters of the whipped cream until all is blended. Transfer the mixture to a fancy glass serving bowl, and chill in the refrigerator until ready to serve. Serve cold.

To Serve

At serving time, garnish with the remaining whipped cream and shaved chocolate curls (see page 127 for chocolate curls). Bring to the table in the serving bowl, and scoop into fancy dessert bowls. Return any leftovers to the refrigerator.

Delightful Chocolate Coffee Mousse

Serves 8 to 10

Note: The finished recipe contains raw eggs.

Melt the chocolate in a saucepan placed in a water bath over low heat, being careful not to get any water in the chocolate. Remove from the heat. Stir in the coffee powder, and set aside to cool to room temperature. Once cooled, beat in the softened butter with a wooden spoon. Beat in the egg yolks one at a time, and set aside again.

In a large bowl, beat the egg whites until soft peaks form. Sprinkle on the sugar, and continue to beat until stiff. Gently fold the chocolate mixture into the egg white mixture until well blended. Pour into a serving bowl, and immediately chill for several hours. Serve cold.

To Serve

Bring to the table, serve immediately, and garnish each serving with whipped cream and chocolate curls or a dusting of cocoa powder. Return any unserved portion to the refrigerator immediately.

11 ounces semisweet chocolate chips or semisweet chocolate broken into pieces

2 tablespoons instant coffee powder

12 tablespoons (1½ sticks) unsalted butter, cut in pieces and at room temperature

5 egg yolks

8 egg whites, at room temperature

3½ tablespoons sugar

Whipped cream for serving

Chocolate curls (see page 127) or cocoa powder for garnish

You will notice that many of the recipes in this book call for a "water bath"—especially when melting chocolate, or for soft puddings and custards. A water bath is simply a larger, shallow pan filled with hot water (to the level specified in the recipe), into which you put the pan or dish that you are cooking in. This technique comes in handy for gentle baking and also works well as a substitute on the stovetop for a double boiler. In either case, the hot water acts as a buffer against harsh direct heat, when tender, loving care is needed. If you want to get really, fancy you can say you cooked your dessert in a "bain-marie."

Coffee Crème Torte

Serves 12 or more

For the Batter:

8 eggs, separated

1½ cups confectioners' sugar

2 teaspoons baking powder

½ cup all-purpose flour

3 tablespoons instant powdered coffee

1 teaspoon vanilla extract

¼ teaspoon cream of tartar

For the Frosting and Filling:

¾ cup all-purpose flour

2/3 cup whole milk

1 cup butter

1 cup granulated sugar

½ cup unsweetened cocoa powder

1 tablespoon instant powdered coffee

1 teaspoon vanilla extract

I use French Vanilla Nut instant coffee for this recipe and I make a cup of that same coffee when I am ready to eat a slice of the cake. Experiment with different instant coffees to find your personal favorite.

Preheat the oven to 350° F. Generously butter and flour three 9-inch-round layer cake pans.

To make the batter, beat the egg yolks very well. Add the confectioners' sugar, baking powder, flour, instant coffee, and vanilla. Mix thoroughly, and set aside. Beat the egg whites with the cream of tartar until stiff peaks form; fold into the batter. Divide the batter among the three prepared cake pans. Bake for 20 minutes. Cool before assembling.

To make the frosting and filling, cook the flour and milk in a saucepan over medium heat, stirring constantly until smooth. Remove from the heat and cool completely. Beat the butter and sugar with an electric mixer until fluffy. Beat in the cocoa powder, coffee powder, and vanilla extract. Add the cooled milk mixture and beat on a high speed until frosting is smooth and fluffy, about 10 minutes. Once the cake has cooled completely, frost each layer and assemble them to make a layer cake. Frost the sides and top.

To Serve

Slice and serve on pretty plates. Put on a pot of coffee.

Mousse au Chocolat

Serves 8

This is a great recipe for the beginner cook.

Mix together 1 cup of the heavy cream, the half-and-half, and the instant pudding. Beat with an electric mixer until the mixture starts to thicken. Whip the remaining cream, and gently fold it into the mixture, stirring just until barely mixed. Do not overwork. Spoon the mousse into stemmed glasses or little custard cups, and chill until serving time.

To Serve

Top with shaved chocolate curls (see page 127), and serve immediately.

> Try this easy dessert with any flavor pudding and see which mousse becomes your favorite—perhaps butterscotch pudding with white chocolate curls or pistachio pudding topped with flaked coconut.

2 cups heavy cream

1 cup half-and-half

1 (4-ounce) package instant chocolate pudding

Chocolate curls for decoration

Orange Dream Pie

Serves 6 to 8

1 single-crust piecrust, crumb or pastry, baked and cooled

1 (6-ounce) can frozen orange juice concentrate, thawed but still cold

1 quart vanilla ice cream, softened

Top each serving with an orange twist to make it fancy. Check out Chapter 8 for piecrust recipes.

Prepare the piecrust according to the package directions or the recipe, and cool completely. Mix together the softened ice cream and juice concentrate. Spoon into the prepared piecrust. Freeze at least 2 hours or overnight.

To Serve

While you are clearing the dinner dishes, pull the pie from the freezer, and let stand at least 10 minutes to soften a little before serving. This makes for easier slicing, plus frozen desserts always taste better just a little thawed.

Crêpes
Serves 4 to 6

Crêpes, or French pancakes, are delicate and tender, and, with a little practice, easy to make. Their versatility suits many dessert combinations. They can be made in advance and assembled at serving time—with the addition of varied sauces and fillings to make wonderful dessert presentations, some of which are served warm and others cold. I have included some serving suggestions and two special recipes on the pages that follow.

The Batter

Basic Crêpe Batter

To make the batter, sift together the flour and salt. Set aside. Combine the beaten eggs with the milk, and slowly add to the flour mixture, beating constantly with a hand mixer or wire whisk. Beat until the batter is very smooth, with no lumps. Beat in the melted butter. The batter should be very smooth and should be the consistency of light cream.

For perfect crêpes, pour the batter through a sieve into a clean bowl, then cover and let rest for 30 minutes in the refrigerator. Batter can be made up to one day in advance, if desired, but it may need to be thinned with 1 or 2 tablespoons of milk.

1 cup all-purpose flour

¼ teaspoon salt

3 eggs, beaten well

1¼ cups whole milk

2 tablespoons butter, melted

Dessert Crêpe Batter

For dessert crêpes, add the confectioners' sugar to the basic flour/salt mixture. Add the optional liqueur when you add the melted butter. This will make a sweet batter for dessert-style crêpes. If you don't want to use liqueur, you could experiment by adding just a little flavoring extract such as vanilla, almond, or maple extracts, among others, if you wish.

2 tablespoons confectioners' sugar

2 tablespoons liqueur, such as Grand Marnier, brandy, or rum (optional)

The Cooking

Heat 1 tablespoon butter in a nonstick skillet over medium-high heat until foamy. Make crêpes one at a time by pouring a scant ¼ cup of batter into the skillet for each crêpe. Spread the batter as thin as possible by rotating the pan until the bottom is covered with the batter. Cook quickly until the bottom is lightly browned and the pancake is set, or about 1 minute. Turn and gently brown the second side, about 1 minute more. Remove and place on a sheet of waxed paper. Proceed with a second crêpe, and then another, melting in more butter each time. When the crêpes are cool, stack them between the layers of waxed paper. Wrap the stack, and store in the refrigerator. Crêpes may be made in advance, wrapped, and refrigerated for up to 5 days, or wrapped airtight and frozen for 1 month.

Most likely your first crêpe will not be as pretty as the rest, as it seasons the pan for the rest of the batch. I call this a "test crêpe" and always serve it to myself as a little snack while I'm making the rest of the batch.

Easy Your-Choice Dessert Crêpes

Serve 2 crêpes per person

Here are some suggested combinations to fill and garnish your crêpes for easy but elegant desserts. If your crêpes are small, allow 2 per person; if they are large, allow 1 per person. If you don't feel like making your crêpes from scratch, you can find packaged, ready-to-serve crêpes in the freezer or refrigerator section of the grocery store.

Fill the crêpes with seasonal fresh fruit, such as sliced strawberries or peaches, macerated with a little sugar. Roll up, and garnish with sweetened whipped cream.

Reverse the order, and fill the crêpes with sweetened whipped cream. Roll up, and garnish with the fruit on top.

Fill the crêpes with slightly softened ice cream. Roll up, and drizzle with a compatible sauce. Some tasty combinations are:

1. Vanilla ice cream/chocolate sauce

2. Coffee ice cream/chocolate sauce

3. Strawberry ice cream/strawberry sauce

4. Butter pecan ice cream/caramel sauce

5. Mint-chip ice cream/hot fudge sauce

6. Chocolate ice cream/hot fudge sauce

7. Spumoni ice cream/whipped cream/garnish with chopped pistachios

Make a Sundae Crêpe Buffet. Set out the crêpes, vanilla ice cream, and an assortment of sauces and garnishes. Let each person build their own sundae-style dessert. Garnish with chopped nuts, whipped topping, and a stemmed maraschino cherry.

Brandy Alexander Crêpes

Serves 1 or 2 per person

Note: The finished recipe contains raw egg whites.

1 recipe dessert crêpes (page 39)

For the Filling:

1 (0.25-ounce) envelope unflavored gelatin

²/₃ cup sugar

3 egg yolks, beaten

Pinch of salt

¹/₃ cup brandy

¹/₃ cup crème de cacao

3 egg whites

Sweetened whipped cream for serving

Shaved chocolate for serving (page 127)

A pure delight, these crêpes make a rich and elegant dessert.

Mix the gelatin with ¼ cup water to soften. Combine the mixture with ¹/₃ cup of the sugar, egg yolks, and salt in a saucepan, and stir over low heat until thickened. Fold in the brandy and crème de cacao; chill mixture until syrupy.

Meanwhile, beat the egg whites until stiff with the remaining sugar. Fold the whites into the gelatin mixture to blend. Fill the crêpes with about ¼ to ½ cup of the filling, and roll up; cover with plastic wrap, and refrigerate until serving time.

To Serve

Place 1 or 2 crêpes per serving on pretty dessert plates; top each serving with whipped cream and shaved chocolate.

Paul's Crêpes Suzettes
Serves 4 to 6

Make your pancakes well ahead of time, so you are not flustered or rushed at dessert time. For the sauce, measurements are not really critical; you may adjust the juice, butter, and sugar to your personal liking. The use of a liqueur is purely optional. I prefer my crêpes without the liqueur and a little more orange juice. This is a most sophisticated dessert.

To make the Suzette sauce, melt the butter in a large skillet over medium heat. Add the orange juice, sugar, and zest. Stir and cook until the sugar is dissolved. Using tongs, dip a crêpe in the sauce, turning to coat both sides, and fold it in half. Using the tongs, fold the crêpe in half again, turning it over in the sauce one more time. Push the completely folded and coated crêpe to the side of skillet. Repeat with the remaining crêpes.

After all the crêpes have been folded and arranged in the sauce, gently cook them just until heated through. Using a long-handled ladle, carefully pour on the Grand Marnier, and ignite to flambé the mixture. Cook the mixture until the flame dies down. Serve immediately.

To Serve
Serve this theatrical dessert warm, 2 or 3 folded crêpes per person, on warmed dessert plates, with pan sauces spooned over each serving.

1 recipe dessert crêpes (page 39)

For the Suzette Sauce:

½ stick butter, melted

½ cup freshly squeezed orange juice

2 tablespoons sugar

¼ teaspoon orange zest

1 to 2 tablespoons Grand Marnier (optional)

Flambé safety: Whenever adding and flaming a liquor or wine into a hot recipe, always pour the needed amount into a long-handled ladle or separate measuring cup. NEVER pour the alcoholic ingredient directly from the bottle itself, to avoid the risk of explosion! Slide the liquid into the pan and the heat of the pan should ignite it. If not, carefully ignite it with a long-handled match or lighter. Gently cook the dessert until the flame goes out completely before serving. Or you can light the liquid in the ladle and pour it, while flaming, over the warm dessert. Again, let it extinguish completely before serving.

Puff Pastry for Cream Puffs

Makes about 10 to 12 large or 20 to 24 mini puffs, suitable for filling

For the Puff Pastry:

½ cup butter

1 cup flour

¼ teaspoon salt

4 eggs, at room temperature

For the Cream Puffs:

Sweetened whipped cream for filling

Confectioners' sugar for dusting

Cream puffs—a cloud-puff of heaven.

Preheat the oven to 375°F (for mini puffs) or 425°F (for large puffs). Grease a cookie sheet.

To make the puff pastry, bring the butter and 1 cup of water to a boil in a large saucepan. Add the flour and salt all at once. Reduce the heat to low, and stir until the mixture forms a ball. Remove from the heat, and cool slightly. Add the eggs, one at a time, beating until smooth and shiny after each addition. Drop by teaspoonfuls or tablespoonfuls, depending on size you want, onto the prepared cookie sheet, placing them 3 inches apart.

Bake the miniature puffs at 375°F for 35 minutes. Bake the larger puffs at 425°F for 15 minutes, and then reduce the heat to 325°for 25 minutes more. Remove the puffs from the oven, and turn off the heat. Split the puffs open by slicing off about one-third of the puff from the top, and return to the warm oven for 20 minutes to dry out their interiors. Remove from the oven, and cool before filling.

Before filling, check the interiors of the puffs for any soft dough; gently remove this dough (if any) to make perfect puff pastry shells. You are now ready to fill them.

Fill the puffs with sweetened whipped cream just before serving time so the puffs don't become soggy; replace the tops.

To Serve

Dust the puffs with confectioners' sugar tapped through a sieve. Serve.

When dusting with confectioners' sugar, always tap it through a sieve to get out any lumps and to distribute the sugar evenly.

Éclairs

Makes about 12 to 14

These éclairs are divine with their homemade custard filling and homemade frosting—and well worth the effort.

Make, bake, and cool your puff pastry according to directions on page 44 (for the larger puffs) with only one change—instead of making your puffs round, fashion your pastry into elongated shapes, about 1 inch wide, ¾ inch thick, and 4 inches long. (If you have a pastry bag, you may use it, but it is not necessary, as I have always just done this by hand.) After baking, set aside to cool and rest until filling and serving time.

To make the custard filling, in a saucepan, mix together the sugar, flour, cornstarch, and salt. Using a wire whisk, gradually stir in the milk to blend. Cook over medium heat, and stir until the mixture thickens and comes to a gentle boil. Continue cooking and stirring with the whisk for 2 or 3 minutes longer. Remove the saucepan from the heat, and stir a little of the hot custard mixture into the beaten egg yolks, stirring constantly to temper them. Add the tempered egg mixture back into the custard mixture in the saucepan, stirring constantly. Return the saucepan to the heat, and continue to cook just until the mixture comes back to a boil. Remove from the heat again, and stir in the vanilla. Let cool.

Once cool, beat the custard mixture until smooth, and gently fold in the whipped cream to lighten the filling. You are now ready to fill your éclair puffs. Otherwise, store the filling in the refrigerator until serving time.

To make the chocolate frosting, heat the butter, chocolate, and milk in a heavy saucepan over medium-low heat. Remove from the heat, and beat in the confectioners' sugar. Stir in the vanilla. If the frosting is too thick, whisk in a little more milk; if it is too thin, add a little more sugar.

For the Puff Pastry:

1 recipe Puff Pastry (page 44)

For the Custard Filling:

²/₃ cup sugar

2 tablespoons all-purpose flour

2 tablespoons cornstarch

Pinch of salt

3 cups whole milk

2 egg yolks, lightly beaten in a small bowl

2 teaspoons vanilla extract

1 cup heavy cream, whipped

For the Chocolate Frosting:

½ tablespoon butter

1 ounce unsweetened chocolate

3 tablespoons whole milk

1 cup confectioners' sugar

¼ teaspoon vanilla extract

To Serve

Just before serving, fill the puffs generously with custard filling, replace the tops, and frost with chocolate frosting or drizzle with chocolate syrup, if you choose not to make your own frosting.

If you want a version that's a little easier than the one above, just follow these suggestions:

Easy Éclair Filling

Prepare a (3.5-ounce) box instant vanilla pudding mix with ¼ cup less milk than the directions calls for, so it is a little stiffer. Fold in whipped topping instead of whipped cream to lighten the filling. Voila! Instant filling!

Easy Éclair Topping

Use a chocolate syrup or a canned chocolate frosting instead of making your own.

My Honey's Apple Cake
Serves 12

This honey-sweetened cake is one of my husband's favorite desserts. What's that old saying, "Sweets for the sweet"?

Preheat the oven to 350°F. Lightly grease a 9 x 13-inch baking pan.

To make the cake, beat together the first five ingredients in a large bowl. In a separate bowl, sift together the dry ingredients. Add the dry mixture to the wet mixture, and beat well. Fold in the walnuts and apples. Spread the batter in the prepared pan.

Bake 45 minutes or until cake tests done. Remove from the oven.

Meanwhile, make the topping. Combine all the ingredients in a heavy-bottomed saucepan, and heat over medium heat. Boil for 2½ minutes. Pour the topping over the cake while it is still warm from the oven.

To Serve
Serve cake straight from the pan with scoops of ice cream on the side.

For the Cake:

3 eggs, beaten

2 cups granulated sugar

1 cup olive oil

¼ cup honey

1 teaspoon vanilla extract

3 cups sifted all-purpose flour

1 teaspoon baking powder

½ teaspoon baking soda

1 teaspoon salt

2 teaspoons ground cinnamon

¼ teaspoon ground nutmeg

1 cup walnuts, chopped

3 cups Granny Smith, Fuij, or Rome apples, peeled and chopped

Ice cream for serving (optional)

For the Topping:

¼ pound (1 stick) butter

1 cup light brown sugar, packed

¼ cup whole milk

¼ cup honey

Butterscotch Nut Torte

Serves 12

For the Torte:

6 egg yolks

1½ cups granulated sugar

1 teaspoon baking powder

½ teaspoon salt

2 teaspoons vanilla extract

2 teaspoons almond extract

6 egg whites

2 cups graham cracker crumbs

1 cup pecans, chopped

For the Frosting:

2 cups heavy cream

3 tablespoons confectioners' sugar

For the Butterscotch Sauce:

¼ cup butter, melted

1 tablespoon all-purpose flour

1 cup brown sugar

¼ cup orange juice

1 egg, beaten

1 teaspoon vanilla extract

Several whole toasted pecans for garnish

This torte is best if made the day before and left overnight to firm up.

Preheat the oven to 350°F. Grease two 9-inch-round layer cake pans.

To make the torte, beat the egg yolks well. Combine the sugar, baking powder, and salt, and add to the yolks. Add the vanilla and almond extracts, mixing well. Beat the egg whites until stiff, and fold into the yolk mixture. Fold in the graham cracker crumbs and pecans. Pour the batter into the prepared pan.

Bake for 30 to 35 minutes. Remove from the oven, and let cool completely before frosting.

To make the frosting, whip the heavy cream while gradually adding the confectioners' sugar. Spread the frosting between the layers and on the sides and top.

To make the sauce, beat together the butter and flour. Add the remaining ingredients plus ¼ cup water, and cook over low heat until thickened, stirring constantly. Remove from heat, and cool thoroughly. Pour the sauce over the frosted torte, drizzling over the top and down the sides. Cool for several hours.

To Serve

Cut into slices, and add a few toasted whole pecans as garnish.

Cherry Pretzel Torte

Serves 12

This is a great recipe for the beginner cook.

Heat the butter over medium heat, and when melted, add the pretzels and sugar. Reserve ¾ cup for the topping, and press the remaining mixture into a 9 x 13-inch pan. Blend the cream cheese and confectioners' sugar together. Prepare the whipped topping according to the package directions, and fold it into the cream cheese mixture. Spread half of the mixture over the crust. Cover with the pie filling; put the remaining cheese mixture on top. Garnish with the reserved pretzel mixture, and refrigerate.

To Serve

Use a sharp knife to cut into slices. Pretzels in the crust tend to get hard, so using a good sharp knife is important. Clean the knife between slices.

1 cup (2 sticks) butter

2 cups coarsely crushed pretzels

¾ cup granulated sugar

1 (8-ounce) cream cheese, softened

½ cup confectioners' sugar

2 (2-ounce) envelopes whipped topping mix

32 ounces canned cherry pie filling

Breanne's Chocolate Chip Cheesecake

Serves 12

1½ cups finely crushed crème-filled chocolate sandwich cookies

¼ cup butter, melted

3 (8-ounce) packages cream cheese, softened

1 (14-ounce) can sweetened condensed milk

3 eggs

2 teaspoons vanilla extract

1 cup mini chocolate chips, divided

1 teaspoon all-purpose flour

This cheesecake is sooo good!

Preheat the oven to 300°F.

Combine the cookie crumbs and butter; press firmly into the bottom of a 9-inch springform pan.

Beat the cream cheese until fluffy in a large mixing bowl. Add the sweetened condensed milk, and beat until smooth. Add the eggs and vanilla, and mix well. In a small bowl, toss ½ cup of the chocolate chips with the flour until the chips are well coated; stir into the cream cheese mixture. Pour the mixture into the prepared pan. Sprinkle the remaining chocolate chips evenly over top.

Bake for 60 minutes, or until the cake springs back when lightly touched. Cool to room temperature, and refrigerate until well chilled.

To Serve

Unclip and remove the side of the springform pan. Garnish the cheesecake as desired. Cut into slices. Refrigerate leftovers.

Read your labels closely, making sure you buy sweetened condensed milk and not evaporated milk by mistake… it's an easy mistake to make if you are in a hurry.

Milk Chocolate Pecan Bars
Serves 16

How can something so simple taste so good?

Preheat the oven to 350°F. Grease a 9 x 13-inch baking pan.

Combine the flour, brown sugar, baking soda, and salt in a large bowl; mix well. Cut in the butter using a pastry blender or two knives until the mixture resembles fine crumbs. Press evenly into the prepared pan. Bake for 10 minutes before adding the topping.

Meanwhile, to make the topping, melt the chocolate chips in the top of a double boiler over hot but not boiling water; remove from the heat, and set aside. In a small bowl, combine the eggs, brown sugar, vanilla, and salt; beat for 2 minutes, using an electric mixer at high speed. Add the melted chocolate, and mix well. Stir in ½ cup of the pecans. Pour the topping over the cookie base; sprinkle with the remaining ½ cup of pecans. Continue baking for 20 minutes more. Cool completely before serving.

To Serve

Using a sharp, clean knife for easy slicing, cut the mixture into 2 x 1-inch bars, and serve on a platter.

For the Bars:

1 cup all-purpose flour

½ cup firmly packed brown sugar

½ teaspoon baking soda

¼ teaspoon salt

¼ cup butter, softened

For the Topping:

2 cups milk chocolate chips

2 eggs

¼ cup firmly packed brown sugar

1 teaspoon vanilla extract

¼ teaspoon salt

1 cup chopped pecans

Easy Meringue Dessert Shells

Makes about 6 shells

2 egg whites, at room temperature

½ cup sugar

½ teaspoon vanilla extract

¼ teaspoon cream of tartar

⅛ teaspoon salt

If you use this recipe or the one on the next page, there will be no mystery to making good meringue shells. They truly are easy to do.

Preheat the oven to 250°F.

Using an electric mixer, beat the egg whites until foamy. Gradually beat in the sugar. Gradually add the remaining ingredients, beating until the egg whites are stiff. Drop by large spoonfuls onto an ungreased cookie sheet. Use the back of a spoon to make an indentation in the center of each.

Bake on the center rack for 45 minutes, or until dry. Turn off the oven, and leave the meringues in there overnight.

If you don't want to leave them in overnight, make them earlier in the day, and leave them in the turned-off-oven for several hours instead. Store on the kitchen counter until serving time.

To Serve

Place individual meringue shells on dessert plates, and fill with any desired filling—pudding, custard, fruit, ice cream—the list is endless. Fill the shells just before serving, to avoid shells becoming soggy.

No-Fail "Next Day" Meringue Shells for Any Dessert
Makes 12 shells

There's something magic about meringue shells filled with a scrumptious filling of your choice. They are like little fairy mountain peaks to delight children and adults alike.

Preheat the oven to 400° F. Line a baking sheet with brown paper or parchment paper.

Beat the egg whites with cream of tartar until frothy. Gradually beat in the sugar, adding a little at a time, until stiff and glossy. Mound the egg white onto the prepared baking sheet, and, using the back of a spoon, press a "well" into each mound. Put the baking sheet in the oven, turn off the heat, and walk away. Let the meringues stand overnight in the oven—do not open the oven door. Do not peek, just trust in the process.

The next day, remove the shells from the oven, and store them on the kitchen counter until you're ready to fill and serve.

To Serve
Fill just before serving with one of the following (added to shells in the order the ingredients are given):

Filling for Strawberry Schaum Tortes
Vanilla ice cream

Trimmed fresh strawberries, sliced and sweetened with a little sugar

Whipped cream

Filling for Coffee Café Meringues
Coffee ice cream

A drizzle of chocolate sauce

Whipped cream

Shaved chocolate curls (see page 127)

6 egg whites, at room temperature

½ teaspoon cream of tartar

2 cups sugar

Gail's Chocolate Meringue Pie Divine

Serves 8, using a 10-inch pie plate

For the Meringue Bottom Layer:

4 egg whites, at room temperature

¼ teaspoon cream of tartar

1 cup sugar

For the Chocolate Filling:

6 ounces chocolate chips or chopped semi-sweet chocolate

Dash ground cinnamon

4 egg yolks

1 teaspoon vanilla extract

1 cup heavy cream

2 tablespoons sugar

For the Garnish:

Additional whipped cream

Dusting of ground cinnamon or chocolate curls

There is only one word to describe this pie—divine!

Preheat the oven to 300°F.

To make the bottom layer, beat the egg whites until stiff but not dry. Gradually beat in the cream of tartar and then sugar until the meringue becomes glossy. Spread in a 10-inch pie plate, building up the sides, and making a well in the center for the filling.

Bake the "meringue crust" for 1 hour. Set the baked shell aside to cool.

Meanwhile, to make the filling, melt the chocolate in the top of a double boiler over simmering water or in a saucepan set in a water bath. Remove from the heat, and stir in the cinnamon. Beat in the egg yolks one at a time. Beat in the vanilla. Set the filling aside to cool. Beat the cream and sugar until stiff; fold into the cooled chocolate filling. Pour the filling into the meringue shell, and refrigerate until serving time.

To Serve

Garnish each wedge with whipped cream and a dusting of cinnamon or chocolate curls (see page 127 for chocolate curls).

Pastel Fudge-Filled Meringues

Makes 5 dozen

Sweet and delicate, these meringue cookies make a special dessert.

Preheat the oven to 250°F. Line several cookie sheets with brown paper or parchment paper.

Beat the egg whites with the cream of tartar and salt until soft peaks form. Add sugar, 1 tablespoonful at a time, and beat after each addition until *very* stiff. Mix in the almond extract. Drop the egg white mixture from a teaspoon onto the prepared cookie sheets. Shape into small walnut-sized mounds, and make a depression in the center of each cookie. Bake for about 30 minutes. Cool.

Meanwhile, to make the filling, melt the white chocolate in a saucepan over low heat. Remove from the heat, stir in 1 tablespoon water, the confectioners' sugar, the cream cheese, and the vanilla, and beat until smooth. Divide the filling into three parts. Tint one part pink, one part green, and one part yellow, using just a drop or two of food coloring for each color.

To Serve

Fill the meringues with the assorted fillings. Arrange on a platter and serve.

For the Meringues:

2 egg whites, at room temperature

1/8 teaspoon cream of tartar

1/8 teaspoon salt

1/2 cup granulated sugar

1/4 teaspoon almond extract

For the Filling:

6 ounces white chocolate

1/2 cup confectioners' sugar

1 (3-ounce) package cream cheese, softened

1 teaspoon vanilla extract

Red, green, and yellow food coloring, 1 to 3 drops each

White chocolate cannot officially be called "chocolate" because it does not contain cocoa solids made from the inner bean's chocolate liquor, which is needed to make actual chocolate. Good white chocolate contains cocoa butter, sugar, milk solids, vanilla extract, and lecithin. Make sure when buying white chocolate that it contains cocoa butter, as some inferior brands contain vegetable fat instead. White chocolate should be ivory-colored and it is rich and creamy.

Meringue Pistachio Fudge Drops

Makes 5 dozen

For the Meringues:

2 egg whites, at room temperature

1/8 teaspoon cream of tartar

1/8 teaspoon salt

1/2 cup granulated sugar

1/4 teaspoon almond extract

For Filling:

1/4 cup butter

1/2 cup chocolate chips

2 tablespoons confectioners' sugar

2 egg yolks

2 tablespoons chopped pistachios

Chopped pistachios are a must for these little cookies.

Preheat the oven to 250°F. Line several cookie sheets with brown paper or parchment.

To make the meringues, beat the egg whites with the cream of tartar and salt until soft peaks form. Add the sugar, 1 tablespoon at a time, beating after each addition, and beat until very stiff. Mix in the almond extract. Drop the egg white mixture from a teaspoon onto the prepared cookie sheets. Shape into small walnut-sized mounds, and make a depression in the center of each cookie. Bake for about 30 minutes. Cool.

Meanwhile, to make the filling, melt the butter with the chocolate chips in a saucepan over low heat. Be sure to stir the filling constantly so it doesn't burn. Beat the egg yolks slightly, and stir in the sugar. Blend into the chocolate mixture. Cook over very low heat for 1 minute, stirring constantly. Remove from the heat, and stir until cooled.

To Serve

Fill each meringue with a teaspoon of filling; sprinkle with chopped pistachios.

Three

March

*"The stormy March has come at last,
with winds and clouds and changing skies..."
—William Cullen Bryant*

Recipes

March brings our first inklings of spring and the tempting treats that are changing with the seasons.

Apricot Coconut Balls

Apricot Manhattan Mousse

Cile's Pineapple Cheese Pie

Linda's Pineapple Cream Pie

Postcard-Perfect Key Lime Pie

Poppy Seed Pound Cake

Chocolate Chip Cake

Alicia's Peanut Layer Cake

Texas Butter Bars

Angie's Peanut Butter Bars

Chocolate Peanut Buddy Bars

Sautéed Bananas

Kay's Strawberry Crêpe Blintzes

Caleb's Favorite Cherry Crêpes

MaryAnn's Famous Chocolate Mint Brownies

Best Carrot Cake

Cheese Squares

Grandma Scherer's Cannoli

Peaches and Cream Cheesecake

Betty's Éclair Cake

Apricot Coconut Balls

Makes about 1½ dozen

2 cups moist shredded coconut

1½ cups dried apricots, ground

⅔ cup sweetened condensed milk

1 cup confectioners' sugar for rolling the balls

Fruit-packed, tart-sweet confections are ideal for children and adults alike.

Blend together the coconut and apricots in a large bowl. Stir in the sweetened condensed milk. Blend well. Shape the mixture into small balls, and roll in the confectioners' sugar to coat well.

To Serve

Let stand uncovered until firm. Arrange in a candy dish or on a decorative plate.

Apricot Manhattan Mousse

Serves 8

Cool, light, and sweet, this dessert is sure to please.

Place the puréed apricots in a bowl, and add the sugar and lemon juice. Stir until the sugar dissolves. Soak 1½ teaspoons of the gelatin in 1½ tablespoons cold water, and dissolve over hot water. Add to the apricot mixture. Pour the mixture into two freezer trays or two similar shallow trays and refrigerate.

Whip the cream until it holds its shape, and add the sugar and vanilla. Soak the remaining gelatin in 1½ tablespoons cold water, and dissolve over hot water. Cool, and fold into the whipped cream. Spread the whipped cream mixture over the chilling apricot mixture, and transfer to the freezer.

To Serve

When frozen, scoop into fancy dessert dishes, and serve with a dab of whipped cream on top.

2½ cups canned apricots, drained and forced through a sieve

½ cup granulated sugar

6 tablespoons lemon juice

3 teaspoons gelatin

1½ cups heavy cream

½ cup confectioners' sugar

1½ teaspoon vanilla extract

Mousse is a French word that means "froth" or "foam" and is defined as a rich, light, fluffy, smooth confection that can be sweet or savory, hot or cold. Sweet mousses are usually flavored with chocolate or fruit purée and gelatin can be used to set the mousse. Chocolate mousses are usually made with egg yolks, and sometimes unsalted butter, whereas lighter fruit mousses use egg whites and cream.

Cile's Pineapple Cheese Pie

Serves 6 to 8

1 (8-ounce) package cream cheese, softened

¼ cup sugar

1 cup heavy cream, whipped

1½ cups canned crushed pineapple, well drained

1 graham cracker crust, baked according to package instructions and cooled (or use one of our recipes; see page 174)

Whipped cream for garnish (optional)

This dessert is as easy as it is fabulous.

Using an electric mixer, blend together the cream cheese and sugar. Fold in the whipped cream and pineapple until blended. Pour the filling into the cooled graham cracker crust. Chill at least 2 hours to set.

To Serve

Cut into wedges, and serve. Garnish with additional whipped cream, if desired.

> Back when my mother-in-law was cooking, canned pineapple dominated the dessert scene—probably because cooks didn't have access to as many fresh fruit dessert options as we have today. However, pineapple desserts still provide a refreshing treat when we want something light and not too sweet.

Linda's Pineapple Cream Pie

Serves 6 to 8

Pineapple pie has as many variations as there are cooks, and all of the desserts are delicious. This easy recipe is perfect for the beginner cook.

Mix together the pineapple, beaten sour cream, and instant pudding. Pour into the graham cracker crust. Chill for at least 2 hours before serving.

To Serve

Cut into wedges, and serve chilled.

> If sour cream is whipped slightly before adding any other ingredients, it will remain perfectly smooth and won't "break."

1 (20-ounce) can crushed pineapple

1 (16-ounce) container sour cream, beaten slightly

1 (3.9-ounce) box instant vanilla pudding

1 baked and cooled (9-inch) graham cracker crust

Postcard-Perfect Key Lime Pie

Makes 6 to 8 servings

Note: The finished recipe contains raw eggs.

For the Crust:

1 baked 9-inch single piecrust

For the Filling:

1 (14-ounce) can sweetened
condensed milk

4 egg yolks

½ cup fresh lime juice

½ teaspoon grated lime zest

1 egg white, beaten stiff

For the Meringue Topping:

3 egg whites

½ teaspoon cream of tartar

6 tablespoons sugar

When separating the 4 eggs for this recipe, put 4 yolks together in one bowl, 1 white in another bowl, and 3 whites in a third bowl. If possible, use Key limes for this dessert.

Preheat the oven to 350°F.

To make the filling, blend together the condensed milk, egg yolks, lime juice, and zest. Gently fold in the 1 beaten egg white. Pour the filling into the prepared shell.

To make the meringue, beat the 3 egg whites and cream of tartar until stiff. Add the sugar, 1 tablespoon at a time, beating well after each addition. Spread the meringue evenly over the top of the filled pie, making sure to cover the entire filling.

Bake just until the meringue is golden brown, about 15 minutes. Remove from the oven, and cool completely on the counter. Once cool, refrigerate until ready to serve.

To Serve

Serve chilled. Keep any leftovers in the refrigerator. This dessert is best if eaten the day it's made.

A memory from many vacations past, this dessert takes me back to sun-filled days in a little beach house balanced on stilts beside a seashell-strewn beach, followed by leisurely, seaside dinners of local fare. Years ago, I bought myself a souvenir post card, so I wouldn't forget one of Florida's most famous desserts, Key lime pie, which, at my insistence, we enjoyed after many of those vacation dinners.

Poppy Seed Pound Cake
Serves 10

Poppy seeds add a nutty, rich taste and are a perfect addition to pound cake.

Preheat the oven to 350°F. Grease and flour a 10-inch tube pan.

Combine all the ingredients except the confectioners' sugar. Add 1 cup water, and using an electric mixer, beat for 2 minutes. Pour into the prepared pan.

Bake for 45 to 55 minutes. Cool completely before unmolding from the pan.

To Serve
Dust the completely cooled cake with confectioners' sugar shaken through a sieve. Slice and serve.

When dusting with confectioner's sugar, make sure the item you are dusting has completely cooled, so that the sugar does not dissolve and disappear into the surface. Shake or tap the sugar through a sieve to provide even and lump-free distribution. It is best to do your dusting just prior to serving to keep the decoration fresh and delicate for presentation.

1 (18-ounce) box yellow layer cake mix

1 (3-ounce) package vanilla instant pudding

½ cup vegetable oil

4 eggs

¼ cup poppy seeds

2 to 3 tablespoons confectioners' sugar for garnish

Chocolate Chip Cake
Serves 12

1½ cups sugar

²/₃ cup shortening

1 teaspoon salt

1 teaspoon vanilla extract

3 cups all-purpose flour

3 teaspoons baking powder

1 cup whole milk

1 cup semisweet chocolate chips plus additional for garnish

5 egg whites, at room temperature

White frosting of your choice

A hidden layer of melted chocolate chips under the frosting makes this cake doubly delicious.

Preheat the oven to 350° F. Grease and flour an 8-inch tube pan.

Blend the first four ingredients together and set aside. Sift together the flour and baking powder, and, alternating with the milk, add the flour to the first mixture, stirring to combine. Stir in ½ cup of the chocolate chips. Beat the egg whites to stiff peaks, and fold them into the batter. Pour the batter into the prepared tube pan.

Bake for 60 minutes. Remove from the oven, and sprinkle the remaining ½ cup chocolate chips on top of the cake. Return to the oven just long enough to melt the chips. Remove from the oven, and while still warm, spread the melted chips with a spatula to make an even layer. Cool the cake, and remove from the tube pan before frosting.

To Serve
Frost with a white frosting of your choice. Cut into slices and put each on a plate with a few chocolate chips as garnish.

A little tip when whipping egg whites: Use a chilled glass bowl for firm peaks. Make sure your bowl and utensils are squeaky clean—they should not contain any residual fat, oil, or moisture. Use room temperature egg whites, and make sure the whites do not contain specks of yolk. Begin beating on low speed and work up to high speed, continuing until the egg whites have increased in volume and form peaks when the beaters are removed. The phrase "soft peaks" means the whites are curling over, and "firm peaks" means the peaks will stand straight up. If you overbeat, the mixture will tend to liquefy again. The eggs should not be beaten until after all the other ingredients are ready, as they will fall if whipped too early and left to stand while you are working with the other ingredients.

Alicia's Peanut Layer Cake

Serves 12

Note: The finished frosting for this cake contains raw egg yolk.

Serve this extravagant cake for a special occasion.

Preheat the oven to 350°F. Grease and flour three 9-inch-round cake pans.

To make the cake, cream together the shortening and peanut butter. Gradually add the brown sugar, beating well. Add the eggs, one at a time, beating well after each addition. In a separate bowl, combine the flour, baking powder, and salt. Add the flour mixture to the creamed mixture alternately with the milk, beginning and ending with the flour mixture, mixing until well combined after each addition. Stir in the vanilla. Pour the batter into the prepared pans.

Bake for 18 to 20 minutes. Cool in the pans for 10 minutes. Remove from the pans, and cool completely on wire racks before frosting.

To make the frosting, cream together the butter and peanut butter. Add the egg yolks, beating well. Gradually add the confectioners' sugar alternately with the half-and-half, beating well after each addition. Stir in the vanilla, and set aside.

Toast the coconut in a large dry skillet over low heat, stirring constantly, until golden brown. Remove from the heat, add the chopped peanuts, and set aside. Spread the frosting between the layers, sprinkling 1/3 cup of the coconut/peanut mixture on each of the bottom two layers after frosting them. Assemble the layers, and frost the top and sides of cake. Sprinkle the remaining coconut/peanut mixture on the top and sides of the frosted cake.

For the Cake:

½ cup shortening

¼ cup creamy peanut butter

2¼ cups packed brown sugar

3 eggs

3 cups all-purpose flour

1 tablespoon baking powder

½ teaspoon salt

1¼ cups plus 1½ teaspoons whole milk

For the Frosting:

½ cup (1 stick) butter, softened

3 tablespoons creamy peanut butter

2 egg yolks

2 cups confectioners' sugar

¼ cup plus 1 tablespoon half-and-half

1 teaspoon vanilla extract

1 cup flaked coconut

1 cup roasted peanuts, chopped

To Serve

Cut the cake into tall slices, revealing all the fabulous layers. Be sure to store any leftovers in the refrigerator.

Toasting the coconut in a dry skillet on your stove top for several minutes brings it to a golden brown and intensifies its flavor.

Two ways to tell if your cake is done:

1. Insert a toothpick into the center of the baking cake—if it pulls out clean, the cake is done.

2. Lightly tap the top of the baking cake with your finger—if the cake springs back, it is done.

Texas Butter Bars
Makes 2 dozen

The rich but delicate flavors of butter and almond combine to make a fabulous cookie.

Preheat the oven to 350°F. Lightly grease a 10 x 15-inch baking pan.

Cream together the butter, sugar, and egg yolk using an electric mixer until light and fluffy. Add the flour, mixing well. Press the dough evenly into the prepared pan. Press a layer of sliced almonds lightly into the top of the dough. Brush with the egg white.

Bake for 40 to 50 minutes, or until golden brown.

To Serve
Cut into squares, and remove from the pan while still hot.

1 cup (2 sticks) butter, softened

¾ cup sugar

1 egg yolk

2 cups all-purpose flour

1 egg white

1 cup sliced almonds

Angie's Peanut Butter Bars
Makes 16

For the Batter:

1 cup shortening

1 cup granulated sugar

1 cup brown sugar

1 cup peanut butter

2 eggs

1 cup all-purpose flour

1 teaspoon baking soda

½ teaspoon salt

1 teaspoon vanilla extract

1 cup old-fashioned rolled oats

½ cup chopped nuts

For the Topping:

¾ cup granulated sugar

½ cup peanut butter

½ cup whole milk

½ cup chocolate chips

Additional chopped nuts for sprinkling (optional)

These are perfect to tuck into a lunchbox or to serve as an afternoon pick-me-up with a glass of cold milk.

Preheat the oven to 325°F.

To make the batter, cream together the shortening, granulated sugar, brown sugar, and peanut butter. Add the eggs, and beat well. Add the flour, baking soda, salt, and vanilla. Beat well. Stir in the rolled oats and chopped nuts. Pat into a 9 x 13-inch baking pan. Bake for 25 to 30 minutes.

Meanwhile, to make the topping, combine the granulated sugar, peanut butter, and milk in a saucepan. Heat over medium heat, and boil for 3 minutes; set aside. As soon as the pan comes out of the oven, sprinkle on the chocolate chips. Let them soften, then pour on the hot topping, and, using a spatula or dinner knife, spread to smooth. Sprinkle with additional chopped nuts, if desired. Cool.

To Serve
Cut into squares, and place on a plate with a few chocolate chips as garnish.

When cutting bar cookies and brownies, too, wait until the cookies have cooled. Use a sharp knife, and cut gently, using a sawing motion to avoid crumbling—a steak knife works perfectly for this. Keep the blade clean between cuts.

Chocolate Peanut Buddy Bars
Makes 12

Chocolate and peanut butter—need I say more? You'll be everybody's buddy when you make these.

Preheat the oven to 350°F.

Beat together the peanut butter and butter in a large bowl until smooth, about 1 minute. Add the sugar, eggs, and vanilla; beat until creamy. Blend in the flour and salt. Stir in 1 cup of the chocolate chips. Spread into a 9 x 13-inch baking pan.

Bake for 25 to 30 minutes or until the edges begin to brown. Immediately sprinkle the remaining chocolate chips over the cookie layer. Let stand 5 minutes, or until the chips become shiny and soft. Using a spatula or dinner knife, spread the softened chips evenly over the top. Cool completely.

To Serve
Cut into bars and serve.

1 cup peanut butter

6 tablespoons butter, softened

1¼ cups sugar

3 eggs

1 teaspoon vanilla extract

1 cup all-purpose flour

¼ teaspoon salt

2 cups chocolate chips

Sautéed Bananas

1 to 2 bananas serves 1

1 to 2 firm, ripe bananas per serving

About 1 tablespoon butter per banana

About 1 tablespoon brown sugar per banana

Sour cream for serving

Additional brown sugar for serving

This simple dessert has the most inviting aroma while cooking—not to be outdone by its sensational combination of tastes, temperatures, and textures.

Peel the bananas, and either leave them whole or cut them in half lengthwise, but do not slice them. Melt the butter in a skillet over medium-heat, and gently cook the bananas. While cooking, sprinkle on the brown sugar to melt and glaze the bananas. Gently brown the bananas on all sides until they are well glazed, warmed through, and the brown sugar has melted completely. Be careful not to overcook them, or the bananas will get too soft and lose their shape. Using a spatula, transfer the bananas immediately to warm serving plates, and drizzle with any remaining pan juices, if desired.

To Serve

Top each serving of warm bananas with a generous dollop of cool sour cream and an additional sprinkling of brown sugar over the sour cream. The brown sugar will dissolve into the sour cream, making a kind of caramelized mixture.

Kay's Strawberry Crêpe Blintzes

Serves 4 to 6

If you don't want to make your own sauce, buy a jarred strawberry sauce and fold in a tablespoon of sherry and/or tablespoon of lemon juice to make it seem homemade. Serve the sauce at room temperature or warmed in the microwave, and garnish with a few slices of fresh strawberries, if available.

To make the cream cheese filling, cream all 6 ingredients together until fluffy using an electric mixer, and set aside.

To make the sauce, cook the strawberries and cornstarch mixture together over low heat until thickened; use warm or at room temperature.

To Serve

Wrap each crêpe around about 3 tablespoons of filling, and drizzle with sauce. Garnish each serving with fresh strawberries, if desired. Serve immediately.

For the Crepes:

1 recipe dessert crêpes (pages 39–40) or ready-made crêpes, about 2 per serving.

For the Cream Cheese Filling:

16 ounces cream cheese, softened

½ cup margarine, softened

½ cup confectioners' sugar

2 tablespoons whole milk

2 tablespoons sherry

1 teaspoon vanilla extract

For the Strawberry Sauce:

2 (10-ounce) packages frozen sliced and sweetened strawberries and their juice, thawed

2 tablespoons cornstarch, softened in ¼ cup water

For the Garnish:

Fresh strawberries, sliced and sweetened with a little sugar, as desired.

Caleb's Favorite Cherry Crêpes

Serves 4 to 6

Note: The finished recipe contains raw egg.

For the Crêpes:

1 recipe dessert crêpes
(pages 39–40)

**For the Cottage Cheese
Filling:**

1 tablespoon butter

1 egg yolk

2 tablespoons sugar

1 cup cottage cheese, forced
through a sieve or blended
smooth in a blender or food
processor

1 egg white, beaten stiff

For the Cherry Sauce:

1 tablespoon cornstarch

1 (16-ounce) can dark, sweet
pitted cherries, drained and juice
reserved

¼ cup brandy (optional)

To make the filling, cream together the butter, egg yolk, and sugar. Fold in the cottage cheese, stirring until well combine. Stir in the beaten egg white. Refrigerate until serving time.

To make the sauce, mix the cornstarch with a little of the reserved cherry juice until blended. Combine this with the remaining cherry juice in a saucepan, and cook over low heat, stirring constantly, until thickened. Stir in the cherries, and warm through. If desired, flame the brandy in a long-handled ladle, and add to the sauce; the sauce is ready when the flame extinguishes.

To Serve

Roll each crêpe around 2 or 3 tablespoons of cheese filling. Top with the warm cherry sauce. Serve immediately.

Variations

For equally delicious versions of this recipe, substitute a filling of whipped cream, vanilla ice cream, or crème Chantilly (page 128) in place of the cheese filling presented here.

MaryAnn's Famous Chocolate Mint Brownies
Makes 24

You'll never have leftovers with this brownie recipe!

Preheat the oven to 350°F. Grease and flour a baking sheet with sides (see below).

To make the first layer, combine the ingredients in a large bowl in the order given; beat until smooth. Spread in the prepared pan. Bake for 20 minutes. Remove from the oven to cool for 10 minutes.

Meanwhile, to make the second layer, cream together the ingredients in the order given until smooth. Spread over the cooled brownie layer. Refrigerate for 20 minutes.

To make the third layer, heat the butter and chocolate chips in a small saucepan, stirring until melted and blended. Spread evenly over all as a final topping. Return to the refrigerator for another 5 to 10 minutes to set the topping.

To Serve
Remove from the refrigerator, cut into bars, and serve.

> A baking sheet with sides is also called a "jelly-roll pan." The most commonly used jelly-roll pan for household baking has dimensions of 15½ x 10½ x 1 inch. There is a larger pan available, (sometimes used to make sheet cakes), which measures 17 x 11 x 1 inch, and some professional pans are even larger than that.

For the First Layer:

½ cup butter, melted

1 cup granulated sugar

4 eggs

½ teaspoon baking powder

1 cup all-purpose flour

16 ounces chocolate syrup

For the Second Layer:

½ cup butter, softened

2 cups confectioners' sugar

2 tablespoons whole milk

1 teaspoon peppermint extract

Few drops green food coloring

For the Third Layer:

½ cup butter

1 cup chocolate chips

Best Carrot Cake
Serves 12

For the Cake:

4 eggs

2 cups granulated sugar

1 cup olive oil

2 cups all-purpose flour

2 teaspoons baking powder

2 teaspoons ground cinnamon

½ teaspoon salt

½ teaspoon baking soda

1 teaspoon vanilla extract

1½ cups pecans, chopped

3 cups finely grated carrots,

For the Cream Cheese Frosting:

½ cup butter, softened

8 ounces cream cheese, softened

1 pound confectioners' sugar

1 teaspoon vanilla extract

I do believe the saying is "carrots are good for your eyes." So I say, let's eat some of this good cake!

Preheat the oven to 350°F. Grease a 9 x 13-inch baking pan.

To make the cake, beat together the eggs and sugar until smooth. Add the olive oil, and beat for 1 minute. Sift together the flour, baking powder, cinnamon, salt, and baking soda, and add to the egg mixture a little at a time, mixing well after each addition. Mix in the vanilla; fold in the pecans and carrots. Spoon the batter into the prepared pan.

Bake for 1 hour, or until a toothpick inserted in the center comes out clean. Remove from the oven, and cool completely before frosting.

To make the frosting, beat the butter and cream cheese together until fluffy. Slowly add the sugar, and when it is incorporated, add the vanilla, beating until creamy. Spread on the cooled cake.

To Serve
Cut into squares, and serve.

Cheese Squares
Makes 12 to 16

This is a treat I take to work on different occasions, and my coworkers give me rave reviews every time!

Preheat the oven to 350°F. Grease and flour a 9 x 13-inch baking pan.

Spread out 1 package of the rolls in the prepared pan, smoothing together any seams to make one solid layer fitting the dimensions of the pan. Combine the softened cream cheese, egg yolk, 1 cup sugar, and the vanilla. Beat well. Spread over the rolled-out dough in the pan. Top with the remaining package of rolls, again making a single layer to fit the dimensions of the pan.

Beat the egg white until foamy. Brush on top of the rolls. Sprinkle with the remaining ¼ cup sugar and the walnuts.

Bake for 40 minutes, or until golden brown. Remove from the oven, and refrigerate until chilled.

To Serve
Cut into squares.

2 (8-ounce) tubes crescent rolls

2 (8-ounce) packages cream cheese, softened

1 egg, separated

1¼ cup sugar, divided

1 teaspoon vanilla extract

½ cup walnuts, chopped

Grandma Scherer's Cannoli

Makes 24

For the Cannoli Shells:

1½ cups sifted all-purpose flour

2 tablespoons sugar

¼ cup shortening

1 egg yolk

¼ cup dry white wine

Several cups vegetable oil for frying

For the Cheese Filling:

32 ounces ricotta cheese, drained of excess moisture

1 cup sugar

1 teaspoon vanilla extract

3 ounces eating chocolate, crushed into small pieces, or mini chocolate chips

For the Garnish:

¼ cup shelled pistachios, chopped

Confectioners' sugar, for dusting

This is a family recipe handed down from my grandmother. You will need cannoli forms and a little cooking savvy to pull this dessert off—but the final result is well worth it. You can purchase metal cannoli tubes at a specialty cooking supply store or order them online. These usually come in sets of four. If you wish to make your own forms, as my Grandma Scherer did, use a ⅞-inch wood doweling cut into 5-inch lengths. These homemade dowels work almost as well as commercially bought tubes.

Sift together the flour and sugar. Cut in the shortening. Stir the egg yolk into the wine, and add to the flour mixture. Mix until stiff. Divide the pastry dough in half; roll it out as thin as paper. Cut into 3½-inch squares. Place a cannoli form diagonally on a pastry square, from point to point. Draw the remaining 2 corners loosely over the cannoli form. Moisten the underside of the overlapping corner with the wine mixture; press the corners together. Repeat with the remaining pastry squares.

Heat ½ to ¾ inches oil in a large skillet to 375°F. Fry the cannoli shells in batches for 2 to 3 minutes, turning occasionally, until golden brown all over. Using tongs, carefully remove each cannoli shell from the oil, and immediately slide it off the form while still hot. Drain on paper towels, and cool completely before filling.

To make the filling, cream together the ricotta and sugar until smooth. Fold in the vanilla and chocolate. Use a pastry tube or teaspoon to fill the shells with the cheese mixture. Fill the shells close to serving time so they remain crisp. Sprinkle the ends with the chopped pistachios.

To Serve

Dust with confectioners' sugar, and serve.

If you have an electric skillet, it works great for deep-frying in hot oil. Set the dial for the temperature needed; for the cannolis, set at 375°F, and heat the depth of oil called for. Fry a test cookie to make sure the oil is at the necessary temperature before starting a whole batch. And always use extreme care when working with hot oil! Make sure the skillet is on a stable countertop and that the cord is tucked away safely.

Peaches and Cream Cheesecake

Serves 8

When they're in season, you can substitute fresh peaches for the canned.

Preheat the oven to 350°F. Grease a 10-inch pie pan.

To make the bottom layer, combine the flour, milk, pudding mix, baking powder, salt, butter, and egg in a large bowl. Using an electric mixer, beat for 2 minutes. Pour the batter into the prepared pan. Place the drained peaches on the bottom layer.

To make the top layer, combine the cream cheese, ½ cup of sugar, and 3 tablespoons of the reserved peach juice. Using an electric mixer, beat for 2 minutes. Spoon over the peaches to within ½ inch of the edge. Sprinkle lightly with the remaining 1 tablespoon sugar and the cinnamon.

Bake for 35 to 40 minutes. The filling will appear soft. Cool on the counter; then refrigerate until firm.

To Serve

Serve by the slice with additional sliced peaches for garnish.

For the Bottom Layer:

¾ cup all-purpose flour

½ cup whole milk

1 (3½-ounce) package non-instant vanilla pudding mix

1 teaspoon baking powder

½ teaspoon salt

3 tablespoons butter, softened

1 egg

For the Middle Layer:

1 (20-ounce) can sliced peaches, drained and juice reserved

For the Top Layer:

1 (8-ounce) package cream cheese, softened

½ cup plus 1 tablespoon sugar

1 tablespoon ground cinnamon

Sliced peaches for garnish

Betty's Éclair Cake

Serves 12

For the Batter:

½ cup (1 stick) butter

1 cup all-purpose flour

4 eggs

For the Filling:

2 (3½-ounce) packages instant vanilla pudding mix

1 (8-ounce) package whipped cream cheese, softened

For the Topping:

8 ounces nondairy whipped topping

6 ounces chocolate syrup

This cake will melt in your mouth.

Preheat the oven to 350°F.

To make the batter, combine the butter and 1 cup water in a saucepan. Heat over medium heat until the butter is melted. Add the flour, and stir until the mixture forms a ball, about 30 seconds. Cool for 5 minutes. Add the eggs, beating in one at a time. Spread in a 9 x 13-inch glass baking dish. Bake for 30 minutes, and set aside to cool.

To make the filling, prepare the pudding according to the package directions. Mix in the cream cheese. Spread the filling over the cooled pastry base. Top with the nondairy whipped topping. Refrigerate for 15 minutes before drizzling with chocolate syrup. Continue to refrigerate until serving time.

To Serve

After the cake is firm, cut it into squares, and serve. Clean your knife after each piece for a smooth cut.

Four

April

"April is a promise that May is bound to keep."
—*Hal Borland*

Recipes
Desserts become lighter and our dreams brighter.

Papaya with Blueberries and Whipped Cream Dessert Sauce

  • Whipped Cream Dessert Sauce

Baked Fresh Pineapple with Whipped Cream Dessert Sauce

Brandied Peach Mousse

Natilla de Piña Mexicana (Mexican Pineapple Custard)

Lemon Meringue Pie

Alicia's Pineapple Torte

Dianne's New York–Style Cheesecake

Sammy's Twinkie Torte

Individual Baked Custards

Individual Crème Brûlées

Flan

Fruit Cup Ambrosia

Sara's Pistachio Torte

Orange Chiffon Pie

Orange Cream Cheese Cookies

Chocolate Orange Blossoms

Angie's Cherry Bars

Lemon Strawberry Bombe Traviata

Lemon Crumb Squares

Daisies

Papaya with Blueberries and Whipped Cream Dessert Sauce

½ papaya serves 1

Fresh papayas, at room temperature

Fresh blueberries, about ¼ cup per serving

Whipped Cream Dessert Sauce, refrigerated (recipe follows), about ¼ cup per serving

1 egg

3 tablespoons sugar

⅛ teaspoon salt

¾ teaspoon vanilla extract

¼ cup butter, melted and cooled

1 cup heavy cream, beaten stiff

As close to serving time as possible, peel, halve, and seed the papayas. You may serve each person a papaya half, or you may arrange slices on a dessert plate. Fill halves, or top slices, with blueberries.

To Serve

Spoon the dessert sauce over all, and serve immediately.

Whipped Cream Dessert Sauce

Note: This finished sauce contains a raw egg.

Papaya is exotic, and with this dessert sauce it becomes sublime!

Beat the egg very well with the sugar. Fold in the remaining ingredients in the order given. Store in the refrigerator until ready to serve.

If you don't wish to use the accompanying Whipped Cream Dessert Sauce, this dessert tastes equally as good topped with the Simple Whipped Crème Chantilly (page 128).

Baked Fresh Pineapple with Whipped Cream Dessert Sauce

Serves 4 to 6

Tart and refreshing—this makes a great dessert after a rich meal. Have your grocer help you pick the ripest, sweetest pineapple possible.

Preheat the oven to 325°F.

Using a very sharp chef's knife, halve the pineapple lengthwise, being careful to cut through the top also. Cut each half lengthwise into 2 or 3 wedges, leaving a portion of the top on each wedge for decoration, if possible. Place each wedge core side up and slice the fibrous core away from the fruit by running a knife just under the core, along the length of the wedge. Place the wedges in a single layer, peel side down, in a baking dish, and sprinkle with rum, then sugar.

Bake until the wedges are warmed through, about 20 minutes.

To Serve

Serve the pineapple wedges warm from the oven, topped with Whipped Cream Dessert Sauce (page 80). Use about ¼ to ½ cup per serving. Serve with dessert forks and sharp knives. If you wish, you can score the pineapple wedges beforehand so that it's easier for your guests to cut bite-size pieces away from the peel.

> If you don't wish to use the accompanying Whipped Cream Dessert Sauce, this dessert tastes equally as good topped with the Simple Whipped Crème Chantilly (page 128).

1 fresh whole pineapple, untrimmed and with top

About 1 tablespoon rum per serving

About 1 tablespoon sugar per serving

Whipped Cream Dessert Sauce (page 80)

Brandied Peach Mousse

Makes 3 cups

1 cup heavy cream

2 cups canned peaches, drained,
½ cup syrup reserved

⅓ cup sugar

⅓ cup peach brandy

⅛ teaspoon almond extract

Whipped cream for serving

This is an easy no-cook dessert with elegant results.

Whip the cream in a blender, and transfer it to a bowl. Put the remaining ingredients into the blender, and purée until smooth. Carefully fold this mixture into the whipped cream. Pour the mixture into a mold or a freezer tray, and freeze until firm.

To Serve

Scoop the frozen dessert into fancy dessert dishes, and top with a dab of whipped cream. Be sure to let your guests know that this dessert contains brandy.

Natilla de Piña Mexicana (Mexican Pineapple Custard)

Serves 4 to 6

This is a souvenir recipe from a Mexican vacation.

Mix the cornstarch with ¼ cup of the milk in a saucepan, stirring until it dissolves. Add the remaining milk, egg yolks, sugar, and pineapple flavoring, and cook over low heat, stirring constantly, until the mixture thickens and coats a spoon. Remove from the heat; stir in the pineapple purée. Pour the custard into dessert cups or stemmed glasses, and refrigerate until serving time.

To Serve

Place the cups or glasses on doily-lined dessert plates, adding a wafer cookie to each plate. You may garnish each serving with a mint leaf or a little whipped cream, if you wish.

Variations

You could serve the *natilla* (custard) as a filling in meringue shells (see pages 62 and 63 for Meringue Shell recipes) or as a filling in rolled crêpes (see pages 39–40 for Crêpe Batter Recipe).

2 tablespoons cornstarch

2 cups whole milk, divided

4 egg yolks

4 tablespoons sugar

½ teaspoon pineapple flavoring or almond extract

1 cup canned pineapple, drained and puréed

Wafer cookies for serving

Mint leaves or whipped cream for garnishing (optional)

Lemon Meringue Pie

Serves 6 to 8

Note: The final recipe contains raw eggs.

4 eggs, separated, with 1 white set aside

1 (10-ounce) can sweetened condensed milk

Juice and zest of 2 lemons

1 baked and cooled piecrust

6 tablespoons sugar

½ teaspoon cream of tartar

You may substitute 1 cup whipped cream for one of the egg whites for a richer filling.

Preheat the oven to 350°F.

Beat 1 egg white until stiff. Mix the condensed milk, egg yolks, lemon juice, and the beaten egg white (or 1 cup whipped cream, if you prefer) to make a light filling. Pour the filling into the cooled piecrust.

Beat the 3 remaining egg whites until stiff, gradually adding the sugar and cream of tartar. Gently mound and spread the meringue over the lemon filling, sealing the filling by spreading the meringue to the edge of the crust.

Bake only until the meringue is delicately browned, for 5 to 10 minutes. Remove from the oven, and cool on a rack. Once cooled, refrigerate until ready to serve.

To Serve

Cut into heavenly wedges, and serve. Return any remaining pie to the refrigerator.

When spreading meringue over a pie filling, make sure to touch the meringue up to the sides of the crust. This "marriage" prevents the meringue from shrinking away from the edge of the pie during baking. Take care to not overcook the meringue, as it will bead and sweat and lose some of its delicate quality. Less is more in the case of baking meringue.

Alicia's Pineapple Torte

Serves 6 to 8

Maraschino cherries add color to this delicious dessert.

Preheat the oven to 250°F. Generously butter a 9-inch glass pie plate.

To make the meringue, beat the egg whites with the salt until they hold a stiff peak. Gradually add the sugar. Beat until glossy and the sugar is well combined with the egg whites. Add the vinegar and vanilla, and blend well. Spread the meringue around and out to the edges of the prepared pie plate. Make a depression in the center of the meringue. Bake at 250°F for 30 minutes. Increase the temperature to 300°F, and continue baking for 30 minutes. Remove from the oven, and set aside to cool before filling.

To make the pineapple filling, soften the gelatin in ¼ cup cold water. Bring the pineapple juice to a boil in a saucepan over medium heat. Add the softened gelatin, and stir to dissolve. Chill just until the mixture begins to set. Fold together the chilled pineapple mixture, confectioners' sugar, vanilla, and whipped cream. Add the pineapple chunks. Pour into the meringue crust. Top with the maraschino cherry slices and chopped pecans, as desired.

To Serve

Refrigerate for several hours. When firm, cut into slices for serving.

For the Meringue:

3 egg whites

¼ teaspoon salt

1 cup granulated sugar

2 teaspoons vinegar

2 teaspoons vanilla extract

For the Filling:

1 tablespoon unflavored gelatin

1 cup pineapple juice, chilled

2 tablespoons confectioners' sugar

1 teaspoon vanilla extract

1 cup heavy cream, whipped

1½ cups drained pineapple chunks

¼ cup pecans, chopped

¼ cup maraschino cherries, sliced

Dianne's New York–Style Cheesecake

Serves 8 to 10

1 (8-ounce) package cream cheese, softened

½ cup plus 1 tablespoon sugar

1 tablespoon lemon juice

¾ teaspoon vanilla extract

Pinch of salt

2 eggs

1 graham cracker crust, uncooked

1 cup sour cream

This is cheesecake with a capital C!

Preheat the oven to 325°F.

Beat the softened cream cheese until fluffy. Gradually beat in ½ cup of the sugar, the lemon juice, ½ teaspoon of the vanilla, and the salt. Beat in the eggs, one at a time. Pour the filling into the piecrust.

Bake for 30 minutes. Meanwhile, mix the sour cream, the remaining 1 tablespoon sugar, and the remaining ¼ teaspoon vanilla together. Spoon over the top of the cheesecake, and bake for 10 more minutes. Remove from the oven, and cool on a wire rack. Refrigerate until well chilled before serving.

To Serve

Slice into small wedges to serve. Store any remaining cheesecake in the refrigerator. For a special treat, you can embellish this cheesecake with a garnish of strawberries, a drizzle of chocolate sauce, or any of a myriad of your favorite toppings. Me, I like it just as is.

My neighbor, Dianne, makes the best cheesecake! I have turned to her recipe many a time when I've wanted good, old New York–deli style, rich, creamy cheesecake. Her recipe never disappoints.

Sammy's Twinkie Torte

Serves 12

How fun is this?

Cut the snack cakes in half lengthwise, and arrange, cream side up, in a 9 x 13-inch baking pan, covering the bottom of the pan in a single layer.

Mix the pudding and milk, stirring until thickened, and pour over the snack-cake layer. Top evenly with the bananas. Pour the strawberries, including any juice over the bananas. Cover with a layer of whipped topping. Shave the chocolate bar using a potato peeler, and sprinkle on top of the whipped topping. Refrigerate the torte for 4 hours before serving.

To Serve

When the torte is completely chilled, cut into squares and serve. Return any leftovers to the refrigerator.

1 (8 to a package) box Twinkies (cream-filled snack cakes)

2 (3.9-ounce) boxes instant vanilla or banana pudding mix

3 cups whole milk

4 bananas, sliced

1 (10-ounce) box frozen sweetened sliced strawberries, thawed

8 ounces whipped topping

1 standard-size Hershey's milk chocolate bar, shaved

Individual Baked Custards

Serves 6

3 eggs, lightly beaten

1/3 cup sugar

Pinch of salt

1 teaspoon vanilla extract

2½ cups scalded whole milk, still warm

Dash nutmeg

Whipped cream for serving (optional)

This is comfort food at its best!

Preheat the oven to 350°F.

Beat together the eggs, sugar, salt, and vanilla in a mixing bowl. Slowly add the scalded milk, stirring constantly. Pour into 6 custard cups or ramekins. Dust each with nutmeg. Place the filled cups in a 9 x 13-inch pan, and fill the pan with hot water to ½ inch below the tops of the cups.

Bake in the water bath on the center rack of the oven for 45 minutes, or until a knife inserted into the custard comes out clean. Cool in the cups to room temperature; then refrigerate still in the cups.

To Serve

Serve each cup as is, or topped with whipped cream, if desired.

Individual Crème Brûlées

Serves 6

Superfine sugar can be found in the baking section of your favorite market.

To Serve

Preheat the broiler. Place the chilled custards on a baking sheet; sprinkle evenly with superfine sugar. Broil just long enough to melt and caramelize the sugar—this takes only 1 to 2 minutes, so don't leave them unattended.

Remove the cups from the broiler, and let them sit just a bit before serving. The sugary glaze will harden like glass, but this is exactly what you want, so that your spoon cracks through the crunchy-rich glaze to the creamy custard underneath.

> Bake the custards in heat-proof ramekins. If the custards have been chilled, remove them from the refrigerator 20 to 30 minutes before putting them under the broiler, to minimize the risk of the ramekins cracking.

1 recipe Individual Baked Custards (page 88), omitting the nutmeg

½ cup superfine sugar

Flan

Serves 8 to 10

1¾ cup sugar, divided

4 cups whole milk

⅛ teaspoon salt

6 eggs, well beaten, at room temperature

1 teaspoon vanilla extract

Brandy or rum for serving

This is perhaps one of the most challenging desserts in this book. Master this and you will be a dessert-maker cum laude.

Preheat the oven to 300°F.

Carefully melt 1 cup of sugar over low heat until deep golden brown. Pour the carmelized sugar into a round cake pan, a shallow mold pan, or an 11-inch flan pan, any of which have a 5- or 6-cup capacity. Spread to coat the bottom and sides of the pan by carefully tilting the pan to distribute the hot glaze evenly. Let cool. Note: Always be extremely careful to avoid burns when working with hot sugar!

In a second saucepan, simmer the milk, the remaining ¾ cup sugar, and the salt until the milk is scalded and the sugar and salt have dissolved. Cool slightly. Add the eggs by slowly drizzling them into the milk mixture. Beat together the egg and milk mixtures, beating *constantly*. After everything is incorporated, continue beating for 3 more minutes. Stir in the vanilla. Pour the custard through a sieve into the sugar-coated mold, and place the mold in a hot water bath halfway up its sides.

Bake for 1½ hours, or until a knife blade inserted near the center comes out clean. Let cool in the original pan, then refrigerate until ready to unmold and serve.

To Serve

To unmold for serving, dip the chilled flan pan into warm water for 5 minutes; this will slightly melt and loosen the caramel glaze. Place a raised-rim serving plate directly over the mold and invert. Jiggle the mold to release the flan onto the plate. Now let the flan sit, unrefrigerated, until it reaches room temperature. Bring the flan to the table, ignite a bit of brandy or rum in a long-handled ladle, and pour it over the flan. When the flame dies, cut the flan into wedges, and serve with a spatula onto dessert plates. Return any leftovers to the refrigerator.

Fruit Cup Ambrosia
Makes 4

Use extra-fancy, long-stemmed maraschino cherries to garnish each serving. Look for the coconut in the baking section of your market.

Mix the orange sections, grapefruit sections, and grape halves in a glass bowl, cover, and refrigerate until serving time.

To Serve

Spoon the refrigerated fruit into your finest stemmed glasses or fancy sherbet glasses. Peel and slice the banana, and divide evenly among the glasses. Drizzle a tablespoon or two of ginger ale over each serving. Sprinkle each serving with a liberal amount of sweet flaked coconut. Top with a stemmed cherry, and serve.

2 fresh oranges, sectioned

1 fresh grapefruit, sectioned

1 cup seedless grapes, halved

1 banana

8 tablespoons ginger ale for serving

4 tablespoons sweet flaked coconut for serving

4 whole long-stemmed maraschino cherries for serving

I always think "ladies' luncheon," "wedding shower," "holiday brunch," "spa-vacation breakfast," or "pampering day" when I think of this dish. Just the word *ambrosia* conjures up dreamy luxury. In Greek mythology, ambrosia was thought to be food of the gods, and eating it made one immortal. Either starting or ending a meal, Fruit Cup Ambrosia is a delicate treat to whet or cleanse the palate and set a healthful scene.

Sara's Pistachio Torte

Serves 8 to 10

For the Crust:

1½ cups graham cracker crumbs

1 cup butter, softened

½ cup chopped pistachios, divided

For the Filling:

1 (3.9-ounce) package pistachio pudding mix

1½ cups cold whole milk

1 (8-ounce) container nondairy whipped topping plus extra for serving (optional)

This dessert is as easy and tasty as it is pretty, and it's a great recipe for a beginner cook.

To make the crust, mix the graham cracker crumbs, the butter, and ¼ cup pistachios. Press into the bottom of a 9 x 13-inch baking pan. Refrigerate.

To make the filling, mix the pudding mix and milk. Reserve ½ cup of the pudding, and pour the rest into the chilling crust. Fold the remaining pudding into the nondairy whipped topping, and spread that on top of the torte. Top with the remaining ¼ cup pistachios, and refrigerate for at least 1 hour before serving, or overnight.

To Serve

This torte is best when refrigerated overnight—a nice convenience when you are having a party. When ready to serve, cut into squares, and transfer to dessert plates with a spatula. Top with additional whipped topping, if desired.

Orange Chiffon Pie

Serves 8

This recipe makes a refreshing pie.

Heat the orange juice in a saucepan over low heat until it simmers. Stir in the lemon gelatin to dissolve. Add the sugar, and stir to dissolve. Cool the mixture until nearly set.

Beat the evaporated milk with the lemon juice until stiff. Fold this into the gelatin mixture, and pour it into the prepared crust. Chill at least 1 hour, or until set.

To Serve

Cut into wedges, and garnish each serving with whipped cream and an orange slice.

Variations

You may substitute pineapple juice or apricot juice for different flavors. You could also top the pie with a meringue (see directions for meringue topping on page 62 or page 216).

1¼ cups orange juice

1 (3-ounce) package lemon gelatin

1 cup sugar

1 cup evaporated milk

1 tablespoon lemon juice

1 (9-inch) piecrust, baked and cooled, or 1 (9-inch) graham cracker crust, baked and cooled

Whipped cream and orange slices for serving

Orange Cream Cheese Cookies

Makes about 2 dozen

½ cup (1 stick) butter

½ cup sugar

1½ ounces cream cheese, softened

1 egg yolk

1 teaspoon vanilla extract

1 tablespoon frozen orange juice concentrate, thawed

Grated zest of 1 orange

1½ cups all-purpose flour

½ teaspoon baking powder

¼ teaspoon salt

The cream cheese makes these delicate cookies rich and tender.

Beat the butter and sugar, using an electric mixer, until fluffy. Beat in the cream cheese and egg yolk. Add the vanilla, orange juice concentrate, and orange zest, blend, and set aside. Sift together the flour, baking powder, and salt; fold into the orange mixture to blend. Cover the dough in plastic wrap, and refrigerate for 1 hour.

Preheat the oven to 350°F.

Drop the dough by teaspoonfuls onto cookie sheets. Bake for 10 minutes.

To Serve

Serve on a favorite cookie plate.

> When making citrus zest, grate the outer peel of the fruit on the finest side of your grater or use a Microplane. Grate off just the colored part of the peel—leave any white pithy part behind, because it is bitter.

Chocolate Orange Blossoms

Makes 4 dozen

These are so fun!

Beat the granulated sugar, brown sugar, shortening, butter, and cocoa in a large mixing bowl, using an electric mixer until light and fluffy. Add the orange zest, vanilla, and egg, blending well. Stir together the flour, baking soda, and salt; fold into the dough mixture to blend. Cover the dough with plastic wrap, and refrigerate 1 hour for easier handling.

Preheat the oven to 375°F.

Shape the dough into 1-inch balls, and roll each in granulated sugar. Place the balls 2 inches apart on ungreased cookie sheets.

Bake for 10 to 12 minutes, or until set. Remove from the oven, and immediately top each cookie with a candy kiss, pressing down firmly so the cookie cracks around the edges. Remove cookies from the baking sheets, and transfer to wire racks to cool.

To Serve

Place on a cookie platter to serve.

Variation

When buying chocolate kisses, you might want to try different kinds, such as the ones with almonds inside, to add a different flavor to the cookies.

½ cup granulated sugar plus extra for rolling dough

½ cup packed brown sugar

½ cup shortening

½ cup butter, softened

¼ cup unsweetened cocoa powder

1 tablespoon grated orange zest

1 teaspoon vanilla extract

1 egg

1¾ cups all-purpose flour

1 teaspoon baking soda

¼ teaspoon salt

48 milk chocolate candy kisses

Tips for storing baked cookies:

- Cool cookies completely before stacking and storing in an airtight container, such as a cookie tin.
- Stack the cookies in single layers with waxed paper between the layers to prevent sticking.
- Store like-flavored cookies together to maintain proper taste and texture.
- Store soft cookies and crisp cookies separately to maintain their proper texture.
- Store most cookies at room temperature for 1 to 2 weeks, or frozen for up to 6 months. Store cookies containing cream cheese in the refrigerator.

Angie's Cherry Bars

Makes 36

For the Crust:

1¼ cups all-purpose flour

½ cup brown sugar

½ cup butter-flavored shortening

½ cup walnuts, chopped fine

½ cup flaked coconut

For the Filling:

2 (8-ounce) packages cream cheese, softened

⅔ cup granulated sugar

2 eggs

2 teaspoons vanilla extract

1 (21-ounce) can cherry pie filling

½ cup walnuts, chopped fine

Make these bars the night before, and the next day they're firmly set and ready to go.

Preheat the oven to 350°F. Grease a 9 x 13-inch baking pan.

To make the crust, combine the flour and brown sugar in a mixing bowl. Cut in the shortening until crumbs form. Add the walnuts and coconut, mixing well. Remove ½ cup of the mixture, and reserve. Press the remaining crumbs in the bottom of the pan. Bake the crust for 12 to 15 minutes, or until the edges are lightly browned.

Meanwhile, to make the filling, beat the cream cheese, granulated sugar, eggs, and vanilla until smooth. Spread over the hot baked crust.

Return to the oven, and bake for 15 minutes more. Spread the cherry pie filling over the cheese layer. Combine the walnuts and the ½ cup reserved crumbs; sprinkle over the pie filling.

Return to the oven and bake 15 minutes longer. Remove from the oven, and let cool to room temperature before refrigerating for several hours.

To Serve
Cut into 2 x 1½-inch bars.

Lemon Strawberry Bombe Traviata

Serves 8 to 10

This frozen dessert is as pretty as a picture.

To make the outer layer, chill a 6- to 8-cup mold or bowl in the freezer until it is very cold. Remove the mold from the freezer, and, working quickly, press the sherbet evenly into the mold to make about a ¾-inch layer, lining the entire mold. Return to the freezer to set. Fill a large bowl with ice, and set aside.

To make the custard filling, bring the sugar and ½ cup water to a boil, and boil for 5 minutes. Set aside to cool. In the top of a double boiler over hot water, using an electric mixer, beat the egg yolks thoroughly. Continuing to beat, slowly drizzle in the cooled sugar syrup until blended. Change to a wire whisk, and slowly stir in the cup of strawberry purée until the mixture becomes somewhat thick. Remove the custard from the heat, and set the pot in the bowl of ice to quickly cool the mixture, stirring all the while.

When cool, fold in the stiffly whipped cream. Remove the sherbet-lined mold from the freezer, and pour the custard mixture into the center. Freeze until firm for several hours or overnight.

To Serve

Unmold onto a chilled serving plate by dipping the mold in hot water and counting to ten before inverting it onto a plate. Or invert it onto a plate, wrap the mold in a hot towel (my favorite way), and jiggle a little until the mold releases. In either case, return the unmolded bombe to the freezer to stay firm until serving time. To serve, cut like a layer cake, and garnish with additional whipped cream, sliced strawberries, and/or blueberries.

For the Outer Layer:

1 quart lemon sherbet, slightly softened

For the Custard Filling:

¾ cup sugar

4 egg yolks

2 to 3 cups strawberries, puréed in blender and forced through a sieve (to make 1 cup purée)

2 cups heavy cream, whipped until stiff

For the Garnish:

Additional whipped cream

Fresh strawberries and/or blueberries

I've always been a bit intimidated by molded desserts, such as Bombe Traviata, and the seemingly mystical process of getting the finished product out of the mold. And I must admit I breathe a sigh of relief when the dessert has dislodged itself successfully onto the serving plate. To ease this unmolding process I can recommend a few tips: (1) spray the mold lightly with a flavorless nonstick cooking spray before filling; (2) make the dessert well in advance to ensure the filling is properly firm, frozen, molded, and set before you attempt to unmold and serve; and (3) use simple-shaped molds, without a lot of nooks and crannies. Follow these tips and with a little practice, you'll be a pro.

Lemon Crumb Squares

Makes 9

1½ cups all-purpose flour

1 teaspoon baking powder

¼ teaspoon salt

1 (15-ounce) can sweetened condensed milk

1 teaspoon lemon juice

1 cup brown sugar

²/₃ cup butter

1 cup rolled oats

Mint leaves for garnish

A great taste for old or young, this is a crowd pleaser every time.

Preheat the oven to 350°F. Grease an 8 x 8-inch-square pan.

Sift together the flour, baking powder, and salt; set aside. Combine the condensed milk and lemon juice, and set aside to thicken. Cream the brown sugar and butter together; add the rolled oats and the flour mixture to make a crumb-style crust. Reserve one-third of the crumb mixture for the topping.

Pat the crust into the prepared pan. Spread on the condensed milk/lemon juice mixture, and cover with the reserved crumbs.

Bake for 25 to 30 minutes. Remove from the oven, and leave in the pan until firm.

To Serve

Cut into squares, garnish each portion with mint leaves, and place on a plate.

Daisies

Makes about 4½ dozen

This is a good recipe to make at Easter time.

Preheat the oven to 350°F. Lightly grease several cookie sheets.

Cream the butter, adding the sugar gradually. Beat in both the uncooked and cooked egg yolks. Blend in the vanilla, then the flour, and then the salt. Generously flour a work surface, and roll out the dough to ¼ inch thick. Using a daisy-shaped or similar cookie cutter, cut out cookies, and place them on the prepared cookie sheets. Brush the cookies with the beaten egg, and sprinkle the centers with walnuts.

Bake for 10 to 15 minutes, or until golden brown. Cool on wire racks.

To Serve

Arrange the cookies on a cookie platter to show off the design.

> This recipe appears in the month of April for a very specific reason. If you'll notice, it uses the yolks of already cooked eggs—and when do we usually have those hanging around? Easter, of course. I don't suppose the Easter Bunny might be hinting that he would like you to make him a batch of Daisies (his favorite cookie, by the way) before he scurries off into the month of May.

1 cup butter

¾ cup sugar

1 egg yolk

5 hard-boiled egg yolks, mashed

1 teaspoon vanilla extract

2 cups all-purpose flour

¼ teaspoon salt

1 egg, beaten

½ cup finely chopped walnuts

Five

May

"Hard is the heart that loved naught in May."
—Geoffrey Chaucer

Recipes
Who doesn't love the budding desserts of May?

Strawberries Cardinal

• Crêpes Cardinal

Peach Melba

Versatile Raspberry Cardinal Dessert Sauce

Electric Skillet Peach Melba

MaryAnn's Raspberry Squares

Rhubarb Whip

Rhubarb Pie with a Twist

Rhubarb Crunch

Barbara's Rhubarb Cake

• Barbara's Cranberry Cake

Rhubarb Marshmallow Cream Torte

Tart Strawberry Mousse

Liz's Lemon Curd Tart

Applesauce Tea Cake

Chocolate Torte Royale

Breanne's Golden Torte

Dirt Cake

Coconut Oatmeal Cookies

Bachelor Button Cookies

Italian Butter Cookies

Velvet Angel Cake

Strawberries Cardinal

Sauce serves 6 to 8

1½ quarts fresh strawberries, cleaned and hulled; larger ones cut in half

For the Cardinal Sauce:

1 (10-ounce) box frozen raspberries, thawed

2 teaspoons lemon juice

2 tablespoons sugar

2 tablespoons Grand Marnier

Whipped cream for garnish

The strawberries are the star of this pretty dessert.

Mash the raspberries and their juice through a sieve. Discard all the seeds and residue remaining in the sieve. To the purée, add the lemon juice, sugar, and Grand Marnier, stirring until all is blended and dissolved into a brilliantly colored sauce.

To Serve

Arrange the strawberries on dessert plates or in shallow bowls. Drizzle with the sauce, and, garnish with whipped cream.

Crêpes Cardinal

Strawberries drizzled with Cardinal Sauce is a very pretty dessert and wonderful on its own—but for an extra, extra, extra treat you can make crêpes cardinal. Fill crêpes (page 39–40) with whipped cream or crème Chantilly (page 128), and roll up; store in the refrigerator until serving time. Slice the strawberries, and place on top of the crêpes. Drizzle Cardinal Sauce over all for the final touch.

Peach Melba

1 peach half serves 1

It is said that this dish was created in the 1890s by an admiring chef for an opera singer named Dame Nellie Melba.

To skin your fresh peaches, plunge them into boiling water for about 30 seconds. Remove with a slotted spoon, and plunge them into ice water to stop the cooking. The peel will come right off. Halve each peach, and remove the pit.

To Serve

Place a scoop of slightly softened rich vanilla ice cream in a fancy dessert bowl or sherbet-style stemmed glass. Top with a peach half. Drizzle with Versatile Raspberry Cardinal Dessert Sauce to taste, and serve.

Ripe fresh peaches or canned freestone peach halves, drained

1 generous scoop of rich vanilla ice cream per serving

Versatile Raspberry Cardinal Sauce (recipe follows on next page)

Freestone peaches: When buying canned peach halves. look for "freestone" on the label. Freestones are a large, succulent variety of peach with wonderful flavor and a pretty red center surrounding the pit. If it's not the season for fresh peaches, canned freestones are the way to go. They got their name because the stone is "free" and can easily be removed, leaving all the flesh behind. On the other hand, the more commonly used clingstone, or cling, peaches, are smaller, harder to pit, have a little less flavor, and are less decorative for presentation.

Versatile Raspberry Cardinal Dessert Sauce

Makes 2 cups

1 (10-ounce) box frozen raspberries, thawed

2 tablespoons sugar

2 tablespoons Grand Marnier

2 teaspoons lemon juice

Use this wonderful sauce, named for its brilliant color, to garnish slices of pound cake, New York–style cheesecake, lemon sherbet, strawberry ice cream, parfaits, special sundaes, or crêpes. Fill crêpes with peach ice cream or fresh sliced peaches, drizzle with the sauce, and you have **Crêpes Melba***!*

Purée the raspberries and any juice in a blender. Press through a sieve to remove seeds and any pulp, discarding them. Add the sugar, Grand Marnier, and lemon juice to the purée. Mix to blend, and use as a dessert sauce, which may be served either cold or warm.

Electric Skillet Peach Melba

1 peach half serves 1

Serve the peaches warm and glazed, topped with slightly softened vanilla ice cream to melt all over. Yum!

Using a low to medium heat setting, melt the butter in the electric skillet. Purée the raspberries and any juice in a blender. Press through a sieve to remove seeds and any pulp, discarding them. Add the raspberry purée, lemon juice, and sugar to the skillet, and stir to blend. Heat and stir the mixture to make a sauce. Add the peaches, and continue to cook until glazed, warmed through, and tender. Turn off the heat, and stir in the Grand Marnier, if using. Serve warm.

To Serve

Place a peach half in each dessert dish. Top with a scoop of slightly softened vanilla ice cream. Distribute any pan sauce equally between servings. Serve immediately.

> If your fresh peaches aren't quite ripe enough for your liking, poach them in a little water or white wine to soften. Chill and proceed with the recipe.

> If you don't have an electric skillet, don't let that stop you from making this delicious warm dessert! Just modify the recipe by using a nonstick skillet over low to medium heat on your stove top.

1 tablespoon butter or nonstick cooking spray

1(10-ounce) box frozen raspberries, thawed, 2 teaspoons fresh lemon juice

2 tablespoons sugar

Fresh peaches, skinned, or canned freestone peach halves, drained

2 tablespoons Grand Marnier (optional)

Vanilla ice cream for serving

MaryAnn's Raspberry Squares
Makes 24

2 egg whites

1/3 cup butter

1 cup all-purpose flour

1/3 cup granulated sugar

2 egg yolks

1/4 teaspoon cream of tartar

2/3 cup confectioners' sugar

1 cup almonds, finely chopped and toasted

1/3 cup seedless red raspberry preserves

This recipe makes 81 square inches of pure cookie delight.

Preheat the oven to 350°F.

Bring the egg whites to room temperature in a mixing bowl, and set aside. In another mixing bowl, beat the butter using an electric mixer on medium to high speed, about 30 seconds or until softened. Add about half the flour; add the sugar and egg yolks. Beat on medium to high speed until thoroughly combined, scraping the sides of the bowl occasionally. Stir in the remaining flour. Press the crust mixture into an ungreased 9 x 9 x 2-inch baking pan. Bake for 15 minutes.

Meanwhile, thoroughly wash and dry the beaters to make the meringue topping. Add the cream of tartar to the egg whites, and beat on medium speed until soft peaks form. Gradually add the confectioners' sugar, beating until stiff peaks form and the tips stand straight. Gently fold in the chopped almonds. Set the meringue topping aside.

Spread the preserves over the top of the crust. Carefully spread the meringue topping over the preserve layer. Return the squares to the oven, and bake for about 20 minutes more, or until the top is golden brown. Remove from the oven, and cool in the pan on a wire rack.

To Serve
Cut into squares. Store in the refrigerator.

Variation
You can use peach or apricot preserves instead of the raspberry preserves, as these make wonderful bar cookies too!

When beating egg whites for meringue, make sure all utensils and the bowl are squeaky clean, completely grease free, and completely dry. The egg whites should be at room temperature for achieving maximum volume and must contain absolutely no yolk or bits of shell—the slightest bit of yolk will prevent the whites from beating properly. Add the sugar slowly, only after soft peaks have begun to form, and continue beating to desired stiffness.

Rhubarb Whip

Serves 6

Note: The final recipe contains raw egg whites.

Nothing speaks of spring more than rhubarb.

Combine the rhubarb and 1 cup water in a saucepan, and cook over medium-low heat for 10 minutes. Purée the rhubarb in a blender, and return to the saucepan. Add the sugar, gelatin, and salt, and cook over medium-low heat until dissolved. Stir in the vanilla. Chill the mixture until slightly thickened. Add the egg whites, and beat until mixture is very light and doubled in size. Chill until set.

To Serve

Mound the chilled mixture into dessert dishes or stemmed glasses, and top with sweetened strawberries to taste. Garnish with whipped cream, if desired.

2 cups chopped rhubarb stalks

2/3 cup sugar

1 (0.25-ounce) envelope unflavored gelatin

1/8 teaspoon salt

1/4 teaspoon vanilla extract

2 egg whites at room temperature

1 pint sweetened strawberries for serving

Whipped cream for garnish (optional)

For an eggless version of this dessert, whip the chilled rhubarb mixture until fluffy, and fold into sweetened whipped cream.

Rhubarb Pie with a Twist

Serves 8

1 recipe double piecrust (page 170), substituting ice-cold orange juice for the ice water called for

3 cups rhubarb stalks, cut into 1-inch pieces

1 ¼ cups sugar

1 teaspoon grated orange zest

3 tablespoons all-purpose flour

Pinch of salt

2 tablespoons butter

Vanilla ice cream for serving

The use of orange juice instead of water in the crust adds a special detail to this delicious pie.

Preheat the oven to 400°F. On a floured surface, roll out the bottom piecrust, and place it in the pie plate.

To make the filling, gently toss the rhubarb with the sugar, orange zest, flour, and salt mixture to coat. Mound in the piecrust. Dot the filling with dabs of the butter. On a floured surface, roll out the top crust. and cut it into strips. Lay the strips over the filling, and weave in a basket pattern to make a lattice-style top crust. Crimp the top and bottom crusts together all around the edge to make a fluted rim.

Bake on the center rack for 50 minutes, or until the filling is bubbly and tender. Remove from the oven, and cool on a wire rack.

To Serve

Serve at room temperature with slightly softened vanilla ice cream.

Set your pie on a foil-lined baking sheet to catch any sugary drips that might spill over while the pie is baking.

Rhubarb Crunch

Serves 12

If your rhubarb is too tart, add more granulated sugar to suit your taste or add some strawberries to the diced rhubarb—this will sweeten the mixture.

Preheat the oven to 350°F.

To make the crumb mixture, mix together the flour, sugar, cinnamon, and oats. Work in the melted butter until the mixture resembles coarse crumbs. Press half of the crumbs in a 9 x 13-inch pan. Cover with the diced rhubarb, and set aside.

To make the fruit mixture, combine the granulated sugar, cornstarch, 1 cup water, and the vanilla in a small saucepan. Cook, stirring, until thick and clear. Pour over the diced rhubarb. Top with the remaining crumb mixture.

Bake for 1 hour. Cool completely, and refrigerate for several hours.

To Serve

Cut into slices. Top with nondairy whipped topping, if desired.

> Did you know that the rhubarb plant is actually a vegetable, even though the stalks are used and cooked like a fruit? So the next time you want your kids to "eat their veggies," serve them a rhubarb dessert!
>
> Use only the pinkish-red stalks and *never* the leaves, as they are toxic. Never consume rhubarb leaves in any form.

For the Crumb Mixture:

1 cup all-purpose flour

1 cup packed brown sugar

1 teaspoon ground cinnamon

¾ cup old-fashioned rolled oats

½ cup (1 stick) butter, melted

For the Fruit Mixture:

1 cup granulated sugar

2 tablespoons cornstarch

1 teaspoon vanilla extract

4 cups diced rhubarb stalks

Nondairy whipped topping for serving (optional)

Barbara's Rhubarb Cake

Serves 8 to 9

2 cups brown sugar, divided

½ cup shortening

1 egg

1 cup buttermilk or soured milk
(page 157)

2 cups all-purpose flour

1½ cups cubed rhubarb stalks

1 teaspoon vanilla extract

1 teaspoon ground cinnamon

Whipped cream for serving

This recipe makes a fabulous tart yet sweet cake.

Preheat the oven to 350°F. Grease an 8-inch-square cake pan.

Beat together 1½ cups of the brown sugar and the shortening until fluffy. Blend in the egg, buttermilk, flour, rhubarb, and vanilla, in that order. Pour into the prepared pan. Mix the remaining ½ cup brown sugar with the cinnamon, and sprinkle evenly over the top of the batter. Bake for 35 minutes. Let cool in the pan.

To Serve

Cut into squares, and serve slightly warm with whipped cream.

Barbara's Cranberry Cake

Barbara sometimes replaces the rhubarb in her recipe with an equal amount of fresh cranberries for her equally delicious cranberry cake. Served with whipped cream, either cake makes a wonderful dessert. Served with cold unsalted butter, either recipe also makes a great coffee cake for a leisurely breakfast or brunch.

> Shortening is a solid fat used in food preparation—especially baking—and is made of hydrogenated vegetable oil. Shortening needs no refrigeration and can lengthen the shelf life of baked goods when substituted for butter. Shortening has a higher smoke point than butter or margarine. It has a 100 percent fat content, compared to 80 percent for butter and margarine.

Rhubarb Marshmallow Cream Torte

Serves 12

Four layers make this dessert a real treat.

Preheat the oven to 350°F.

Combine the flour, butter, and confectioners' sugar. Mix and press into 9 x 13-inch baking pan. Bake for 20 minutes.

Boil the rhubarb in just enough water to keep it from scorching. As it cooks, add the sugar, and stir to dissolve. Add the strawberry gelatin, and continue to cook over medium heat until the gelatin dissolves and the rhubarb is fork tender. Let the mixture cool; spread over the crust to set.

Whip the cream and add the marshmallows. Spread evenly over the set gelatin layer. Whip the pudding mix with the milk, and spread over the marshmallow layer. Refrigerate for several hours, or until completely set.

To Serve

Cut into wedges, and serve on pretty plates with a few fresh strawberries.

2 cups all-purpose flour

1 cup (2 sticks) butter, softened

½ cup confectioners' sugar

2 cups ½-inch long pieces rhubarb stalks

1 cup granulated sugar

1 (3-ounce) package strawberry gelatin

1 cup heavy cream

2 cups miniature marshmallows

1 (3½-ounce) package instant vanilla pudding

1 cup whole milk

Fresh strawberries for garnish

Tart Strawberry Mousse

Serves 6

2 cups strawberries, washed and hulled

¼ cup sugar

1 teaspoon grated lemon zest

1 (0.25-ounce) envelope unflavored gelatin

1 tablespoon lemon juice

½ cup orange juice

1 cup sour cream

Sweetened whipped cream for serving

Strawberries were my mother's favorite and this treat always pleased her. Today, I make it for my family, just as she did for hers.

Mash the strawberries in a large bowl, and add the sugar and lemon zest; set aside. Soften the gelatin in ¼ cup cold water, then dissolve over boiling water. Remove from the heat, and add the lemon juice and orange juice, mixing well. Add the gelatin mixture to the strawberry mixture, and stir well. Chill.

When the mixture is almost set, using an electric mixer beat until light and foamy. Gently fold in the sour cream. Pour the mixture into six individual fancy molds, and chill until firm, or spoon into dessert glasses, and chill until firm.

To Serve

Top with sweetened whipped cream, and serve.

Liz's Lemon Curd Tart
Makes 1 (9- to 10-inch) tart or 24 tartlets

This recipe was given to me by a wonderful check-out lady at my favorite gourmet grocery store in Vancouver, Washington. She saw me buying lemon curd, we struck up a conversation, and she offered me this recipe.

Blend the sugar and egg yolks in a saucepan. Add the lemon juice gradually, stirring continuously. Cook over low heat, stirring constantly, until the mixture coats the back of the spoon. (This process takes time, so be patient and *do not* let the mixture boil.)

Remove from the heat. Skim off any foam, and cool slightly. Stir in the butter and lemon zest to blend. Cool completely, stirring often to keep a film from forming on top. When cool, fill the pastry shell or tartlet shells to the rim. Refrigerate until ready to serve.

To Serve
Cut the tart into slim wedges or serve tartlets individually, and garnish with kiwi slices and/or a thin curl or twist of lemon. Strawberries and blueberries make good garnishes for this tart. Return any leftovers to the refrigerator.

Lemon curd may be sealed and vacuum-packed in sterilized jars (see page 201 for stove-top method) to give as gifts or to save for future use. Straight from the jar, it may also be used as a spread on scones, muffins, tea biscuits, or toast. Once the jar has been opened, store it in the refrigerator.

1 cup sugar

6 egg yolks

½ cup lemon juice

½ cup (1 stick) butter

1 to 1½ tablespoons grated lemon zest

1 pastry shell or 24 individual tartlet shells, prebaked and cooled

Kiwi slices, lemon peel, strawberries, or blueberries for garnish

Applesauce Tea Cake
Serves 8

½ cup granulated sugar

¼ cup butter

¼ cup brown sugar

2 eggs

1 cup applesauce

1 tablespoon lemon juice

1½ cups sifted all-purpose flour

1 teaspoon baking soda

⅛ teaspoon salt

1 teaspoon ground cinnamon

½ teaspoon ground cloves

½ cup raisins

½ cup dates, chopped

½ cup walnuts, chopped

Confectioners' sugar for dusting

My sister introduced me to this fabulous recipe when we would get together for tea and catch up on everything new in our lives.

Preheat the oven to 350°F. Grease a loaf pan.

Using an electric mixer, in a mixing bowl, beat the granulated sugar, butter, and brown sugar together until creamy. Beat in the eggs one at a time. Stir in the applesauce and lemon juice; set aside.

Sift together the flour, baking soda, salt, and spices. Stir the fruits and nuts into the flour mixture. Add the dry mixture to the wet mixture, and blend. Pour into the prepared pan.

Bake for 45 minutes. Allow to cool in the pan for 5 minutes before removing.

To Serve
When completely cooled, dust with confectioners' sugar, and cut into slices.

Chocolate Torte Royale

Serves 8

This is a rich dessert—so good that you won't believe you made it all by yourself!

Preheat the oven to 250°F. Butter a pie pan. To make the piecrust, beat the egg whites using an electric mixer until stiff. Add the salt and vinegar. Gradually beat in the sugar and cinnamon, turning the mixer speed to high speed after half of the sugar has been added. Spread the meringue in the prepared pie pan. Bake for 1 hour; turn the heat off, and allow the meringue shell to stand in the oven another hour. Remove from the oven and let cool.

Meanwhile, to make the filling, melt the chocolate chips in the top of a double boiler over simmering water. Spread about 2 tablespoons of the melted chips in the bottom of the meringue shell before continuing with the filling. Combine the egg yolks with the water, and add to the remaining melted chocolate. Set aside to cool. Beat the cream until stiff, and beat in the sugar and cinnamon. Spread half of the whipped cream mixture over the chocolate layer in the shell. Fold the chocolate filling into the remaining whipped cream to incorporate; pour over all to make the top layer of the torte. Refrigerate until completely set.

To Serve

Cut into slices, and top each slice with shaved chocolate.

For the Piecrust:

1/3 cup egg whites (about 3)

1/2 teaspoon salt

2 teaspoons vinegar

1 1/3 cups sugar

1/2 teaspoon ground cinnamon

For the Filling:

1 1/2 cups chocolate chips

3 egg yolks, beaten

1/3 cup water

2 cups heavy cream

1/2 cup sugar

1/4 teaspoon ground cinnamon

For the Garnish:

Shaved chocolate from a candy bar

Breanne's Golden Torte
Serves 12

For the Cake:

12 egg yolks

½ cup hot water

1⅛ cups granulated sugar

1 teaspoon vanilla extract

1 ¼ cups cake flour

1 tablespoon baking powder

1 teaspoon salt

For the Frosting:

2 cups confectioners' sugar

½ cup whole milk

2 eggs

¼ teaspoon salt

½ teaspoon vanilla extract

6 tablespoons butter

4 ounces unsweetened chocolate

A rich and delicious torte.

Preheat the oven to 325° F.

To make the filling, beat the egg yolks until thick and lemon-colored; add the hot water, and beat until lightened. Add the sugar gradually, followed by the vanilla. Sift together the cake flour, baking powder, and salt three times. Fold the dry ingredients into the egg yolk mixture. Divide evenly among 3 ungreased layer cake pans.

Bake for 30 minutes. Cool completely before frosting.

To make the frosting, place the sugar, milk, eggs, salt, and vanilla in a bowl over ice water. Stir until the egg yolks are broken; set aside. Carefully melt the butter and chocolate in the top of a double boiler over simmering water. Add to the sugar mixture, and beat until the frosting holds its shape. Frost in between the cooled layers, and stack them one on top of another. Frost the sides and top of the cake.

To Serve
Slice and serve on dessert plates.

For easier frosting of a cake, always let your cake layers cool completely before frosting them, or you may find you have problems with the layers breaking or crumbling. If you do have trouble, you can piece it back together with extra frosting and no one will ever know.

Dirt Cake

Serves 12

This cake is a fun way to surprise your guests.

Wash the garden trowel and clay flower pot well, because you are going to use them to serve the dirt cake. Plug or cover the hole in the bottom of the pot. The plastic lid from a coffee can works well for this.

Cream together the butter, cream cheese, and confectioners' sugar; set aside. Mix together the milk, instant pudding, and nondairy whipped topping. Blend the butter/cream cheese mixture into the pudding mixture. Layer the pudding mixture and the crushed cookies alternately in the clay pot, starting and ending with cookie layers so you have "dirt" on the top. Refrigerate overnight.

To Serve

Decorate with the clean plastic flowers, and serve with a trowel.

1 garden trowel

1 new clay flowerpot, 6 or 7 inches high

1¼ cup butter, softened (but not melted)

8 ounces cream cheese, softened

1 cup confectioners' sugar

3½ cups whole milk

2 (3-ounce) boxes instant French vanilla pudding

12 ounces nondairy whipped topping

1 (18 ounce) package crème-filled chocolate sandwich cookies, crushed

1 bunch of newly purchased plastic flowers

Coconut Oatmeal Cookies

Makes about 3½ dozen

1¼ cups sifted all-purpose flour

1 teaspoon baking powder

1 teaspoon baking soda

½ teaspoon salt

½ cup shortening

½ cup packed brown sugar

½ cup granulated sugar

2 eggs

1 teaspoon vanilla extract

1 tablespoon whole milk

1 cup flaked coconut

1 cup quick-cooking rolled oats

These are just good cookies!

Preheat the oven to 350°F. Grease several baking sheets.

Sift together the flour, baking powder, baking soda, and salt; set aside. Using an electric mixer at medium speed, cream together the shortening, brown sugar, and granulated sugar in bowl until light and fluffy. Add the eggs, one at a time; beating well after each addition. Blend in the vanilla and milk. Gradually add the flour mixture to the creamed mixture, blending well. Stir in the coconut and oats. Drop by rounded teaspoonfuls onto the prepared baking sheets.

Bake for 10 to 12 minutes.

To Serve

Place cookies on a platter and serve.

When you come across the term "shortening" in a recipe, it can mean vegetable shortening (such as solid Crisco), lard, oleo, butter, margarine, any mixture thereof, or any *solid fat* used for baking. Each type of solid fat has a different melting point, so always try to use the specific one (or ones) called for in the recipe. Do not substitute butter for shortening.

Bachelor Button Cookies

Makes 4½ dozen

Having a bachelor party? Serve these fun cookies. A bit of trivia: in European folklore, the bachelor button flower (also known today as cornflower, or boutonniere flower) was considered to be a good luck charm, worn on the lapel by romantic young men courting their ladies. If the flower faded too fast, it was sadly taken as a sign that their love would go unrequited by the intended lady.

Preheat the oven to 375°F. Sift together the flour, baking powder, and salt. Add the coconut, almonds, and cherries, and mix well; set aside. Cream the butter well; add the sugar gradually and continue creaming until light and fluffy. Add the egg and vanilla; mix well again. Add the flour mixture gradually to the creamed mixture, mixing well after each addition. Drop by teaspoonfuls onto baking sheets.

Bake for 9 minutes. Once cooled completely, store the cookies in an airtight container.

To Serve

Place cookies on a cookie platter.

2 cups sifted all-purpose flour

2 teaspoons baking powder

⅛ teaspoon salt

½ cup unsweetened shredded coconut

½ cup thinly sliced blanched almonds

½ cup candied cherries, cut into small pieces

¾ cup butter, softened

1 cup packed brown sugar

1 egg, well beaten

1 teaspoon vanilla extract

Italian Butter Cookies

Makes 4 dozen

1 pound (4 sticks) unsalted butter, softened to room temperature

1 egg

1 egg yolk

1 cup confectioners' sugar

1/8 teaspoon salt

1 tablespoon almond extract

4 1/2 cups all-purpose flour

Confectioners' sugar for garnish

To assure tender cookies, do not overwork the dough.

Preheat the oven to 325°F.

Cream the butter until light and fluffy, using an electric mixer. Add the egg, egg yolk, confectioners' sugar, and salt, and cream for 10 minutes. Add the almond extract and flour, and mix until completely incorporated, but do not overwork. The dough will be very soft. Using generous tablespoons of dough, shape each cookie into a 1/2-inch-thick crescent shape, leaving 1 inch of space between each cookie on the baking sheet.

Bake on ungreased cookie sheets for 20 to 30 minutes, or until the cookies are light golden brown. Remove from the oven, and immediately place on waxed paper sprinkled with confectioners' sugar. Sift additional confectioners' sugar on top of the cookies while they're still warm.

To Serve

Place on a cookie platter, and serve with milk.

Some tips for the perfect cookie

- For uniform baking and browning, heat in the oven must circulate freely around the cookies. Leave at least two inches of room on all sides of the pan for this purpose.

- Make your cookies uniform in size, and always leave at least one inch of space between cookies on the baking sheet, unless otherwise noted.

- When storing cookies, always make sure they are completely cooled before transferring them to a cookie tin, cookie jar, or other container.

Velvet Angel Cake

Serves 12

Use this cake to show off your favorite homemade frosting.

Preheat the oven to 325°F.

Beat the egg yolks with an electric beater, slowly adding 1 cup sugar, until smooth. Add the vanilla and the boiling water. Sift together the flour and baking powder, and add to the yolk mixture, blending well; set aside.

Beat the egg whites with the salt. Add the remaining 1 cup sugar gradually, beating well after each addition. Turn the yolk mixture into the egg white mixture, folding very lightly, until incorporated. Pour the batter into an ungreased angel cake pan.

Bake for 1 hour. Cool at least 10 minutes before removing from the pan.

To Serve

Slice the cake, top with fresh fruit, if desired, and serve. Or transfer the cake to a serving platter, and frost with your favorite frosting.

6 eggs, separated

2 cups sugar

1 teaspoon vanilla extract

1 cup boiling water

2½ cups all-purpose flour

1½ teaspoons baking powder

¼ teaspoon salt

Cut-up fresh fruit for garnishing (optional)

Six

June

"If a June night could talk, it would probably boast that it invented romance."
—Bern Williams

Recipes
A month for lightness and play, romance and open air.

Rum Raisin Ice Cream

Baked Coconut Soufflé

Grand Marnier Soufflé

Chocolate Kahlúa Soufflé

Simple Whipped Crème Chantilly

Baked Peach Pudding

Mother's Pineapple Whipped Cream Cake

MaryAnn's No-Bake Cheesecake

Mom's Strawberry Cake

Fruit Cocktail Cake

MaryAnn's Lemon Layer Cake

Lemon Cake

Chocolate Lemon Torte

Chocolate Jimmy Cake

Magic Cookie Bars

Angie's Ranger Cookies

Cherry Oat Dessert Squares

Six Dessert Sauces from MaryAnn

- Coffee Scotch Sauce

- Nutty Coffee Scotch Sauce

- Chocolate Mint Sauce

- Instant Dessert Sauce

- Lemon Dessert Sauce

- Golden Sauce

Mom's Glazed Pound Cake

Rum Raisin Ice Cream

Makes 1 quart

1 cup golden raisins

½ cup light rum

1 quart French vanilla ice cream

How easy and elegant is this?

Combine the raisins with the rum in a small bowl, and let stand overnight to plump. The next day, let the vanilla ice cream soften slightly. Drain off any excess rum, and fold the raisins into the slightly softened ice cream. Return the ice cream to the freezer to harden. Store in the freezer as you would any store-bought ice cream.

To Serve

Serve in fancy dessert cups with a fancy cookie on the side of each serving. Accompany with a cup of good coffee.

I first experienced rum raisin ice cream during a stay at the Waldorf-Astoria hotel in New York City. My mother knew how much I loved it and somehow figured out this delicious way to replicate it. This remains one of my favorite comfort desserts to this day. Thanks, Mom!

Baked Coconut Soufflé

Serves 8

Light and delicately sweet, this makes the perfect dessert for any special occasion.

Preheat the oven to 350°F. Butter a 1½-quart soufflé dish.

Scald the milk in the top of a double boiler over boiling water. Add the tapioca, and cook until the granules turn clear. Stir in the butter; cool slightly. Combine the egg yolks, vanilla, sugar, salt, and ¾ cup of the coconut. Add to the milk mixture, beating all the while. Mix well. Fold in the egg whites. Pour into the buttered soufflé dish and place it in a pan of hot water to a depth halfway up the soufflé.

Bake for 30 minutes. Sprinkle with the remaining coconut, and bake another 20 to 30 minutes, or until the soufflé is puffy and firm. The soufflé will deflate after it's pulled from the oven and begins to cool—this is normal.

To Serve

Serve in fancy dessert dishes, sprinkled with toasted coconut for garnish.

2 cups whole milk

⅓ cup granulated tapioca

2 tablespoons butter

3 egg yolks, beaten well

1 teaspoon vanilla extract

⅓ cup sugar

¼ teaspoon salt

1½ cups shredded coconut, divided

3 egg whites, beaten until stiff

Extra shredded coconut, toasted, for garnish

Grand Marnier Soufflé

Serves 6

Note: This finished recipe contains tempered but not fully cooked egg yolks.

⅞ cup sugar

4¼ tablespoons Grand Marnier

4 egg yolks

1 cup heavy cream

Whipped cream for serving (optional)

Wafer cookies for serving (optional)

This dessert is incredibly rich and smooth. Note that when cooking this, it is very important to beat constantly while adding the warm syrup to the beaten egg yolks—this is called "tempering" and it prevents the eggs from curdling and beginning to turn solid. It also keeps the mixture silky smooth and perfectly blended.

Combine 1 cup water, the sugar, and 1¼ tablespoons of the Grand Marnier in a saucepan, and cook to "thread stage" (250°F) to make a syrup. Beat the egg yolks until lemon colored, light, and fluffy. Continuing to beat constantly, pour the syrup mixture in a very thin stream into the egg yolks, until the mixture becomes cool. Whip the cream stiff, and fold in the remaining 3 tablespoons Grand Marnier. Gently fold this mixture into the yolk mixture until nicely incorporated. Transfer the soufflé mixture to 6 individual stemmed glasses, and refrigerate at least 4 hours.

To Serve

Place each dessert glass on a doily-lined dessert plate. Add a wafer cookie to each serving, if you wish. Garnish with additional whipped cream, and serve with long-handled spoons (your iced-tea spoons are perfect for this).

Chocolate Kahlúa Soufflé

Serves 6

Note: This finished recipe contains tempered but not fully cooked egg yolks.

Combine the gelatin and ¼ cup water in a saucepan, and when it is softened, add the Kahlúa and 3 tablespoons of the sugar. Mix and stir constantly over low heat until all is dissolved. Add the chocolate, and continue stirring until melted and the mixture is blended. Remove from the heat.

Beat in the egg yolks, one at a time, beating well after each addition. Set aside to cool. Beat the egg whites and salt until stiff but not dry. Add 5 tablespoons of the remaining sugar gradually, beating constantly, until very stiff. Gently fold the meringue mixture into the chocolate mixture. Whip the heavy cream until stiff with the remaining ⅛ cup sugar. Fold into the chocolate mixture. Transfer to stemmed glasses and chill overnight.

To Serve

Serve chilled with a garnish of whipped cream and/or chocolate curls.

⅝ teaspoon unflavored gelatin

¼ cup Kahlúa

8 tablespoons plus ⅛ cup sugar

4½ ounces semisweet chocolate, chopped, or chocolate chips

3 eggs, separated

Pinch of salt

1 cup heavy cream

Shaved chocolate curls (optional)

Whipped cream for garnishing (optional)

To make **Chocolate Curls,** gently slide your potato peeler down the side of a room-temperature chocolate candy bar or a block of baker's chocolate. This makes a wonderful garnish on any dessert for which you desire additional chocolate flavor.

Simple Whipped Crème Chantilly

Makes about 2 to 3 cups filling or topping for fancy desserts

1 cup heavy cream

1 tablespoon confectioners' sugar

1 tablespoon sweet cream sherry

Use when you want to add that extra touch.

Whip the cream and sugar in a very cold bowl using an electric mixer with very cold beaters until almost thickened to desired consistency. Add the sherry, and finish beating until just stiff. Do not overwhip or the sauce may separate. Store in the refrigerator.

To Serve

Use as a delicate filling for crêpes, meringue shells, cream puffs, or éclairs or as a topping on fruits or pound cake.

> Whipped Crème Chantilly makes an excellent (non-egg) substitute topping for desserts calling for the Whipped Cream Dessert Sauce (which includes raw egg).

Baked Peach Pudding

Serves 6

A bit of comfort food…

Preheat the oven to 350°F and butter a 1½-quart baking dish. Pour the milk over the bread crumbs; set aside to cool. Add the sugar, eggs, nutmeg, and salt; mix. Fold in the peaches. Pour into the prepared baking dish; dot with the butter. Bake for about 25 minutes or until the peaches are tender and the pudding is set.

To Serve

Serve in glass dishes with a dash of nutmeg on top.

2 cups whole milk, scalded

2 cups whole wheat bread crumbs

⅔ cup sugar

2 eggs, beaten

⅛ teaspoon nutmeg

⅛ teaspoon salt

2 cups fresh peaches, peeled (see page 192) and sliced (or canned peaches if fresh are not available)

2 tablespoons butter

Dash nutmeg for garnish

Mother's Pineapple Whipped Cream Cake

Serves 8 to 10

For the Cake:

2¼ cups all-purpose flour

1½ cups sugar

1 tablespoon baking powder

1 teaspoon salt

½ cup vegetable oil

5 egg yolks

¾ cup pineapple juice

8 egg whites

½ teaspoon cream of tartar

For the Filling and Frosting:

2 cups chilled heavy cream

1 (20-ounce) can crushed pineapple, thoroughly drained and chilled

Light but sweet, pineapple desserts make the perfect ending after rich meals. There's something very clean and refreshing about pineapple.

Preheat the oven to 350°F.

Sift together the flour, sugar, baking powder, and salt. Make a well in the center, and add, in the order given, the oil, egg yolks, and pineapple juice, beating until silky-smooth. In a separate large bowl, beat the egg whites with the cream of tartar until stiff. Gently pour the flour mixture evenly over the stiff egg whites. Fold gently to incorporate. The final batter should be very light.

Bake in an ungreased 10-inch tube pan for 1 hour. Remove from the oven, and invert the tube pan to cool. Meanwhile, whip the chilled cream until stiff, and gently fold in the very well-drained and chilled crushed pineapple. Store the mixture in the refrigerator, and frost the cake shortly before serving time.

To Serve

Shortly before serving, split the cooled cake into two layers. Fill and frost with the chilled whipped cream-pineapple mixture. Once the cake is filled and frosted, refrigerate until serving. Slice generous portions onto dessert plates, and serve immediately. Return leftovers to the refrigerator.

MaryAnn's No-Bake Cheesecake
Serves 12

This cheesecake is so creamy that no one will believe it's not baked.

Crush the vanilla wafers, and mix with the melted butter. Pat the crust into a 9 x 13-inch pan; set aside. Combine the cream cheese, sour cream, sugar, and vanilla. Using an electric mixer, beat until creamy. Fold in the nondairy whipped topping, And spoon over the vanilla wafer crust. Refrigerate until firm.

To Serve
Cut into slices, and top with your favorite fruit, if desired.

1 (16-ounce) package vanilla wafers

½ cup butter, melted

2 (8-ounce) packages cream cheese, softened

1 (16-ounce) container sour cream

²/₃ cup sugar

1 tablespoon vanilla extract

1 (16-ounce) container nondairy whipped topping

Fresh fruit for garnish (optional)

Mom's Strawberry Cake

Makes 12 servings

1½ cups mini marshmallows

1½ cups sugar

½ cup butter, softened

2½ cups all-purpose flour

3 teaspoons baking powder

¼ teaspoon salt

1 cup whole milk

1 teaspoon vanilla extract

3 eggs

3 cups strawberries, sliced

1 (3-ounce) package strawberry gelatin

Sweetened whipped cream for serving

This was one of my Mom's favorite desserts—a confection made in heaven.

Preheat the oven to 350°F. Grease a 9 x 13-inch pan and line the bottom of the pan with the marshmallows.

Cream together the sugar and butter; set aside. Mix together the flour, baking powder, and salt; set aside. Mix the milk with the vanilla and eggs; set aside. Combine all the mixtures, mix together well, and distribute the batter over the marshmallows. Combine the strawberries and gelatin. Spoon the strawberry mixture evenly over the batter. Bake for 45 to 50 minutes. Cool before serving.

To Serve

Top with whipped cream, and watch everybody ask for seconds!

Fruit Cocktail Cake
Serves 16

This is a wonderful family-style dessert to follow a midweek meal.

Preheat the oven to 350°F. Grease a 9 x 13-inch baking pan.

Combine the flour, granulated sugar, salt, baking soda, and baking powder, and mix well. Beat the egg, and add it to the dry mixture. Toss the fruit cocktail with a little flour to coat, and add; stir in the reserved juice. The batter will be quite thin compared to other cakes. Pour the batter into the prepared pan and top with the ½ cup brown sugar and ½ cup nuts.

Bake for 30 to 35 minutes.

To Serve
Let cool and cut into squares. You can serve this cake plain or topped with nondairy whipped topping. Keep leftovers in the refrigerator.

> Here's a hint for baking with fruits and nuts: To stop them from sinking to the bottom of a cake, coat them with a little flour, shaking off any excess. Then put them in the preheating oven for 2 minutes, while it's warming up, to set the flour coating. The fruit or nuts are now ready to use in the recipe.

For the Cake:

1 cup plus 2 tablespoons all-purpose flour

1 cup granulated sugar

1 teaspoon salt

1 teaspoon baking soda

1 teaspoon baking powder

1 egg

1 (24-ounce) can fruit cocktail, drained and half of the juice reserved

For the Topping:

½ cup brown sugar, packed

½ cup walnuts or pecans, chopped

Nondairy whipped topping (optional)

MaryAnn's Lemon Layer Cake

Serves 12

For the Bottom Layer:

1 cup all-purpose flour

½ cup pecans, chopped

¼ cup butter, softened

For the Filling:

1 (8-ounce) package cream cheese, softened

1 cup confectioners' sugar

1 cup nondairy whipped topping

For the Top Layer:

3 cups whole milk

2 (3.5-ounce) packages instant lemon pudding

1 (0.25-ounce) envelope unflavored gelatin

1 cup nondairy whipped topping, or more, if desired

This luscious dessert can be made up to two days in advance and stored, covered, in the refrigerator.

Preheat the oven to 350°F.

To make the bottom layer, combine the flour, pecans, and butter, and press evenly into the bottom of a 9 x 13-inch baking pan. Bake for 15 minutes. Remove from the oven, and cool to room temperature.

To make the filling, combine the cream cheese, confectioners' sugar, and nondairy whipped topping in a mixing bowl, blending well. Spread this mixture over the cooled crust.

To make the top layer, mix together the milk, lemon pudding, and gelatin. Layer on top of the cream cheese filling. Refrigerate to set the layers, and serve chilled.

To Serve

Top cake with the remaining nondairy whipped topping, if desired, using 1 cup or more. Slice and serve. Return any leftovers to the refrigerator.

> Desserts, bar cookies, tortes, and other baked goods that are made with cream cheese should always be stored in the refrigerator, and any leftovers should be refrigerated after serving.

Lemon Cake

Serves 12

This cake is a crowd pleaser because it's a very showy dessert. It makes a great cake to take along to a friend's house for that special party.

Preheat the oven to 350°F.

To make the cake, sift together the flour, baking powder, and salt; set aside. Cream the butter and sugar thoroughly. Add the egg yolks. Next add the flour mixture, and finally, add the milk and lemon extract. Fold in the stiffly beaten egg whites. Divide the batter evenly among three 9-inch-round cake pans.

Bake for 25 minutes. Remove from the oven, and cool completely before filling and frosting.

Meanwhile, to make the filling, cream the butter, sugar, and eggs together in a mixing bowl. Set the bowl over a saucepan of boiling water, and stir constantly until heated through. Add the lemon juice and zest, and continue to heat until the mixture thickens. Remove the filling from the heat, and let cool.

When both the cake and filling are cool, spread the filling between the layers of the cake. Frost the top and sides of the cake with a frosting of your choice. Refrigerate the cake until serving time.

To Serve

Cut in slices to reveal the layers inside, and serve on a cake plate. Return leftovers to the refrigerator.

For the Cake:

2 cups all-purpose flour

1 tablespoon baking powder

¼ teaspoon salt

6 tablespoons butter

2 cups sugar

6 egg yolks, well beaten

6 egg whites, beaten stiff

1 teaspoon lemon extract

7 tablespoons whole milk

For the Filling:

½ cup butter

1½ cups sugar

3 eggs

Juice and grated zest of 2 lemons

For the Frosting:

Your choice, ready-made or one of the recipes in this book (see index)

Chocolate Lemon Torte

Serves 12

For the Cake:

Cocoa powder for dusting

½ cup butter, softened

2 cups granulated sugar

4 eggs

4 ounces unsweetened chocolate, melted

2 cups all-purpose flour, sifted

2 teaspoons baking powder

½ teaspoon salt

1¼ cups whole milk

2 teaspoons vanilla extract

For the Frosting:

½ cup butter, softened

4 cups confectioners' sugar

3 ounces semisweet chocolate, melted

1 egg

1 teaspoon vanilla extract

⅛ teaspoon salt

1 tablespoon grated lemon zest

1 cup walnuts, chopped

1 ounce chocolate, shaved, for garnish

Thin layers of rich, firm-textured fudge cake with a chocolate-lemon frosting and shaved chocolate pieces—what a combo!

Preheat the oven to 350°F. Grease the sides of three 9-inch-round cake pans; dust with the cocoa. Line the bottoms of the pans with brown paper or parchment paper.

Combine the butter and sugar in a mixing bowl, and beat until light and fluffy. Beat in the eggs, one at a time. Add the unsweetened chocolate, and blend thoroughly. Sift together the flour, baking powder, and salt. Combine the milk and vanilla. Add the dry ingredients alternately with the wet to the creamed mixture, beating well after each addition. Divide the batter evenly among the three pans.

Bake for 30 minutes, or until a toothpick inserted in the center comes out clean. Cool for 5 minutes before removing from the pans. Cool thoroughly on racks before frosting.

Meanwhile, to make the frosting, in a mixing bowl, cream the butter with 1 cup of the confectioners' sugar, the semisweet chocolate, and the egg. Add the remaining 3 cups confectioners' sugar, vanilla, salt, and lemon zest. Using an electric mixer, beat until smooth. Mix to a spreadable consistency, adding more milk if necessary. Spread on the cooled layers, and sprinkle each layer with walnuts. Stack and finish frosting the cake. Garnish with shaved chocolate.

To Serve

Let the frosting set before slicing and serving.

Here's a hint for that perfect frosting: Add a pinch of baking soda to your frosting recipe. It will stay moist and prevent cracking until the last piece of cake has been eaten.

Chocolate Jimmy Cake

Serves 12

Coffee lovers, this cake is for you. Jimmies are the little chocolate sprinkles found in the baking and decorating section of your market.

Preheat the oven to 375°F. Grease and flour a 10-inch tube pan.

Cream the butter in a mixing bowl, using an electric mixer; add the confectioners' sugar, and mix well. Add the egg yolks one at a time, beating well after each addition; set aside. Mix together the baking powder and flour. Add the flour mixture alternately with the coffee to the creamed mixture, mixing after each addition. Stir in the chocolate jimmies, pecans, and vanilla. Fold in the egg whites. Pour the batter into the prepared pan.

Bake for 60 minutes. Cool the cake completely before removing it from the pan.

Meanwhile, to make the frosting, cream all the ingredients together until smooth. Mix to a spreadable consistency, adding more milk, if necessary. Frost the cake, and garnish as desired.

To Serve

Present the cake on a cake plate, slice, and serve.

I sprinkle on multi-colored jimmies for a colorful look, but you could just as readily garnish with dark chocolate curls, shaved coffee-flavored chocolate, crushed pecans, or a crumbled Skor candy bar. Each garnish gives the subtly coffee-flavored cake a different presentation and appearance.

For the Cake:

1 cup butter, softened

2 cups confectioners' sugar

4 egg yolks

2 teaspoons baking powder

2 cups all-purpose flour

1 cup strong coffee, cooled

1 cup chocolate jimmies

½ cup pecans, chopped

1 teaspoon vanilla extract

4 egg whites, beaten until stiff but not dry

For the Frosting:

1 (8-ounce) package cream cheese, softened

2 cups confectioners' sugar

4 tablespoons whole milk

1 teaspoon vanilla extract

Extra jimmies for sprinkling (optional)

Magic Cookie Bars

Makes 16

½ cup butter

1½ cups graham cracker crumbs

1 (14-ounce) can sweetened condensed milk

1 (6-ounce) package semisweet chocolate morsels

1 (3.5-ounce) can flaked coconut

1 cup pecans, chopped

What kid (or adult, for that matter) doesn't love a little magic?

Preheat the oven to 350°F.

Melt the butter in a 9 x 13-inch baking pan while the oven is preheating; swirl to coat the bottom of the pan. Sprinkle the graham cracker crumbs evenly over the melted butter. Pour the sweetened condensed milk evenly over the crumbs. Top evenly with the remaining ingredients in the order given. Gently press down.

Bake for 25 to 30 minutes, or until lightly browned. Remove from the oven, and cool thoroughly before cutting.

To Serve

Cut the cooled bars into squares. Store, loosely covered, at room temperature.

Let the new baker in your house try this recipe as one of his or her first baking projects. It's simple to follow and the results will please any novice baker. I make this recipe on a rainy day with my granddaughters and they are so proud of their dessert. This is a great opportunity to teach oven safety, measuring skills, use of pot holders and equipment, setting a timer, and team cooperation.

Angie's Ranger Cookies
Makes 3 dozen cookies

Let's face it, a good cookie recipe never goes out of style.

Preheat the oven to 350°F. Grease several cookie sheets generously.

Cream together the shortening, granulated sugar, brown sugar, eggs, vanilla, and salt in a large mixing bowl. Mix together the flour, rolled oats, cereal, coconut, baking soda, and baking powder, and incorporate into to the sugar mixture. Mix well. Drop the dough in rounded tablespoonfuls on the prepared sheets about 3 inches apart.

Bake for about 13 minutes. Cool the cookies on wire racks.

To Serve
Place on your favorite cookie platter.

1 cup shortening

1 cup granulated sugar

1 cup brown sugar

2 eggs, well beaten

1 teaspoon vanilla extract

½ teaspoon salt

2½ cups all-purpose flour

1 cup rolled oats

1 cup puffed rice cereal

1 cup shredded coconut

1 teaspoon baking soda

1 teaspoon baking powder

Cherry Oat Dessert Squares

Makes 9 to 12

1 cup chopped walnuts

1 cup quick-cooking rolled oats

¾ cup all-purpose flour

½ cup butter, softened

⅓ cup sugar

½ teaspoon ground cinnamon

1 (21-ounce) can cherry pie filling

Need a last-minute dessert? Try this one, and you will be pleasantly surprised at how fast it is to make and how good it tastes! A great recipe for the novice cook.

Preheat the oven to 375°F.

Mix together the walnuts, oats, flour, butter, and sugar in a large bowl until crumbly. Reserve 1½ cups. Press the remainder into the bottom of a 9-inch-square baking pan. Stir the cinnamon into the cherry pie filling, and spread over the crust. Sprinkle the reserved crumbs evenly over the top, and press in lightly.

Bake for 20 to 25 minutes, or until lightly browned.

To Serve

Cool. Cut into squares, and place on plate.

Six Dessert Sauces from MaryAnn

A choice of a homemade sauce can transform any plain-Jane dessert into an enticing treat. Serving suggestions are included.

Coffee Scotch Sauce
Makes 2 cups

Pour the corn syrup into a bowl. Blend in the pudding mix, instant coffee, and cinnamon. Gradually add the evaporated milk, stirring constantly. Allow the mixture to stand about 10 minutes before using.

To Serve
Serve over ice cream or pound cake. Store in the refrigerator.

Nutty Coffee Scotch Sauce
Prepare as directed above (in the directions for Coffee Scotch Sauce), adding ½ cup chopped pecans or walnuts.

Chocolate Mint Sauce
Prepare as directed above (in the directions for Coffee Scotch Sauce), using chocolate-flavored pudding, omitting the instant coffee and cinnamon, and adding ½ teaspoon mint extract.

Instant Dessert Sauce
Makes 3½ cups

Pour the milk and light cream into bowl. Add the sugar, vanilla, and pudding mix. Prepare as directed on the package. Allow the mixture to set for about 5 minutes. Just before serving, stir the sauce until creamy.

¾ cup light corn syrup

1 (4-ounce) package butterscotch instant pudding

2 tablespoons instant coffee granules

¼ teaspoon ground cinnamon

¾ cup evaporated milk

2½ cups whole milk

½ cup light cream

2 tablespoons sugar

½ teaspoon vanilla extract

1 (3.5-ounce) package instant pudding, any flavor

To Serve

Serve over fruit that is fresh, canned, or frozen; slices of plain cake; or gelatin desserts, selecting the pudding flavor as needed. Store in the refrigerator.

Lemon Dessert Sauce

Prepare Instant Dessert Sauce as directed, omitting the vanilla and using lemon instant pudding. Add 1 teaspoon grated lemon zest. Serve over fresh or canned pear halves topped with crème de menthe (optional); or serve over baked apples.

1½ cups orange juice

1 (3.5-ounce) package vanilla pudding

Pinch of salt

Golden Sauce

Makes 1¾ cups

Pour the orange juice into a mixing bowl. Add the pudding mix and salt. Slowly beat with an electric mixer at low speed just until well blended, about 2 minutes. Let stand to thicken slightly.

To Serve

Serve over gingerbread or ice cream. Store in the refrigerator.

Mom's Glazed Pound Cake

Serves 8

The hint of lemon in the cake and orange in the frosting makes this a special cake.

Preheat the oven to 350°F. Grease and flour a 12-inch loaf pan.

To make the cake, combine all the cake ingredients in a mixing bowl, and using an electric mixer, beat well. Pour the batter into the prepared pan.

Bake for 1 hour.

Meanwhile, to make the glaze, heat the butter, sugar, and orange juice in a small saucepan, stirring until the sugar dissolves and all is blended. Remove the cake from the oven, and pour the glaze over top while the cake is still in the pan. Cool for 1 hour in the pan, and remove it from the pan.

To Serve

Cut into slices. Top with fresh strawberries, if desired, and serve.

Variation

Drizzle a dessert chocolate sauce on each serving plate and lay the cake on top of the sauce. Top with another drizzle of sauce and an orange twist for decoration. Orange and chocolate go great together.

For the Cake:

6 eggs

1½ cups butter, softened

2½ cups confectioners' sugar

2 cups all-purpose flour

1 teaspoon vanilla extract

1 tablespoon lemon juice

For the Glaze:

¼ cup butter

⅔ cup granulated sugar

⅓ cup orange juice

Fresh strawberries for garnish (optional)

Seven

July

"Let them eat cake..."
—Marie Antoinette

Recipes
Summer is busting out all over. It's time for neighborhood and family get-togethers, reunions and block parties, picnics and potlucks.

Mrs. Miller's Chocolate Cake

Miracle Whip Chocolate Cake

My Milky Way Cake

Mandarin Orange Cake

Swiss Chocolate Cake

Chocolate Angel Food Cake

- Magic Chocolate Frosting

- Chocolate Mint Frosting

- Chocolate Marshmallow Frosting

- Chocolate Filling Sauce

Eddie's Lemon Birthday Cake

Ron's Jell-O Cake

Auntie's Fruit Grunt

Whipped Cream 101

Sour Milk 101

Crème Fraîche 101

Ice Cream 101 (for à la mode style)

MaryAnn's Lemon Torte

A Peach of a Pie

Paula's Yogurt Pie

Glazed Strawberry Kiwi Cream Cheese Tart

Banana Berry Brownie Pizza

Strawberry or Peach Shortcake

Fresh Berries Supreme

Fresh Berries with Cream

Banana Delight

Mrs. Miller's Chocolate Cake

Serves 12 to 16

For the Cake:

2 cups all-purpose flour

2 cups granulated sugar

2 teaspoons ground cinnamon

1 teaspoon baking soda

½ cup vegetable oil

¼ cup margarine

4 teaspoons unsweetened cocoa powder

1 cup room-temperature water

½ cup soured milk (see page 157)

2 eggs, beaten

1 teaspoon vanilla extract

For the Glaze:

¼ cup margarine

6 tablespoons whole milk

1 tablespoon plus 1 teaspoon unsweetened cocoa powder

1 (1-pound) box confectioners' sugar

1 teaspoon vanilla extract

Dusting of cocoa powder or chocolate curls, for garnish (optional)

This makes a wonderful sheet cake for large gatherings, buffet tables, picnics, and bake sales. It's easy to transport and ever so delicious to eat. You may be tempted, but do not use butter instead of margarine.

Preheat the oven to 375°F. Grease a 10½ x 15½-inch jelly-roll pan.

Mix together the flour, sugar, cinnamon, and baking soda, in a large bowl; set aside. In a saucepan, bring to a boil the oil, margarine, cocoa, and 1 cup water, stirring to combine. Pour over the flour mixture, and mix together; set aside. Mix together the soured milk, beaten eggs, and vanilla; add to the cake batter, and mix. Pour the batter into the prepared pan.

Bake for 15 to 20 minutes, or until a knife or toothpick inserted into the center comes out clean.

Meanwhile, to make the glaze, bring the margarine, milk, and cocoa to a boil, stirring well. Add the sugar and vanilla, and mix until smooth. Remove the cake from the oven, and transfer it to a wire rack. Spread the boiled frosting onto the hot cake to glaze; leave to cool on the wire rack. Dust the completely cooled cake with cocoa or shaved chocolate for decoration, if desired.

To Serve

Cut the sheet cake into serving-size squares, and serve.

Miracle Whip Chocolate Cake
Serves 12

Who would've thought that Miracle Whip would taste so great in a cake? You'll get rave reviews every time you make this moist and fun cake.

Preheat the oven to 350°F. Grease and flour a 9 x 13-inch baking pan.

To make the cake, sift together the first four ingredients. Add the remaining ingredients in the order given, mixing after each addition. Pour the batter into the prepared pan.

Bake for 30 minutes, or until the cake springs back when touched lightly. This cake may be frosted while hot.

To make the frosting, mix together the sugar, cornstarch, chocolate, and salt in a saucepan. Add the water, and cook over low heat until thick, stirring constantly. Stir in the butter and vanilla until blended and glossy. Spread on the cake while the frosting is still hot.

To Serve
To serve, cut into squares.

For the Cake:

2 cups all-purpose flour

1 cup sugar

4 tablespoons unsweetened cocoa powder

2 teaspoons baking soda

1 cup Miracle Whip

1 cup water

1½ teaspoons vanilla extract

⅛ teaspoon salt

For the Frosting:

1 cup sugar

3 tablespoons cornstarch

2 ounces unsweetened chocolate, chopped

⅛ teaspoon salt

1 cup boiling water

3 tablespoon butter, softened

1 teaspoon vanilla extract

My Milky Way Cake
Serves 8

5 (2.05-ounce) Milky Way bars

½ cup butter

1 cup sugar

⅓ cup buttermilk

1¼ cups all-purpose flour

⅛ teaspoon salt

⅛ teaspoon baking soda

2 eggs

1⅛ teaspoons vanilla extract

½ cup pecans, finely chopped

Serve with an ice-cold glass of milk.

Preheat the oven to 275°F. Melt 1½ of the candy bars with the butter, stirring until blended. Add the sugar and beat until creamy. Add the buttermilk. Combine the flour, salt, and baking soda, and add to the batter mixture. Continue mixing. Add the eggs, one at a time, beating well after each addition. Add the vanilla. Chop the remaining candy bars, and fold into the batter. Fold in the chopped pecans, and mix well.

Bake in a loaf pan for 2 hours, checking for doneness at 1½ hours. Cool the cake and dust with confectioners' sugar, if desired.

To Serve
Cut with a clean knife into slices, and serve.

Mandarin Orange Cake

Serves 16

Not all things sublime have to be chocolate…

Preheat the oven to 350°F. Grease and flour a 9 x 13-inch baking pan.

To make the cake, mix the ingredients in the order given in a large mixing bowl, and, using an electric mixer, beat well. Pour the batter into the prepared pan.

Bake for 45 minutes. Immediately after removing the cake from the oven, poke holes with a fork down to the bottom of cake pan. Let cool.

Meanwhile, to make the icing, combine all the ingredients in a 3-quart saucepan. Heat the mixture over medium heat, and let boil for 3 minutes, stirring constantly to prevent burning. Remove from the heat, and pour evenly over the cooled cake, letting the icing drizzle down into the holes pierced in the cake.

To Serve

Cool completely before serving. Cut into squares and, if you desire, garnish with a few additional mandarin orange slices on each plate.

For the Cake:

2 cups all-purpose flour

2 cups granulated sugar

2 eggs

2 teaspoons baking soda

2 (12-ounce) cans mandarin oranges, drained

2 teaspoons vanilla extract

1 teaspoon salt

½ cup walnuts, chopped

For the Icing:

1½ cups brown sugar

6 tablespoons butter

6 tablespoons whole milk

Extra mandarin orange slices for garnishing (optional)

To grease and flour a baking pan: With a paper towel, spread about 1 tablespoon of shortening (do not use butter) evenly over the bottom and sides of the pan, covering the surfaces completely with a thin film. Discard any extra unused shortening; the amount you need depends on the size of the pan. Put 1 or 2 tablespoons of flour in the pan; tilt and tap the pan to evenly distribute the flour over all the greased surfaces. Shake out any excess flour, and discard.

Only grease and flour a pan when it is called for; if it's not mentioned, it's not needed, such as in chiffon and angel cakes, baked in a tube pan.

Swiss Chocolate Cake

Serves 12

For the Cake:

½ cup shortening

1 teaspoon vanilla extract

¾ teaspoon salt

1½ cups granulated sugar

2 eggs, unbeaten

1 ounce chocolate, melted

2 cups cake flour

2½ teaspoons baking powder

1 cup evaporated milk

For the Frosting:

1 (8-ounce) package cream cheese, softened

4 tablespoons milk

2 cups confectioners' sugar

1 ounce chocolate, melted

½ teaspoon vanilla extract

Whipped cream for garnish (optional)

If you have a craving for chocolate, this recipe is for you!

Preheat the oven to 350°F.

To make the cake, combine the shortening, vanilla, and salt in a large mixing bowl, and beat together. Add the sugar gradually, and cream together after each addition. Add the eggs one at a time, blending after each addition. Blend in the chocolate. Sift together the flour and baking powder. Add the flour mixture and milk alternately to the batter, blending after each addition. Pour the batter into two 8-inch-square baking pans.

Bake for 25 to 30 minutes. Cool.

Meanwhile, to make the frosting, combine all the frosting ingredients together, and beat until smooth. Spread the frosting on the cooled cake.

To Serve

Garnish cake slices with whipped cream, if desired.

The recipe calls for cake flour—but what if you only have all-purpose flour on hand? Here's the solution: for each cup of cake flour needed, mix together ⅞ cup all-purpose flour with 2 tablespoons cornstarch; then sift five times to lighten and completely combine the mixture.

Chocolate Angel Food Cake

Serves 12

Beating egg whites with sugar and cocoa adds a special taste to this cake.

Preheat the oven to 375°F.

Add 1 tablespoon water to the egg whites, and let stand until the mixture reaches room temperature. Sift the sugar and cocoa together; set aside. Sift the flour with the salt; set aside. Beat the egg white mixture until foamy; add the cream of tartar, and continue beating until the mixture holds a peak. Continue beating while slowly adding the sugar/cocoa mixture. Fold in the flour mixture, and add the vanilla, mixing well. Pour the batter into a 10-inch ungreased tube pan.

Bake for 40 minutes, or until the top of the cake springs back when lightly touched. Remove from the oven, and immediately invert the cake to cool thoroughly before removing it from the pan. If your tube pan does not have feet, or the cake has risen too high and touches the counter when inverted, invert the pan over a slim-necked glass bottle, fitted into the center tube—this raises the cake up off the counter so it can cool properly. Cool before frosting.

To Serve

Once it's cooled, run a knife around the side of the pan to loosen the cake. Unmold the cake, remove the center tube, and place the cake on a serving platter. Frost with a chocolate or white frosting. Pick one from our book, try the one that follows, or use a store-bought frosting. Slice and serve.

1½ cups egg whites (about 12)

2 cups sugar

½ cup unsweetened cocoa powder

1 cup cake flour (See note on p. 150 for substituting with all-purpose flour.)

1½ teaspoons salt

1 teaspoon cream of tartar

1 teaspoon vanilla extract

Chocolate or white frosting of your choice

Be careful when you are separating the egg whites that you don't accidentally get any yolk in with the white, which will cause the whites to beat hard and not become fluffy, no matter how long you beat them. I separate each egg over a small bowl and then transfer it. You'd hate to contaminate your batch of whites on the eleventh or twelfth egg!

For angel food cakes, sponge cakes, and chiffon cakes, it is not necessary to grease the baking pan, unless the recipe specifically calls for it. These airy cakes need to cling to the side of the pan to rise properly while baking. The recipe will either simply say "pour the batter into the tube pan" or "pour the batter into an ungreased tube pan."

3 ounces bittersweet chocolate

1⅓ cups condensed milk

Magic Chocolate Frosting

Frosts 1 cake

Don't be afraid to experiment with different extracts for different flavors.

Melt the chocolate in a double boiler. Add the condensed milk, and stir over boiling water for about 5 minutes or until thickened. Stir in 1 tablespoon water. Spread on the cooled cake. Note: If you want a milder-flavored frosting, you may reduce the amount of chocolate to 2 ounces.

Chocolate Mint Frosting

Follow directions for Magic Chocolate Frosting, adding 3 drops of peppermint extract instead of the water.

Chocolate Marshmallow Frosting

Follow directions for Magic Chocolate Frosting, substituting 8 quartered marshmallows for the water.

Chocolate Filling Sauce

Follow directions for Magic Chocolate Frosting, adding between ½ cup to 1 cup hot water, depending upon the consistency desired.

Eddie's Lemon Birthday Cake

Serves 12

Not just for his birthday, Eddie liked to eat this cake any time of the year.

Preheat the oven to 350°F. Grease and flour a 9 x 13-inch baking pan.

To make the cake, mix together the cake mix, gelatin, eggs, water or lemon juice, and oil. Beat until smooth, according to cake-package directions. Pour into the prepared pan.

Bake for 30 to 35 minutes, or until the center of the cake springs back when touched. Let cool 20 minutes. Meanwhile, to make the glaze, combine the confectioners' sugar and the lemon juice. Puncture the cake all over with the tines of a dinner fork. Pour the glaze over the cake, letting it drizzle into the holes.

To Serve

Cut into squares, and serve.

I asked my friend, Janice, to add this recipe to our book in honor of her late son, Eddie. Along with her recipe came this cute story: "I sent this cake to Eddie when he was in the Navy. Every birthday Eddie would ask for this cake, so I baked it in coffee cans (so that it wouldn't be crumbs when he got it) and sent it off to parts unknown. It wasn't until he returned home on leave that he told me the top of each cake had been moldy when it arrived! He said it didn't matter...his shipmates cut off the moldy part and ate it anyway!"

For the Cake:

1 (18-ounce) package yellow layer cake mix

1 (3-ounce) package lemon gelatin

4 eggs

¾ cup water or lemon juice (depending on how lemony you want your cake)

¾ cup vegetable oil

For the Glaze:

¾ cup confectioners' sugar

½ cup lemon juice

Ron's Jell-O Cake

Serves 12 happy kids

1 (18-ounce) box yellow layer cake mix

1 (3-ounce) envelope flavored gelatin of your choice

Whipped cream or nondairy whipped topping for serving

This is a fun kid's dessert. Kids always love the way the gelatin makes patterns throughout the cake.

Preheat the oven according to the baking instructions on the cake mix box. Mix the cake according to the package directions, and bake the cake in a greased and floured 9 x 13-inch baking pan. Remove the cake from the oven, and pierce all over with the tines of a fork. Prepare the gelatin according to the package instructions, and pour over the cake, letting the gelatin run into all the pierced holes. Chill in the refrigerator at least 6 hours to set.

To Serve

Cut into squares, and serve topped with whipped cream or nondairy whipped topping.

Auntie's Fruit Grunt
Serves 6

This is a fun recipe if you are on vacation and berry picking is accessible. Send your kids out to pick a few berries for this wonderful cake. They will be so proud of their part in making this dessert!

Preheat the oven according to the baking instructions on the cake mix box. Butter a loaf pan. Spread the berries in the bottom, and sprinkle them with the sugar. Mix the cake according to the package instructions, and pour over the berries. Bake as directed on the cake mix package. Cool the cake before unmolding.

To Serve
To serve, invert the loaf onto a serving plate, and cut in slices. Top each slice with whipped cream or vanilla ice cream.

If you can't find the smaller cake mix, substitute half of a standard (18-ounce) cake mix—or make two loaf cakes!

1 to 1½ cups freshly picked berries, such as blueberries, blackberries, or red raspberries

¼ to ⅓ cup sugar

1 (9-ounce) box yellow cake mix

Whipped Cream 101

There is nothing more divine than a cloud of perfectly whipped cream to top a dessert.

The best way to whip cream is to prechill the bowl, the beaters, and the cream. Have *everything* as cold as possible. Add 1 or 2 tablespoons of sugar, and, using an electric mixer, beat, starting on low and increasing to high speed as the cream thickens. You can also add a few drops of vanilla extract or a tablespoon of liqueur, if you wish to flavor the cream. Beat just until stiff—do not overbeat, or you will end up with almost-butter.

Sour Milk 101

Souring milk is a handy tip to know, especially when your favorite recipe for that perfectly moist chocolate cake calls for buttermilk... and you don't have any!

Many recipes call for buttermilk—if you don't have it handy, soured milk is the next best thing. To sour milk, use this formula: 1 cup whole milk mixed with 1 tablespoon lemon juice or white vinegar. Let stand 5 minutes to thicken and proceed with the recipe. Sour milk is wonderful in chocolate cake and makes a great substitute anytime for buttermilk.

Crème Fraîche 101

1 cup heavy (whipping) cream mixed with 2 tablespoons buttermilk or yogurt

or

1 cup buttermilk mixed with 2 tablespoons fresh lemon juice

The French cousin of sour cream, crème fraîche makes a wonderful departure from our usual dessert toppings of ice cream, sour cream, whipped cream, and others. And it is very easy to make.

Mix and let stand undisturbed in a small covered glass bowl at room temperature all day or overnight until thickened. Then store in the refrigerator for up to 1 week. Use as a topping in place of whipped cream on desserts.

Ice Cream 101 (for à la mode style)

Next to whipped cream, ice cream is probably the most popular topping with which to garnish a dessert, especially on a piece of pie still warm from the oven; atop a rich, crumbly cobbler, and even beside a thick wedge of chocolate cake. Then, of course, there is the infamously decadent brownie sundae! To serve your desserts à la mode, just follow the simple little tip below for that perfect scoop of ice cream that will add just the right touch to your fabulous dessert.

Soften the ice cream slightly before serving as a topping on dessert; you do not want your ice cream to be rock-hard, but rather rich and slightly melty. To do this, remove the ice cream from the freezer, and let stand for ten or fifteen minutes before garnishing your dessert.

MaryAnn's Lemon Torte

Serves 12

For the Crust:

1½ cups all-purpose flour

1½ cups butter, softened

¾ cup pecans, chopped

For the Filling Layers:

1 (8-ounce) package cream cheese, softened

1 cup confectioners' sugar

4 cups nondairy whipped topping, divided

1 (7-ounce) package instant lemon pudding

3 cups whole milk

Make this the night before so it has time to firm up.

Preheat the oven to 350°F.

To make the crust, mix the crust ingredients together, and pat into a 9 x 13-inch pan. Bake for 20 minutes. Set aside to cool before proceeding.

To make the filling layers, beat together the cream cheese and confectioners' sugar until blended. Fold in 2 cups of the nondairy whipped topping, and spread over the top of the cooled crust. For the next layer, mix the lemon pudding with the milk and let thicken. Spread on top of the cream cheese layer. Top with the remaining 2 cups nondairy whipped topping. Refrigerate until firm, several hours or overnight.

To Serve

Cut into squares, and serve. Return any leftovers to refrigerator.

A Peach of a Pie

Serves 6 to 8

You'll know you've had something truly special when you eat this pie.

Put the fresh peaches into a bowl, sprinkling with sugar to taste as you put them in; let stand 15 minutes. Drain, reserving the sugared juice left in the bowl. Set the peaches aside.

Add enough water to the reserved juice to make 1 cup. (If you are using canned peaches, use their juice.) Heat the juice to boiling, and add the gelatin to dissolve. Remove from the heat, and add ½ cup cold water to cool down the mixture. Cut the ice cream into 6 equal pieces, and stir into the still-warm mixture until melted. Chill the mixture until it mounds slightly. Fold in the reserved peaches, and pour the filling into the prepared piecrust. Chill several hours, or until set.

To Serve

Top with whipped cream. You may slice an additional fresh peach for garnish. Return any leftovers to the refrigerator.

In the summer, this is my absolutely most fabulously favorite pie to serve. I get rave reviews every time. The trick is to find perfectly ripe peaches at the peak of their perfection.

3½ cups peeled and sliced fresh peaches or 1 (2.5-pound) can peach slices, drained, juice reserved

Sugar to taste

1 (3-ounce) package lemon gelatin

1 pint vanilla ice cream

1 (9-inch) piecrust, baked and cooled

Whipped cream for serving

Extra peaches for serving (optional)

Paula's Yogurt Pie

Serves 6 to 8

2 cups yogurt, your choice of flavor

1 cup nondairy whipped topping

1 store-bought graham cracker crust, baked and cooled

Fresh fruits of your choice, such as fresh berries, sliced kiwis, or sliced bananas, for serving

Easy. Colorful. Healthy. Summer-fresh. Delightful.

Mix together the yogurt and nondairy whipped topping; pour this filling into the piecrust. Refrigerate until serving time.

To Serve

When ready to serve, garnish the pie with fresh fruits of your choice. Serve immediately. Return any leftovers back to the refrigerator.

Glazed Strawberry Kiwi Cream Cheese Tart

Serves 8

This tart is best if made and served the same day.

Beat together the cream cheese, sugar, and vanilla until smooth. Spread evenly in the cooled piecrust. Decoratively layer on the sliced strawberries and kiwi slices in a pretty pattern, to cover the filling completely. Gently melt the apple jelly in 1 tablespoon water to make a glaze. Spoon the glaze over the fruit, so that all is completely covered and glistening. Refrigerate until serving time.

To Serve

Cut into wedges, and top with sweetened whipped cream. Return any leftovers to the refrigerator.

Try this tart with either a prebaked pastry crust or a graham cracker crust—see which you like better. Change the topping to strawberries and blueberries for a red, white, and blue pie that's perfect for the Fourth of July!

1 (8-ounce) package cream cheese, softened

½ cup sugar

1 teaspoon vanilla extract

1 single 8- or 9-inch piecrust, baked and cooled

Fresh strawberries, sliced in half (enough to cover half the pie)

Fresh kiwis, peeled and sliced (enough to cover half the pie)

3 tablespoons apple jelly

Sweetened whipped cream for serving

Banana Berry Brownie Pizza

Serves 10 to 12

1 (15-ounce) package brownie mix

¼ cup oil

2 eggs

1 (8-ounce) package cream cheese, softened

¼ cup sugar

1 teaspoon vanilla extract

1 cup fresh strawberry slices

1 cup banana slices

2 ounces semisweet chocolate, melted

Nondairy whipped topping or vanilla ice cream, for serving (optional)

Preheat the oven to 350°F. Grease and flour a 12-inch pizza pan.

Bring ⅓ cup cold water to a boil. Combine the brownie mix, hot water, oil, and 1 of the eggs in a large bowl; mix until well blended. Pour into the prepared pan. Bake 25 minutes.

Meanwhile, in a small mixing bowl, using an electric mixer, beat the cream cheese, sugar, remaining egg, and vanilla at medium speed until well-blended. Pour over the crust to cover. Bake 15 minutes longer. Remove from the oven, and cool.

Top the pizza with the fresh fruit slices; drizzle with the melted chocolate.

To Serve

Cut into wedges, and serve like a pizza. Top with some nondairy whipped topping or a scoop of vanilla ice cream, if desired. Store leftovers in the refrigerator.

When my daughter was in high school and would have sleepovers, she and her girl friends would make this "pizza." I think they had as much fun making it as eating it. The biggest choice would be which fruits to use for topping, so sometimes the pizza would be half and half—"deluxe" on one side and just strawberries or bananas on the other, or maybe a new fruit altogether—who says pineapple doesn't go on pizza!

Strawberry or Peach Shortcake
Serves 8

Cool whipped cream, fresh sweet fruit, warm biscuits—it just doesn't get any better than this for a summer dessert.

Slice the fruit, and sprinkle with a little sugar as you layer it into a bowl; let macerate in refrigerator. (The sugar will dissolve onto the fruit and create a little juice.) Whip the cream until stiff with the remaining 2 to 3 tablespoons sugar, and store in the refrigerator. Just before serving, bake the biscuits according to the package instructions. Assemble the shortcake while the biscuits are still warm.

To Serve
Split the biscuits in half, and place 2 halves on each dessert plate. Top with sugared fruit (and any juices) and then with whipped cream. Serve immediately.

Fresh strawberries or peaches, sliced (enough to fill 8 shortcakes to taste)

Sugar to sweeten fruit plus 2 to 3 tablespoons

1 (16.3-ounce) tube jumbo refrigerator buttermilk biscuits

2 cups heavy cream

Fresh Berries Supreme
Flexible recipe

Fresh strawberries, halved, or
whole blueberries

Brown sugar

Sour cream

How can anything so good be so simple?

Place selected berries in individual berry bowls. Pass brown
sugar and sour cream at the table.

To Serve

Sprinkle each serving with brown sugar, top each with a
dollop of sour cream, and sprinkle just a touch more brown
sugar on the sour cream. This serving style also is wonderful
with fresh peach slices. If you don't have berry bowls, use
pretty little dessert cups, teacups, or sherbet glasses.

Berry bowls are shallow little bowls four to five inches
in diameter, used to serve individual portions of fruit.
If you inherited your grandmother's set of fine china, it
probably includes berry bowls. If not, you can hunt for
them in antique shops or at flea markets. It is fun to pick
them up one or two at a time to make a mixed set.

Fresh Berries with Cream

Flexible recipe

Three ingredients, three stars.

Use the best berries of the season. My favorites are sun-ripened raspberries picked on a summer afternoon, or the little wild strawberries growing out by my mailbox. Gently clean and sort just before serving.

To Serve

Serve at room temperature in delicate little bowls, with half-and-half and table sugar to pass.

Perfectly ripe seasonal berries, preferably freshly picked rather than bought

Half-and-half

Sugar

Raspberries are so delicate that they need to be treated gently. Use them as close to purchase or picking as possible, as they do not keep for more than a day or so. I do not wash them. I just pick them over to sort out any leaves or foreign material. As for chemicals and pesticides, rinsing with water doesn't really do any good, other than to remove dirt particles. If you must rinse, do so just before serving or the berries will lose their texture.

Banana Delight

Serves 12

For the Crust:

1½ cups all-purpose flour

1½ cups butter, softened

½ cup pecans, chopped

For the Filling Layers:

1 (8-ounce) package cream cheese, softened

⅔ cup sugar

1 (12-ounce) container nondairy whipped topping, divided

6 bananas, sliced

2 (3½-ounce) packages instant banana pudding

3 cups whole milk

Extra sliced bananas for serving (optional)

This is a very refreshing treat after a long, hot summer day. Go ahead and treat yourself—relax and enjoy.

Lightly grease a 9 x 13-inch baking pan. To make the crust, mix together the flour, butter, and pecans to form a crust. Spread the crust into the prepared pan, patting down firmly; set aside.

To make the filling layer, using an electric mixer, cream together the cream cheese, sugar, and 6 ounces of the nondairy whipped topping. Spread this mixture over the crust to make the first filling layer. Layer on the banana slices for the second filling layer. In another bowl, combine the pudding and milk, and beat until smooth. Pour the pudding mixture over the banana layer to cover entirely to make the third layer. Top with the remaining nondairy whipped topping to make the final layer. Refrigerate until set and ready to serve.

To Serve

Cut into squares, and gently scoop onto serving plates. You can garnish with a little more sliced banana right at serving time, if you wish. Return leftovers to the refrigerator.

Eight

August

"Chameleons feed on light and air:
Poets' food is love and fame."
—Percy Bysshe Shelley, "An Exhortation"

Recipes
Neither poetry nor prose can express the desserts of August.

No-Fail Formula for the Best Piecrust Ever

Marie's Six-Secret Formula for Summer Fruit Pies

The Cutover Wild Blueberry Pie

Currant-Glazed Strawberry or Raspberry Tart

Crumb Crusts for Pies

- Graham Cracker or Zwieback Crumb Crust

- Chocolate Cookie Crumb Crust

- Gingersnap Crumb Crust

Cherry Cream Cheese Pie

MaryAnn's Lemon Squares

Summer Melon à la Mode

Ice Cream Parfaits Cardinal

Peach Parfait with Blueberries

Baked Peach Custard

Betty's Peach Betty

Bananas Foster

The Rush Hour Cook's Banana Boats

Chocolate Chip Zucchini Cake

Nutritious Zucchini Cookies

No-Fail Formula for the Best Piecrust Ever

2 parts all-purpose flour (about 1 to 1¼ cups for a single crust pie; 2 to 2½ cups for a double crust pie)

1 part lard (found in the refrigerated section of your market; comes wax paper-wrapped like a pound block of butter) or vegetable shortening

Generous pinch of salt

Ice water (about 3 tablespoons or so for a single crust pie; 5 to 6 tablespoons for a double crust pie)

Using a wire pastry cutter or two forks, mix the flour with the lard until the particles are the size of small peas. Add the salt. Add the ice water, 1 tablespoon at a time, mixing just until the dough starts to bind together. Try not to use too much water, and do not overwork the dough; work lightly and quickly.

To Use

Flour a work surface and a rolling pin. Roll out the dough, 1 crust at a time, to about ⅛-inch thick. Gently roll the crust around the rolling pin, lift, and place over a pie plate. Unroll the dough, and pat into the pie plate, with the dough generously draping over the edge. This extra dough will be crimped (pinched) to form the rim of a single crust pie, or crimped together with a top crust, to seal the edges of a double-crust pie. Always pierce the top crust with vent-holes or slits to allow steam to escape.

A generously crimped edge is the sign of a good from-scratch pie. It does take a little practice, but making your own crust can be fun. Just remember not to overwork the pastry, and to use icy-cold water. Fun note: Any remaining scraps can be rolled out by your kids, cut out with cookie cutters, sprinkled with sugar and cinnamon, and baked until crisp on cookie sheets, for a fun treat they can make themselves.

Marie's Six-Secret Formula for Summer Fruit Pies

When you've just picked some berries and don't have a cookbook handy, just remember Grandma's six secrets for your perfect fruit pie.

Bake all fruit pies at 400°F for 45 to 60 minutes.

Use 4 cups fruit and 1 cup sugar for the filling.

Toss the filling with 2 to 3 teaspoons quick-cooking tapioca.

Dot the filling with butter before adding the top crust.

Prick the top crust with a fork to vent.

Serve the pie at room temperature, or slightly warm with ice cream.

A seventh secret: For a pretty pie, brush the unbaked top crust lightly with a little milk or water (just enough to moisten); then sprinkle lightly with a little granulated sugar, and put the pie in the oven to bake.

The Cutover Wild Blueberry Pie

Serves 8

4 cups freshly picked wild
blueberries

1 cup sugar

2 to 3 tablespoons lemon juice

2 to 3 teaspoons tapioca

Pinch of salt

1 recipe double piecrust, made
with lard, using the formula on
page 170

1 tablespoon butter, cut into
pieces, for dotting

Ice cream for serving (optional)

Nothing says summer like a wild blueberry pie!

Preheat the oven to 400°F.

Toss the blueberries with the sugar, lemon juice, half the tapioca, and the salt. Sprinkle the remaining tapioca around the bottom of the piecrust. Pour in the blueberry filling, and dot with the butter. Put on the top crust, and crimp. Cut several slits or prick the crust with fork to vent the crust.

Bake for 45 to 60 minutes. Cool on a wire rack.

To Serve

Cut into wedges (the pie will be juicy), and serve at room temperature or warmed slightly, with ice cream à la mode.

When I was a little girl, around midsummer I used to go blueberry picking with my neighbors. This was quite a privileged invitation, because blueberry spots were guarded like gold within each family. Usually found in a burnt-over clearing from a long-ago forest fire, or a lumber-jacked cutover, the bushes would be shoulder-high with big plump berries and it didn't take long to fill your pail if you timed your visit to the berry patch just right. Those bushes have long been over-grown with poplar and hardwoods, and I've never found another spot quite as good as that one, but I can still remember the taste of that great blueberry pie that was baked with *my* gathered berries.

Currant-Glazed Strawberry or Raspberry Tart

Serves 8

This is the easiest and most spectacular dessert to make, and so luscious. Everyone will ask you for the recipe! If you are a novice cook, you'll wow them with this one!

Bake the pie shell at 450°F for 10 to 12 minutes.

Cool the piecrust completely, and fill it with the whipped cream. Arrange the strawberries or raspberries pointy-side-up (like little mountain peaks) as close together in a single layer as possible on the whipped cream, to cover the whipped cream entirely. Carefully heat the currant jelly and 1 tablespoon water together to dissolve, and make a glaze; this takes only a minute or so, and cool slightly. Pour the glaze over the berries to cover. Refrigerate the tart until serving time.

To Serve

Cut into wedges, and serve. Return any leftovers to refrigerator.

1 single piecrust, unbaked

2 cups heavy cream, sweetened and whipped until stiff

1 pint fresh strawberries, hulled, or raspberries

3 tablespoons currant jelly

Crumb Crusts for Pies

Each recipe makes 1 (8- or 9-inch) piecrust

Of course, you can buy ready-made crusts from your market, or boxed crumb mixes. But sometimes it's fun to make your own from scratch.

1¼ cups crumbs, made from graham crackers or zwieback

6 tablespoons butter, melted

4 tablespoons sugar

Graham Cracker or Zwieback Crumb Crust

Mix together all the ingredients, and pat into a pie plate. For a baked pie shell, bake at 375°F for 6 to 8 minutes; cool before filling. For an unbaked crust, chill for 45 minutes before filling.

1½ cups chocolate wafer crumbs

¼ cup sugar

¼ cup butter, melted

Chocolate Cookie Crumb Crust

Preheat the oven to 450°F. Butter a pie plate. Mix together all of the ingredients, and pat into the prepared pie plate. Bake 5 minutes; cool before filling.

1½ cups gingersnap crumbs

¼ cup softened butter

Gingersnap Crumb Crust

Butter a pie plate. Mix together the crumbs and butter, and press firmly into the prepared pie plate. Chill until set before filling.

To get a uniform crust, pat the shell into a 9-inch pie plate, top with an 8-inch pie plate, and press down firmly. Remove the top pie plate and your piecrust will be evenly formed and ready for you to proceed with the recipe.

Cherry Cream Cheese Pie

Serves 8

This is a delicious pie with almost any crust. Try them all and see which you like best.

To make the filling, beat the cream cheese together with the sugar until fluffy. Blend in the vanilla. Fold in the whipped cream. Spoon the filling into the piecrust. Top with the chilled cherry pie filling. Refrigerate for several hours or overnight.

To Serve

Serve chilled. Return leftovers to the refrigerator.

One single 9-inch piecrust, baked and cooled, or use your choice of a crumb crust from page 174.

For the Filling:

1 (8-ounce) package cream cheese, softened

½ cup confectioners' sugar, sifted

½ teaspoon vanilla extract

1 cup heavy cream, whipped

For the Topping:

1 (20-ounce) can cherry pie filling, well chilled

MaryAnn's Lemon Squares

Makes 9 squares

1 cup all-purpose flour

½ cup butter

¼ cup confectioners' sugar, plus extra for dusting

2 eggs

1 cup granulated sugar

½ teaspoon baking powder

¼ teaspoon salt

2 tablespoons freshly squeezed lemon juice

A true classic, lemon squares are a tasty addition to any cook's cookie repertoire.

Preheat the oven to 350°F.

Cream together the flour, butter, and ¼ cup confectioners' sugar. Press into an ungreased 9-inch square pan. Bake for 20 minutes.

Meanwhile, using an electric mixer, beat together the remaining ingredients until light and fluffy. Pour over the hot crust, and continue baking for 25 minutes more. Cool in the pan.

To Serve

Once cooled, dust lightly with additional confectioners' sugar. Cut into squares, and serve.

Summer Melon à la Mode

Serves 4 to 6

There is just something heavenly about the combination of melon and vanilla ice cream on a summer evening. The number of servings will depend on the size of the melon.

Have your produce manager help you pick a ripe, choice melon. Cut the melon in half lengthwise and, with a spoon, scoop out all of the seeds and discard. Cut the halved melon into generous serving-sized wedges lengthwise.

To Serve

Place the individual wedges on dessert plates. Sprinkle with just a "tidge" of salt (optional) to further enhance the taste of the melon. Place a generous scoop of vanilla ice cream in the center of each melon wedge. Serve immediately.

1 cantaloupe or honeydew melon, at room temperature

Tiny pinch of salt (optional)

Vanilla ice cream for serving

Ice Cream Parfaits Cardinal
Makes 8

For the Sauce:

1 (10-ounce) package frozen raspberries, thawed and drained, syrup reserved

¼ cup sugar

2 tablespoons cornstarch

2 cups sliced fresh strawberries

1 teaspoon lemon juice

For the Layers:

2 cups sour cream

1 to 2 teaspoons sugar (optional)

1 quart French vanilla ice cream or strawberry ice cream

For the Garnish:

Fresh raspberries if available

Whipped cream (optional)

A sundae becomes so much more than a sundae when it's layered in a tall parfait glass.

Put the raspberries in a small bowl. Add enough water to the reserved syrup to make 1 cup. Place the syrup mixture in a saucepan with the sugar and cornstarch, and cook, stirring constantly over medium-high heat to bring to a boil. As the sauce thickens, add the sliced strawberries. Remove from the heat, and stir in the raspberries and lemon juice; chill until serving time.

To make the layers, sweeten the sour cream with the sugar, if desired, and set aside. Soften the ice cream slightly for easy scooping just before serving.

To Serve

In the bottom of each parfait glass, place a scoop of ice cream. Layer on some of the sauce, then some of the sweetened sour cream, then more sauce. Repeat with more ice cream, more sauce, more sour cream, and more sauce. Top with a final (smaller) scoop of ice cream, and garnish with fresh raspberries if available. If you don't have fresh raspberries, you can top with whipped cream and a sliced strawberry or maraschino cherry. Serve with long-handled iced tea or soda spoons.

Peach Parfait with Blueberries

Makes 6

If fresh peaches are unavailable, you can substitute well-drained frozen or canned peaches. Pat dry prior to puréeing.

Combine the peach purée, sugar, honey, and lemon juice in a 2-quart saucepan. Sprinkle the gelatin over the mixture, and let stand 5 minutes. Bring the mixture to a boil, stirring occasionally, over medium-high heat. Remove from the heat, and transfer to a medium-sized bowl. Chill, stirring occasionally, until the mixture begins to thicken, about 1½ hours.

Place the heavy cream in a chilled bowl, and beat until stiff. Fold the whipped cream into the peach mixture. Layer the peach mixture with the fresh blueberries in 6 parfait glasses. Chill the parfaits until set, about 4 hours.

To Serve

Garnish each dessert with a peach slice, several blueberries, and a sprig of mint, if desired.

6 to 7 medium-large fresh peaches, peeled and puréed, to equal 3 cups

¼ cup sugar

1 tablespoon honey

1 tablespoon lemon juice

1½ teaspoons unflavored gelatin

¾ cup heavy cream

2 cups fresh blueberries

Additional peach slices, blueberries, and mint leaves for garnish (optional)

Baked Peach Custard
Serves 9

²/₃ cup sweetened condensed milk

2 cups hot water

¼ teaspoon salt

1 teaspoon vanilla extract

3 eggs, slightly beaten

9 peach halves, fresh or canned

1 teaspoon ground nutmeg

Whipped cream for garnish
(optional)

A luscious peach half hides inside each rich serving of extra creamy custard. If you use canned peaches, drain the halves well before using,

Preheat the oven to 325°F. Grease 9 custard cups.

Blend together the sweetened condensed milk, hot water, salt, and vanilla in a mixing bowl. Add the eggs while stirring rapidly; set aside. Put a peach half into each of the prepared custard cups. Pour the custard on top of the peaches. Sprinkle the tops with the nutmeg. Put the custard cups into a deep pan; fill the pan with hot water to the level of the custard.

Bake about 45 minutes, or until a knife inserted near the center of the custard comes out clean. Cool to room temperature. Refrigerate until serving time.

To Serve
Serve as is, or garnish with whipped cream.

Betty's Peach Betty
Serves 6

When peaches are in season this makes a dessert that is hard to beat. You may make the crumble topping in a food processor rather than by hand, but be careful not to overmix it.

Preheat the oven to 375°F. Butter an ovenproof 2-quart baking dish.

Place the sliced peaches in the prepared dish; sprinkle with the lemon juice.

To make the topping, mix together the first five topping ingredients. Cut in the butter with a wire pastry blender or two forks, until crumbly and evenly mixed. Spread the topping evenly over the peach layer.

Bake for 40 to 45 minutes, or until the peaches are bubbly and fork-tender.

To Serve
Serve warm with ice cream, whipped cream, or crème fraîche (see page 158).

6 to 7 fresh peaches, peeled and sliced

1 tablespoon lemon juice

For the Crumble Topping:

¾ cup all-purpose flour

½ cup granulated sugar

½ cup brown sugar

½ teaspoon ground cinnamon

Pinch of salt

½ cup firm but not hard butter, cut into small pieces

Ice cream, whipped cream, or crème fraîche, for serving

Need a substitute for brown sugar? Here's the formula:

For dark brown sugar: mix together 1 cup white sugar and 1 tablespoon molasses.

For light brown sugar: mix together 1 cup white sugar and 1½ teaspoons molasses.

Bananas Foster

Serves 6

6 tablespoons butter

6 tablespoons brown sugar

6 firm but ripe bananas, peeled and cut on the diagonal into 3 or 4 pieces

½ cup rum or pineapple juice or a mixture of the two

½ teaspoon grated orange zest (optional)

Vanilla ice cream for serving

Thin orange slices, twisted and placed on top as a garnish (optional)

A wow of a dish, and so easy—a lot of bang for your buck!

Heat the butter and brown sugar in a medium-hot skillet over medium heat to make a glaze. Add the banana pieces, and sauté for about 2 minutes to soften, turning to glaze all sides. Reduce the heat to low. Add the rum by using a long-handled ladle, and flambé until the flames die down. (Remember, NEVER, never add liquors to a hot skillet straight from the bottle, unless you want to burn your house down—and then no one will get to enjoy dessert!) Stir in the orange zest, if using.

To Serve

Serve bananas immediately with their sauce, warm, over rich vanilla ice cream in your fanciest dessert dishes. Garnish each dessert with a delicate twist of orange, if using.

Variation

Substitute sliced fresh or canned pineapple for the bananas; sauté and flambé in the above sauce. Serve over thin slices of pound cake topped with ice cream for an equally delicious **Pineapples Foster.**

The Rush Hour Cook's Banana Boats
1 banana serves 1

The next time you go camping or have an outdoor picnic, let the kids make these! Accompany with ghost stories and tall tales.

Peel back the banana peel, but don't remove it completely. Make a slit in the flesh of each banana. Fill the slit with chocolate chips and mini marshmallows. Replace the peel, and wrap the filled banana in foil. Bake over the campfire coals until "ooey-gooey."

To Serve
Remove from the coals, and let cool for a minute or two (remember that marshmallows get very hot). Peel back the foil, and eat warm.

1 banana per serving

1 to 2 tablespoons chocolate chips per serving

1 to 2 tablespoons mini marshmallows per serving

Heavy-duty aluminum foil

A campfire

Chocolate Chip Zucchini Cake

Serves 16

2 cups grated zucchini

½ cup olive oil

1¾ cups sugar

⅓ cup butter, softened

2 eggs

½ teaspoon vanilla extract

½ cup sour milk (see page 157)

2½ cups all-purpose flour

¼ cup unsweetened cocoa powder

1 teaspoon ground cinnamon

1 teaspoon baking soda

½ teaspoon baking powder

¼ cup semisweet chocolate chips

The use of zucchini makes for a nice, moist cake.

Preheat the oven to 350°F. Grease 9 x 13-inch baking pan.

Blend together the zucchini and the olive oil; set aside. Cream together the sugar and the butter until fluffy. Add the zucchini mixture and the eggs, mixing well; set aside. Add the vanilla to the sour milk; set aside. Mix together the flour, cocoa, cinnamon, baking soda, and baking powder. Add the dry ingredients alternately with the sour milk to the zucchini mixture, blending after each addition. Pour the batter into the prepared pan. Sprinkle the top of the batter with the chocolate chips.

Bake for 40 minutes. Cool.

To Serve

Cut into serving-sized squares. This cake tastes really good with a cup of coffee.

Before creaming butter and sugar together, I like to rinse the bowl with boiling water. That way they'll cream faster.

Nutritious Zucchini Cookies
Makes 4 dozen

Who says cookies can't be healthy? These have it all!

Preheat the oven to 350° F. Oil several cookie sheets.

Mix together the zucchini, honey, butter, and beaten egg until well blended; set aside. Sift together the flour, baking soda, spices, and salt. Stir into the creamed butter mixture. Stir in the oats, walnuts, dates, and coconut. Drop by teaspoonfuls on the prepared cookie sheets.

Bake for 10 to 15 minutes, or until lightly browned.

To Serve
Cool the cookies and place on a cookie platter.

1 cup peeled and grated zucchini

2/3 cup honey

1/2 cup butter, softened

1 egg, beaten

1 1/2 cups all-purpose flour

1 teaspoon baking soda

1 teaspoon ground cinnamon

1/2 teaspoon ground nutmeg

1/4 teaspoon ground cloves

1/4 teaspoon salt

1/2 cup rolled oats

1 cup walnuts, chopped

1 cup dates, chopped

1/2 cup shredded coconut

Nine

September

"My tongue is smiling."
—Abigail Trillin

Recipes
The first hints of fall tempt our taste buds.

Peggy's Perfect Plum Cake

Peggy's Prune Whip

Mother's Pineapple Upside-Down Cake

Mom's Glazed Dessert Peaches

• Crockery Version

• Oven-Baked Version

Flambé of Peaches with Sabayon Custard Sauce

• Sabayon Custard Sauce

Captain Jack's Chess Pie

Pumpkin Torte

Chocolate Chip Oatmeal Cake

Chewy Brownies

Chocolate Spice Cake

Buttercream Frosting

Old-Fashioned Caramel Frosting

Chocolate Cupcakes with Seven-Minute Frosting

Cakes in a Jar

Pecan Crunch Cookies

Great-Aunt Betty's Oatmeal Cookies

Great-Aunt Marie's Poor Man's Cookies

Peggy's Perfect Plum Cake

Serves 9

For the Cake:

1 cup all-purpose flour

¼ cup sugar

1 teaspoon baking powder

1 tablespoon vegetable shortening

1 tablespoon butter

9 to 12 fresh blue plums, halved and pitted

For the Topping:

¾ cup sugar

1 teaspoon ground cinnamon

1 tablespoon butter

1 tablespoon all-purpose flour

Whipped cream for serving

This is as homemade as it gets. Warm, rich, old-fashioned, fruity—what else can you ask for?

Preheat the oven to 400°F. Grease generously an 8-inch-square baking pan.

To make the cake, mix together the flour, sugar, and baking powder. Blend in the vegetable shortening and butter to make a crumbly dough. Pat the dough into the bottom and halfway up the sides of the prepared pan. Arrange the halved plums, cut-side up, over the dough, keeping them from touching the sides of the pan.

To make the topping, combine the sugar, cinnamon, butter, and flour, and sprinkle over the plums.

Bake for 10 minutes, and reduce the temperature to 300°F. Bake 40 minutes more. Cover the cake with another pan or with foil, and bake, covered, for 5 minutes more to form a shiny glaze on the top of the plums. Remove the cake from oven, remove cover, and set on a rack to cool.

To Serve

Cut in squares and serve warm or at room temperature, topped with whipped cream.

Peggy's Prune Whip

Serves 6

Note: The finished recipe contains raw egg whites.

Combine the pineapple juice, sugar, and salt in a saucepan, and heat to boiling. Add the prunes and cinnamon. Soften the gelatin in 2 tablespoons cold water, and add to the heated prune mixture; mix thoroughly until gelatin is dissolved. Set aside to cool. When cooled, fold in the whipped cream first, and then fold in the egg whites. Refrigerate in dessert glasses until serving time.

To Serve

Serve chilled. You can sprinkle a dash of cinnamon on each serving, if desired.

¾ cup pineapple juice

⅔ cup sugar

Pinch of salt

1½ cups jarred stewed prunes, pitted and blender-chopped

½ teaspoon ground cinnamon

1 tablespoon unflavored gelatin

1 cup heavy cream, whipped until stiff

2 egg whites, beaten until stiff

This recipe is very old-fashioned and very delicious, a sublime inheritance from my mother. You know, there are many legacies we can leave our children, and I feel my recipe box is one that I can pass on to my daughter and her daughter as well. Really good recipes *never* go out of style and this is one that was (and remains) a favorite of mine to this day.

Mother's Pineapple Upside-Down Cake

Serves 8 to 10

For the Glaze and Fruit:

¼ cup butter, melted

1 cup packed brown sugar

1 (20-ounce) can pineapple rings, drained and juice reserved

Maraschino cherries (1 per pineapple slice)

For the Cake:

1¼ cups all-purpose flour

½ cup granulated sugar

2 teaspoons baking powder

½ teaspoon salt

⅓ cup butter, melted

7 tablespoons reserved pineapple juice

1 egg

Whipped cream for serving

A timeless comfort-food dessert, pineapple upside-down cake is sunny and bright and oh-so-good. My mother always used her well-seasoned cast iron skillet for this recipe!

Preheat the oven to 375°F.

To make the glaze and fruit, cover the bottom of a 10-inch-round baking dish or a 10- to 12-inch cast iron skillet with the melted butter. Sprinkle the brown sugar evenly over the butter. Arrange enough pineapple slices in a single layer on top of the butter-sugar mixture to cover the bottom of the pan Place a cherry in the hole of each pineapple ring. Set the pan aside.

To make the cake, sift together the flour, granulated sugar, baking powder, and salt. Beat in the melted butter, pineapple juice, and egg. Beat for 2 minutes using an electric mixer. Pour the batter evenly over the pineapple-lined skillet.

Bake for 45 minutes. Let the cake cool for at least 5 to 10 minutes before inverting onto a serving platter.

To Serve

Serve warm or at room temperature, topped with whipped cream.

Mom's Glazed Dessert Peaches

1 peach serves 1

Crockery Version

Depending on the size and shape of your slow cooker, you may stack the peaches, if need be.

Butter a slow cooker pot. Peel, halve, and pit the fresh peaches (see page 192 for tips). Place the peaches in the prepared slow cooker pot, pitted sides up. As you arrange them, fill each hollowed center with brown sugar and a dab of butter. Sprinkle with sherry, if desired. Cover with the lid, and cook on high until the peaches are warmed through, glazed, and tender, but still hold their shape, for 1 to 3 hours. Cooking times will vary by slow cooker, the ripeness and size of peaches, and your desired level of tenderness.

To Serve

Serve warm in dessert bowls, with any cooking juices drizzled over the peaches, and a pitcher of half-and-half to pass.

Oven-Baked Version

If you prefer, you can bake the peaches in a 350°F oven rather than using the slow cooker. The cooking time will depend on the size and ripeness of fruit, but do keep an eye on them, checking after 20 minutes or so. You do not want to overcook them. The peaches should be warmed through, tender but not too soft, and should still hold their shape. As in the slow-cooker method, serve warm with half-and-half.

1 fresh peach per person

1 pat butter per peach half

1 pinch brown sugar per peach half

½ teaspoon sherry per peach half (optional)

Half-and-half for serving

Flambé of Peaches with Sabayon Custard Sauce

1 fresh peach (or 2 canned peach halves) serves 1

Fresh peaches, peeled, halved, and pitted, or canned freestone peach halves, drained

1 teaspoon brown sugar per peach half

1 teaspoon butter per peach half

1 sugar cube soaked in brandy per peach half

Preheat the broiler. Arrange the peach halves hollow side up, in a single layer in a broiler-safe pan. Put 1 teaspoon, or more to taste, brown sugar in the center of each peach half. Dot each with butter.

Place under the broiler to warm through and to brown the topping. Bring to the table and place a brandied sugar cube in the center of each peach half. Ignite each sugar cube, and let the flame die off before serving.

To Serve

Serve warm, topped with vanilla ice cream, whipped cream, or chilled Sabayon-Custard Sauce. Allow 2 peach halves per person.

> To easily peel fresh peaches, dip them in scalding water for 30 seconds, remove them with a slotted spoon, and plunge into ice water. Drain, peel, and use in your recipe.

4 egg yolks

¼ cup sugar

¼ teaspoon salt

1½ cups whole milk, scalded

1 teaspoon vanilla extract

Sabayon Custard Sauce

In a saucepan, over a water bath (or in a double-boiler), beat the egg yolks with the sugar and salt. Slowly add in the scalded milk, stirring constantly. Continue stirring and cooking until the mixture thickens enough to coat a spoon. Remove from the heat, and cool; stir in the vanilla. Refrigerate until serving time. Serve as a dessert sauce.

> To scald milk, bring the milk to just under a boil in a saucepan over low heat, stirring occasionally. When small bubbles start to form around the edge of the pot, the milk has been properly heated. Remove from the heat, and use in your recipe while still warm.

Captain Jack's Chess Pie

Serves 8

The rich pastry crust adds to this unique pie.

Preheat the oven to 350°F.

To make the pastry, sift together the flour, salt, and baking powder. Cut in the butter until the size of small peas. Add the milk, 1 tablespoon at a time. Mix until the dough forms a ball. Flour a surface, and roll the dough out to fit a 9-inch deep-dish pie plate. Flute the edge high. Set aside.

To make the filling, cream the sugar and butter. Beat in the flour and cornmeal. Continuing to beat well, add the eggs, milk, lemon juice, and vanilla. Pour the filling into the prepared crust.

Bake about 60 minutes, or until the filling is set. Cool on a wire rack.

To Serve

Serve at room temperature.

For the Rich Pastry:

1 cup all-purpose flour

¼ teaspoon salt

¼ teaspoon baking powder

6 tablespoons firm butter

4 tablespoons cold whole milk

For the Filling:

2 cups sugar

½ cup butter

1 tablespoon all-purpose flour

1 tablespoon yellow cornmeal

5 eggs, beaten well

1 cup whole milk

1½ tablespoons lemon juice

1 teaspoon vanilla extract

Pumpkin Torte
Serves 16

24 graham cracker squares, crushed

½ cup butter, melted

2 cups sugar, divided

2 whole eggs, beaten

1 (8-ounce) package cream cheese, softened

1 (0.25-ounce) envelope unflavored gelatin

1 (16-ounce) can pumpkin purée

3 egg yolks, beaten

½ cup whole milk

1 teaspoon ground cinnamon

¼ teaspoon salt

3 egg whites

Whipped cream or nondairy whipped topping for serving

This torte is a nice departure from traditional pumpkin pie and it makes a spectacular dessert.

Preheat the oven to 350°F.

Mix the graham cracker crumbs, melted butter, and ½ cup of the sugar. Pat into a 9 x 13-inch pan; set aside. To make the second layer, mix the 2 beaten eggs, ¾ cup of the remaining sugar, and the cream cheese. Pour over the crust. Bake for 20 minutes; set aside to cool.

Dissolve the gelatin in ¼ cup cold water, stirring well; set aside. Combine the pumpkin, egg yolks, ½ cup of the remaining sugar, milk, salt, and cinnamon in a saucepan. Cook over medium heat, stirring constantly, until the mixture thickens. Take the pumpkin mixture off the heat, blend in the gelatin mixture, and refrigerate.

Beat the egg whites with the remaining sugar until stiff. Fold into the chilling pumpkin mixture. Pour this final mixture over the cream cheese layer in the crust. Refrigerate the torte until firm, at least 1 hour, before serving.

To Serve
Top with whipped cream or nondairy whipped topping just before serving. Return any leftovers to the refrigerator.

Chocolate Chip Oatmeal Cake

Serves 16

This moist cake is great without frosting.

Preheat the oven to 350°F. Grease and flour a 9 x 13-inch baking pan.

Combine the oats and boiling water. Let stand for 10 minutes. Add the butter, both sugars, and the eggs. Mix together the flour, cocoa, baking soda, and salt, and add to the oat mixture; fold in the chocolate chips. Pour into the prepared pan.

Bake for 30 to 40 minutes. Remove from the oven and cool.

To Serve

Cool before cutting into squares.

1 cup rolled oats

1¾ cups boiling water

½ cup butter

1 cup brown sugar

1 cup granulated sugar

2 eggs

1¾ cups all-purpose flour

2 tablespoons unsweetened cocoa powder

1 teaspoon baking soda

½ teaspoon salt

6 ounces chocolate chips

Chewy Brownies

Makes 8

1 cup all-purpose flour

4 tablespoons unsweetened cocoa powder

2 cups brown sugar

½ cup butter

2 eggs

1½ cups walnuts, chopped

Confectioners' sugar for dusting, sifted

Serve these brownies as is with an ice-cold glass of milk—or for a real treat, top them with vanilla ice cream, chocolate sauce, whipped cream, and a cherry, for an ultimate brownie sundae!

Preheat the oven to 350°F. Line a 7 x 11-inch baking pan with oiled waxed paper.

Sift together the flour and cocoa; set aside. Cream the sugar and butter in a mixing bowl using an electric mixer. Add the eggs, one at a time, beating after each addition. Fold in the flour/cocoa mixture. Add the nuts. Pour into the prepared pan.

Bake for 35 minutes. Remove from the oven, and cool slightly.

To Serve

When slightly cooled, sprinkle with sifted confectioners' sugar. Remove from the pan, and sprinkle the bottom with more sifted confectioners' sugar. When thoroughly cool, cut into squares.

Chocolate Spice Cake

Serves 12

The aromas of cinnamon and nutmeg smell so enticing while this cake is baking.

Preheat the oven to 350°F. Grease a 9 x 13-inch baking pan.

Cream together the sugar and butter. Beat the egg yolks, and add to the creamed mixture. Sift together the flour, cocoa, baking soda, cinnamon, nutmeg, and salt twice, and add to the creamed mixture alternately with the buttermilk, mixing after each addition. Stir in the vanilla. Beat the egg whites until stiff, and fold into the batter. Pour into the prepared pan.

Bake for 50 minutes. Cool before frosting with Buttercream Frosting.

To Serve

Cut into serving-size squares and enjoy.

2 cups sugar

½ cup butter, softened

2 eggs, separated

3 cups all-purpose flour

3 tablespoons unsweetened cocoa powder

2 teaspoons baking soda

2 to 3 teaspoons ground cinnamon, or to taste

½ teaspoon ground nutmeg

¼ teaspoon salt

2 cups buttermilk

1 teaspoon vanilla extract

1 recipe Buttercream Frosting (page 198)

Buttercream Frosting

Makes enough to frost 1 cake

2 cups confectioners' sugar

¼ cup whole milk

Pinch of salt

1 teaspoon butter-vanilla or plain vanilla extract

1 cup vegetable shortening

With this versatile frosting, you can fashion flowers or any design you would like to pipe or mold for fancy cakes. It is great for decorating birthday cakes, wedding cakes, and theme cakes.

Combine the sugar, milk, salt, and butter-vanilla together, and mix well with an electric mixer. Add the shortening, 1/3 cup at a time, mixing well and scraping the bowl after each addition. Beat at medium speed for 8 minutes. When the icing peaks, it is the correct consistency.

To Serve

Frost your favorite cake with this buttery-tasting frosting. Store in a covered container to prevent drying.

Tips for assembling and frosting a cake

1. Cool cake layers completely.
2. Place the bottom (or first) cake layer upside down on a serving plate.
3. Tuck strips of waxed paper under the bottom edges of the cake to keep the platter clean while frosting.
4. Brush any loose crumbs from the cake before applying the frosting.
5. Using a narrow spatula, spread ½ to ⅔ cup of frosting evenly over the top of the layer of cake. Repeat with a second layer, if making a three-layer cake. For a two-layer cake you will need approximately 2 to 2½ cups frosting; for a three-layer cake, approximately 3 to 3½ cups frosting. (These amounts are based on an 8- or 9-inch-round cake.)
6. Place the top cake layer top side up on the cake.
7. Frost with the remaining frosting, doing the sides first and then the top, and merging the two together at the edge.
8. Make decorative swirls in the frosting, using your spatula. Or, after dipping the spatula in hot water, slide it over the frosting to make a smooth surface—particularly nice if decorating the cake with such items as piping or flowers.
9. When you've finished frosting, remove the waxed paper from under the bottom of the cake. Let the cake set for 1 hour before slicing.

Old-Fashioned Caramel Frosting

Makes enough to frost 1 cake

Mix and heat the butter, brown sugar, and cream in a saucepan over medium-high heat, and bring the mixture to a boil. Cook the mixture until it reaches the soft ball stage (235°F to 239°F) on a candy thermometer. Remove from the heat, stir in the vanilla, and beat until thick enough to spread (this can take up to 10 minutes). Let the frosting cool to thicken a little more before using. If the frosting becomes too thick, blend in very hot water, a few drops at a time, until it is a spreadable consistency.

1 cup packed brown sugar

2 tablespoons butter, softened

¼ cup heavy cream

½ teaspoon vanilla extract

If you don't have a candy thermometer, you can test your frosting by dropping a tiny bit of it into cold water. It should keep the form of a ball. If not, keep cooking until it does. Then remove from the heat, and proceed with the recipe.

Chocolate Cupcakes with Seven-Minute Frosting

Serves 18

For the Cupcake Batter:

¼ cup vegetable shortening

1 cup sugar

¼ cup unsweetened cocoa powder

½ cup boiling water

1½ cups all-purpose flour

½ teaspoon baking powder

½ teaspoon baking soda

¼ teaspoon salt

1 egg, beaten

½ cup sour cream

½ teaspoon vanilla extract

For the Seven-Minute Frosting:

2 egg whites

1½ cups sugar

1 tablespoon light corn syrup

1 teaspoon baking powder

½ teaspoon vanilla extract

Nothing beats a homemade chocolate cupcake!

Preheat the oven to 350°F. Grease two standard cupcake pans.

To make the cupcake batter, combine the shortening, sugar, and cocoa, and add the boiling water. Beat until the sugar dissolves. Sift together the flour, baking powder, baking soda, and salt, and set aside. Mix together the egg, sour cream, and vanilla. Add the dry ingredients alternately with the wet ingredients to the shortening mixture, mixing well after each addition. Fill the prepared cupcake pans half full.

Bake for 25 minutes. Cool the cupcakes completely before frosting.

Meanwhile, to make the frosting, combine the egg whites, sugar, corn syrup, and 5 tablespoons cold water in the top of a double boiler set over boiling water. Stir the mixture until the sugar is dissolved, and cook for 2 minutes without stirring. Remove the double boiler from the heat, and with a hand-held mixer, beat the mixture for 7 minutes, or until the frosting holds its shape and stands in peaks. Stir in the vanilla and baking powder, mixing well.

To Serve

Frost and decorate as desired. Arrange the cupcakes on a platter and serve.

> You may add a few drops of food coloring to the frosting, if you wish.

Cakes in a Jar

Makes 6 to 8 small cakes

This is a fun recipe for experimenting. I like to use a spice cake mix best for this recipe, adding a handful of currants or raisins tossed with a little flour to coat to the batter. Use canning glass jars with proper lids, prepped and ready. You might not use them all, but it's best not to be caught short!

1 (18-ounce) box cake mix, your choice

6 to 8 sterilized (1-pint) wide-mouthed, straight-sided Mason or Kerr jars

Stove-Top Method for Sterilizing Jars

Start by putting the jars and lids through the dishwasher, or hand-wash and air-dry them. Then place the jars, mouth end down, along with the lids in a pan filled 1 inch deep with boiling water. Let jars steam, boil, and bubble in the pan for 10 minutes. Using tongs, carefully remove the jars and lids from the water, and invert to air dry, undisturbed, on a clean kitchen towel. Any water remaining in the jars will evaporate out as they sit on your counter.

Cake Preparation

Preheat the oven to 325°F. Generously grease the inside of each sterilized jar with shortening.

Mix your cake according to the package directions. Carefully pour 1 cup batter into each jar; jars should be filled only halfway, as the cake will rise as it bakes. Wipe off any batter that spills onto the rims with a paper towel. Set the jars on a cookie sheet, and bake for about 40 minutes, or until a toothpick inserted into the center comes out clean. Remove the jars one at a time from the oven and *immediately*, while the cake is very hot, screw on a sterilized lid to create a vacuum seal. Make sure the rim of the jar is still clean, wiping with a paper towel, if necessary. This creates a proper seal. Let the jarred cakes cool on the kitchen counter, undisturbed. The lids "ping" as they indent to form their proper seal.

To Serve

Store the sealed cakes in the refrigerator for up to 2 weeks or indefinitely in the freezer. Serve in their jars, letting guests open their own cake from their own jar.

Just for fun, make a cake for each dinner guest. Decorate the jars, add name tags, and use at each table setting as a place card. If your guests are too full for dessert after dinner, they can take their dessert home!

Pecan Crunch Cookies
Makes 3½ dozen

When I first tried this recipe, I was so fascinated by the use of potato chips. Who would've ever thought!

Preheat the oven to 350°F.

Cream together the butter, sugar, and vanilla in a mixing bowl. Add the potato chips and pecans. Stir in the flour. Form the dough into small balls, using about 1 tablespoon dough for each. Place the balls on an ungreased cookie sheet, and press the balls flat with a tumbler dipped in sugar.

Bake for 16 to 18 minutes, or until the cookies are lightly browned. Remove from the oven, and cool.

To Serve
Serve on a pretty cookie plate, and have people try to guess the "secret ingredient."

1 cup butter, softened

½ cup sugar

1 teaspoon vanilla extract

½ cup crushed potato chips

½ cup pecans, chopped

2 cups all-purpose flour

Great-Aunt Betty's Oatmeal Cookies

Makes about 4 dozen

2 cups packed brown sugar

1 cup shortening

2 eggs

1¾ cups all-purpose flour

1 teaspoon baking soda

1 teaspoon salt

¼ teaspoon ground cinnamon

1½ cups quick-cooking rolled oats

1 cup raisins

These cookies are awesome and store beautifully. They seem to be even better the next day. For a variation, substitute sweetened dried cranberries for the raisins.

Preheat the oven to 375°F.

Cream together the sugar and shortening until fluffy. Beat in the eggs. Sift together the flour, baking soda, salt, and cinnamon; add to the creamed mixture, and mix well. Fold in the oats, and stir in the raisins. Drop by rounded teaspoonfuls onto ungreased cookie sheets, leaving room in between for the cookies to spread.

Bake for 10 to 12 minutes.

To Serve

Cool completely and store in airtight container.

Great-Aunt Marie's Poor Man's Cookies

Makes 3 to 4 dozen

Preheat the oven to 350°F.

Combine the sugar, raisins, 1 cup water, shortening, and, salt, and bring to a boil over medium heat; boil for 10 minutes. Remove from the heat, and add the flour, baking soda, cinnamon, and vanilla. Spread the batter in a 9 x 13-inch baking pan.

Bake for 20 minutes. Remove the pan from the oven. While hot, frost with In-a-Pinch Icing. Let cool completely in the pan.

To Serve

Cut into squares for serving.

1 cup sugar

1 cup raisins

½ cup shortening

½ teaspoon salt

2 cups all-purpose flour

1 teaspoon baking soda

1 teaspoon ground cinnamon

1 teaspoon vanilla extract

1 recipe In-a-Pinch Icing (page 20)

Both my Great-Aunt Betty and my Great-Aunt Marie kept their households during the Depression and the World Wars. Undaunted, they were wonderful cooks and created delicious treats with both limited ingredients and limited funds. This recipe is just further proof that it doesn't have to be fancy to be good. I always looked forward to their visits because they each would bring a tin of their delicious cookies, and now I am lucky enough to have their recipes.

Ten

October

"October is crisp days and cool nights, a time to curl up around the dancing flames…"
—John Sinor

Recipes
Hearty desserts begin to warm the chilling nights.

Angie's Baked Apple Dumplings

Betty's Baked Apples

Betty's Apple Betty

Harriet's Hot Cinnamon Apple Crisp

Baked Bananas with Cranberry Sauce

Baked Apple Butter Bananas

Pumpkin Bars with Cream Cheese Frosting

Margarite's Upside-Down Apple Pie

Meringue-Topped Apple Pie

Apple Crumb Pie

• Traditional Double-Crust Apple Pie

• Seven Ways to Sensationalize Your Apple Pie

Old-Fashioned Sour Cream and Raisin Pie

Glenn's Apple Carrot Cake

Apple Butter Cake

Northwoods Cranberry Torte

Elegant but Easy Cranberry Mousse

• Cranberry Mousse Pie

Magic Baked Custard

Angie's Baked Apple Dumplings
Makes 12

2 cups all-purpose flour

2 teaspoons baking powder

1/8 teaspoon salt

2/3 cup plus 4 tablespoons butter

1/2 cup whole milk

6 cooking apples, cored, halved, and peeled

1/2 cup raisins

2 cups brown sugar

1 teaspoon ground cinnamon

1/2 teaspoon ground nutmeg

Half-and-half for serving

Angie makes these dumplings for her two daughters, who love apples. It's my husband's and my favorite, too. Mmm-mmm good; she can make these for me anytime!

Preheat the oven to 375°F.

Sift together the first three ingredients, and cut in 2/3 cup butter with a pastry blender. Gradually add the milk until the soft dough reaches the consistency for rolling out. Flour a surface, and roll dough out to 1/8 to 1/4-inch thick. Cut into twelve equal squares.

Place an apple half in the center of each square, and sprinkle with a few raisins. Bring the corners of the dough to the top of each apple, and press to seal. Place the dumplings in a shallow baking dish. Make a syrup by combining the brown sugar, 2 cups water, and the remaining 4 tablespoons butter, cooking until blended and thickened. Pour over the dumplings. Mix together the cinnamon and nutmeg and sprinkle on each dumpling.

Bake for 30 to 35 minutes.

To Serve
Serve warm with pan juices and pass half-and-half at the table.

Betty's Baked Apples

1 apple serves 1

This is a dish that I fondly remember my mother making every autumn, as soon as the new crop of apples came in. Granny Smith, Gala, Rome Beauties, or Cortlands make great choices for this recipe. The addition of the half-and-half turns the warm apples from delicious to spectacular.

Preheat the oven to 400°F.

Wash and core each apple. Pare off the peel from the top one-quarter of each apple. Fill the hollowed-out cores with the brown sugar, and dot with the butter. Or, fill with one of the optional additions, then add the brown sugar and butter. Place the apples side by side in a baking dish. Fill with water to a depth of ¾-inch around the apples.

Bake for 30 minutes, or until the apples are very tender but still hold their shape. When done, carefully remove the apples from the baking dish with a slotted spoon.

To Serve

Serve warm in dessert bowls, and pass the half-and-half to pour over the apples.

1 cooking apples of your choice, per serving

1 tablespoon brown sugar per serving

1 teaspoon butter per serving

Optional additions: raisins, nuts, dried cherries, pre-sweetened dried cranberries

Half-and-half for serving

Betty's Apple Betty

Serves 6

4 to 5 cups peeled, cored, and sliced tart cooking apples

1 tablespoon lemon juice

For the Crumble Topping:

¾ cup all-purpose flour

½ cup granulated sugar

½ cup brown sugar

½ teaspoon ground cinnamon

Pinch of salt

½ cup firm butter, cut into small pieces

Ice cream, whipped cream, or crème fraîche (see page 158) for serving

Spend an afternoon with your children at a local apple orchard or roadside stand selecting apples for this wonderful dessert! You may make the crumble topping by pulsing in your food processor, rather than mixing by hand, if you wish. But be careful not to overwork the mixture.

Preheat the oven to 375°F. Butter an ovenproof 2-quart square baking dish. Place the apples in the prepared dish; sprinkle with the lemon juice.

To make the topping, mix together the first five ingredients. Cut in the butter with a wire pastry blender or two forks until crumbly and evenly mixed. Spread the topping evenly over the apple layer.

Bake for 40 to 45 minutes, or until the apples are bubbly and fork-tender, and the topping is golden.

To Serve

Serve warm with ice cream, whipped cream, or crème fraîche (see page 158).

Harriet's Hot Cinnamon Apple Crisp

Serves 6

Cinnamon candies add a wonderful zip and zing to make Harriet's apple crisp extra special.

Preheat the oven to 350°F. Butter an 8-inch square pan or a casserole dish.

Mix together the sugar, flour, and butter to make a crumb topping; set aside. Spread the apple slices in the prepared pan. Sprinkle with the cinnamon candies. Cover all with the crumb topping.

Bake uncovered on the center rack, for 40 to 45 minutes, or until bubbly and the apples are fork-tender. Check after 40 minutes to be sure it isn't burning.

To Serve

Serve warm with a garnish of whipped cream or vanilla ice cream.

1 cup sugar

¾ cup all-purpose flour

½ cup butter

6 to 8 Granny Smith apples, peeled, cored, and sliced ¼-inch thick

¼ cup Red Hots or similar cinnamon candies

Whipped cream or vanilla ice cream for garnish

Baked Bananas with Cranberry Sauce

Serves 4

4 bananas, peeled

1½ tablespoons melted butter

⅛ teaspoon salt

¾ cup canned whole berry cranberry sauce

Whipped cream or vanilla ice cream for serving

Beyond the nut bread, beyond the banana split, warmed bananas accompanied with a great glaze or sauce make terrific desserts!

Preheat the oven to 375°F. Butter a baking dish. Place the bananas in the prepared dish. Drizzle with melted butter. Sprinkle with just a slight bit of salt. Pour on the cranberry sauce.

Bake for 15 to 18 minutes, or until the bananas are fork tender but still hold their shape.

To Serve

Transfer each banana to a dessert plate, and spoon the cooking sauce over each. Top with whipped cream or vanilla ice cream. Serve warm.

Baked Apple Butter Bananas

1 banana serves 1

To make this unique dessert, use bananas that are firm and not overly ripe. Look for apple butter where your market stocks jams and jellies.

Preheat the oven to 375°F. Butter a casserole dish.

Spread the bananas with the apple butter, and place in the prepared dish in a single layer.

Bake for 15 to 18 minutes, or until the bananas are just fork tender and still hold their shape.

To Serve

Serve warm with a topping of sour cream or crème fraîche (see page 158).

1 banana per person, peeled

¼ cup apple butter per banana

Crème fraîche or sour cream for serving

Pumpkin Bars with Cream Cheese Frosting

Makes 24

For the Bars:

4 eggs

2 cups sugar

2 cups canned pumpkin purée

¾ cup butter, melted

2 cups all-purpose flour

2 teaspoons baking powder

1 teaspoon baking soda

1 teaspoon ground cinnamon

1 cup walnuts, chopped

For the Frosting:

3 cups confectioners' sugar

1 (3-ounce) package cream cheese, softened

6 tablespoons butter, melted

3 tablespoons whole milk

1 teaspoon vanilla extract

This makes the perfect autumn dessert.

Preheat the oven to 325°F. Grease a 10 x 15-inch baking pan.

To make the bars, mix together the eggs, sugar, pumpkin, and melted butter; set aside. Sift together the flour, baking powder, baking soda, and cinnamon. Add to the egg mixture, and blend. Stir in the chopped nuts. Pour into the prepared pan.

Bake for 25 minutes. Cool in the pan on a wire rack before frosting.

Meanwhile, to make the frosting, combine all of the ingredients, and beat with an electric mixer at low speed until smooth. Spread on the bars when completely cool, or the frosting will break and not have the right texture.

To Serve

Cut into 2½-inch squares. Store leftovers in the refrigerator.

Margarite's Upside-Down Apple Pie

Serves 8

Not for the faint of heart—this is a masterpiece.

Preheat the oven to 400°F.

To make the topping, melt the butter and honey together; spread on bottom of a deep-dish glass pie plate. Sprinkle evenly with the brown sugar and chopped nuts. Lay on the bottom crust, draping over the edge of the pie plate.

To make the filling, scoop the sliced apples into the crust; sprinkle on the granulated sugar, cinnamon, and nutmeg. Dot with the butter. Lay on the top crust, and generously crimp all around the edge. Prick the top crust with the tines of a fork to make vent holes.

Bake for 15 minutes. Reduce the oven temperature to 325°F, and continue to bake for 30 minutes more, or until the apples are tender. Cool the upside-down pie completely on a wire rack.

To Serve

Rewarm the pie in the oven just to loosen the bottom caramel layer; invert onto a serving plate, and unmold from the pie plate. Serve the warm pie caramel-side-up and à la mode.

For the Topping:

¼ cup butter, melted

1 teaspoon honey

½ cup brown sugar, packed

½ cup finely chopped pecans

For the Crust:

Pastry for a deep-dish double-crust pie

For the Filling:

6 cups peeled, cored, and sliced tart apples

½ cup granulated sugar

½ teaspoon ground cinnamon

¼ teaspoon ground nutmeg

1 tablespoon firm butter, cut into little pieces

Vanilla ice cream for serving

Meringue-Topped Apple Pie

Serves 8

For the Filling:

2 eggs, separated

¾ cup sugar

4 large apples, peeled, cored, and chopped

¼ cup chopped almonds

¼ cup chopped raisins

Juice of 1 lemon

1 teaspoon grated lemon zest

1½ tablespoons butter

1 (9–inch) single homemade or commercial piecrust, unbaked

For the Meringue Topping:

3 egg whites

¼ teaspoon cream of tartar

6 tablespoons sugar

The meringue topping for this pie makes a nice change from the traditional double crust so commonly used on apple pie.

Preheat the oven to 400°F. Beat the egg yolks with the sugar. Add the apples, almonds, raisins, lemon juice, and zest. Beat the egg whites until stiff, and fold into the mixture. Pour into the piecrust. Dot the filling with butter.

Bake for 25 minutes.

Meanwhile, to make the meringue, beat the egg whites with the cream of tartar until soft peaks begin to form. Add in the sugar gradually, beating until stiff glossy peaks form. Remove the pie from the oven, and top with the meringue, covering the filling completely, making sure the meringue is touching the edges of the crust all around. Make swirls in the meringue with a spatula. Immediately return the pie to the oven.

Bake until the meringue is golden brown, for 8 to 10 minutes. Remove from the oven, and cool on a wire rack.

To Serve

Serve at room temperature.

> The key to a perfect meringue topping is to spread the meringue all the way to the edge of the crust, sealing it to the crust. This prevents the meringue from shrinking away from the edge. Swirling peaks into the meringue adds to the delicate browning quality. Not overcooking the meringue prevents sweating or beading.

Apple Crumb Pie

Serves 8

There are as many ways to make and enjoy apple pie as there are people to eat it. The following is a suggestion for a simple, traditional, old-fashioned farmhouse apple pie. The serving twist in the variation is my Dad's.

Preheat the oven to 400°F.

To make the filling, toss the sliced apples with the granulated sugar, flour, cinnamon, and nutmeg. Arrange in the piecrust.

To make the topping, mix together the flour, granulated sugar, and brown sugar. Cut in the butter with a wire pastry blender or the tines of a fork until the mixture becomes crumbly. Do not overwork. Sprinkle the topping evenly over the filling.

Bake for 45 to 50 minutes. Remove from the oven, and cool on a wire rack.

To Serve

Serve at room temperature. Add softened ice cream, if desired.

Traditional Double-Crust Apple Pie

Omit the crumble topping, and replace it with a second piecrust. Increase the sugar in the filling to 1 cup, and top the filling with dots of butter. Cover with the top crust, crimp, and vent with fork pricks or slits. Bake at 400°F for 50 minutes. Serve warm or at room temperature with a slice of sharp Cheddar cheese on top—just the way my Dad liked it.

For the Filling:

6 cups peeled, cored, and sliced tart apples

2/3 cup granulated sugar

2 tablespoons all-purpose flour

1/2 teaspoon ground cinnamon

1/8 teaspoon ground nutmeg

1 (9-inch) piecrust

For the Topping:

3/4 cup all-purpose flour

1/4 cup granulated sugar

1/4 cup packed brown sugar

1/3 cup firm butter, cut into pieces

Ice cream for serving (optional)

Seven Ways to Sensationalize Your Apple Pie

Written for 1 pie, using 6 cups apples and 1 cup sugar as filling

Apple pie provides the perfect palette to express your creativity.

Sugar Combinations for Apple Pie
Use:

1 cup granulated sugar

or 1 cup packed brown sugar

or ½ cup each: brown and granulated sugars

Mixed Fruit Apple Pie
Add up to 1 cup:

Raisins, golden raisins, cranberries, sweetened dried cranberries, diced rhubarb, dried cherries; mix with the 6 cups apples.

Cheese Crust Apple Pie

At the end of the baking time, top with thin slices of Cheddar or American cheese; bake 5 to 6 minutes more to melt the cheese over the top crust.

German Apple Pie

At the end of the baking time, pour ½ cup heavy cream into the pie through the vent-slits in the crust; bake 5 to 6 minutes more.

Flavorings for Apple Pie

Add to filling:

Mixture of ½ teaspoon each: ground cinnamon, ground ginger, and ground nutmeg;

or 1 teaspoon vanilla extract or almond extract;

or 1 teaspoon grated orange zest.

Hot Cinnamon Apple Pie

Mix into filling:

¼ cup Red Hots cinnamon candies

Caramel Sundae Apple Pie

Serve with a drizzle of caramel sauce and a scoop of vanilla ice cream.

Old-Fashioned Sour Cream and Raisin Pie

Serves 8

2 eggs

1 cup sour cream

1 cup raisins

²/₃ cup sugar

1 teaspoon ground cinnamon

Pinch of salt

¾ cup chopped pecans

1 (9-inch) prebaked piecrust

Ultrarich, this is a great variation for the pecan-pie lover who wants something just a little bit different.

Preheat the oven to 450°F.

Put the eggs, sour cream, raisins, sugar, cinnamon, and salt in a blender or food processor, and process. Add the pecans, and process 1 minute more until well blended. Transfer the filling to the piecrust.

Bake for 15 minutes, then reduce the temperature to 350°F, and continue baking for 30 minutes more, or until a knife inserted in the center comes out clean. Remove the pie from the oven, and cool.

To Serve

Serve slightly warm or at room temperature, à la mode or as is.

Glenn's Apple Carrot Cake

Serves 12

Glenn likes to make this cake for his friends at work and treat them to a fresh dessert. The pan always comes home empty. Some men aren't chocolate lovers, so this cake is just right for them.

Preheat the oven to 325°F.

Combine the sugar, oil, eggs, and vanilla. Beat well until smooth. Sift together the flour, baking powder, cinnamon, baking soda, and salt, and stir into the wet mixture. Add the carrots, apples, and walnuts. Pour the batter into a 9 x 13-inch baking pan.

Bake for 60 to 70 minutes

To Serve

This is great and tasty without any frosting; just cut into squares, and serve.

2 cups sugar

1½ cups olive oil

4 eggs

1 teaspoon vanilla extract

2 cups all-purpose flour

2 teaspoons baking powder

1½ teaspoons ground cinnamon

½ teaspoon baking soda

⅛ teaspoon salt

1½ cups grated carrots

1½ cups chopped apples

1 cup walnuts, chopped

Five tips to help your oven bake its best:

1. Preheat the oven always, unless specifically noted otherwise.

2. Allow at least 10 to 15 minutes for it to come up to temperature.

3. Bake at the temperature specified in the recipe, rather than trying to "hurry it up" with a higher temperature or "slow it down" with a lower temperature.

4. Don't open the oven door prematurely during baking. If you do, you risk drafts or letting heat escape, which can cause the item to fall, deflate, or not cook properly.

5. Use a clean oven always, void of past drips and spills that can smoke and burn, affecting the outcome and flavor of the dish.

Apple Butter Cake

Serves 8

For the Cake:

1 cup granulated sugar

½ cup butter, softened

4 eggs, beaten

2½ cups all-purpose flour

1½ teaspoons baking soda

1½ teaspoons ground cinnamon

½ teaspoon ground cloves

½ teaspoon ground nutmeg

⅛ teaspoon salt

1 cup buttermilk

1 cup apple butter

For the Quick Caramel Icing:

1 cup brown sugar

½ cup cream

1½ tablespoons butter

½ teaspoon vanilla extract

Preheat the oven to 350°F. Grease a 9 x 13-inch pan.

To make the cake, cream together the sugar and butter until fluffy. Stir in the eggs. Sift together the flour, baking soda, spices, and salt, and add to the egg mixture alternately with the buttermilk. Mix well. Blend in the apple butter. Pour the batter into the prepared pan.

Bake for 45 to 50 minutes. Cool slightly before frosting with **Quick Caramel Icing**.

Meanwhile, to make the icing, combine the brown sugar and cream in a saucepan. Cover, and heat over medium heat for 3 to 4 minutes. Remove the cover, bring to a boil, and let boil for several minutes, stirring occasionally. Stir in the butter. Remove the mixture from the heat, and cool to lukewarm. Add the vanilla, and beat until thick and creamy. Spread on the warm cake.

To Serve

Cut into slices, and serve warm or at room temperature.

Northwoods Cranberry Torte

Serves 8

Note: The finished recipe contains a raw egg.

Living in cranberry country, townsfolk always serve this dessert at our town's fall festival, which, you guessed it, features locally grown cranberries.

Preheat the oven to 375°F.

To make the first layer, combine the graham cracker crumbs, sugar, and butter, and pat into a pie plate. Bake for 8 minutes. Set aside to cool.

To make the second layer, cream together the confectioners' sugar and butter; add the egg, beating well. Spread over the crust.

To make the third layer, mix the fruits and sugar together, and spread over the second layer.

To make the fourth layer, whip together the cream, vanilla, and sugar, and spread over the third layer. Sprinkle the graham cracker crumbs on top. Refrigerate until serving time.

To Serve

Serve chilled. Cut into small slices because this dessert is very rich. Return leftovers to the refrigerator.

For the First Layer:

1 ¼ cup graham cracker crumbs

¼ cup granulated sugar

¼ cup butter, softened

For the Second Layer:

2 cups confectioners' sugar

½ cup butter, softened

1 egg

For the Third Layer:

1 cup finely chopped fresh cranberries

1 cup finely chopped apple

12 ounces crushed pineapple, drained

1 cup granulated sugar

For the Fourth Layer:

1 cup heavy cream

1 teaspoon vanilla extract

1 teaspoon granulated sugar

For the Topping:

1 or 2 graham crackers, crushed to crumbs

Elegant but Easy Cranberry Mousse

Serves 6 to 8

1 (3-ounce) package raspberry gelatin

1 cup boiling water

1 cup cold cranberry juice cocktail

1 cup heavy cream, whipped until stiff

1 cup canned whole berry cranberry sauce

1 teaspoon lemon juice

Whipped cream for serving (optional)

Looking for something on the lighter side to follow a rich dinner? Try this.

Stir the gelatin with the water until the gelatin is dissolved. Stir in the cranberry juice cocktail, and place the mixture in the refrigerator to partially set. When the gelatin begins to set, fold in the whipped cream. Stir together the cranberry sauce and lemon juice, and fold into the mousse mixture. Spoon the mixture into stemmed glasses or dessert cups, and refrigerate until set.

To Serve

Serve chilled, garnished with a dollop of whipped cream, if desired.

Cranberry Mousse Pie

Fill a baked and cooled graham cracker piecrust with the mousse mixture as made above. Refrigerate to firm until serving time. Garnish each slice with a dollop of whipped cream, and serve.

Magic Baked Custard

Serves 6

As your spoon sinks into this custard, you know you're in for a glorious treat.

Preheat the oven to 325°F. Grease a 1-quart casserole or six individual custard cups.

Blend together the condensed milk, vanilla, salt, and 2 cups hot water in a mixing bowl. Gradually add the eggs, stirring rapidly. Pour the custard into the prepared casserole or cups. Sprinkle the top with the nutmeg. Set the casserole or cups into a shallow pan. Fill the pan with hot water to a depth of 1 inch.

Bake about 45 minutes for the 1-quart casserole, or 30 to 35 minutes for the custard cups, or until a knife inserted near the center of the custard comes out clean. Cool to room temperature, and refrigerate.

To Serve

Scoop the larger custard into individual dessert dishes. Place individual custard cups on dessert plates.

$2/3$ cup sweetened condensed milk

1 teaspoon vanilla extract

$1/4$ teaspoon salt

3 eggs, lightly beaten

$1/4$ teaspoon ground nutmeg

Eleven

November

"November always seemed to be the
'Norway' of the year."
—Emily Dickinson

Recipes
Our thoughts turn to harvests and gatherings and memories that last.

Swedish Cardamom Cookies

College Care-Package Ginger Cookies

Breanne's Boiled Cookies

Pecan Pie Bars

Angie's Shortbread Cookies

Cranberry Apple Pie

Gram's Southern Chess Pecan Pie

Frank's Maple Nut Pie

Sweet Potato Pecan Pie

Perfectly Pumpkin Pumpkin Pie

Jan's Carrot Pumpkin Cake with Cream
Cheese Frosting

Pumpkin Walnut Cake

Spice Cake with a Secret

   • Boiled Caramel Frosting

June's Noodle Kugel

Wild Rice Harvest Cake

Mocha Flan with Coffee Sauce

   • Coffee Sauce

Alvina's Brandied Fruit Sauce (Rumtopf)

Neil's Popcorn Cake

Caleb's Cherry Clafouti

June Wallace's Almond Biscotti

Swedish Cardamom Cookies

Makes several dozen

1 cup unsalted butter

½ cup granulated sugar

½ cup brown sugar

1 teaspoon ground cardamom

1 egg, lightly beaten

4 cups all-purpose flour

The dough makes a thin, delicate cookie.

Preheat the oven to 375°F.

Cream together the butter and both sugars. Add the remaining ingredients in the order listed, beating to make a stiff dough; the dough should not be sticky at all. Shape the dough into small balls, using about 2 teaspoons dough per ball, and place on ungreased cookie sheets. Press flat with the floured or sugared bottom of a drinking glass.

Bake for 10 minutes. Cool before serving.

To Serve

Serve these subtly spicy cookies with a warming cup of tea. Store extra in airtight tins.

Native to India, cardamom is a member of the ginger family and has a slight peppery taste. White cardamom is traditionally used in Scandinavia to flavor cookies, stollen, and other festive foods. You can find this unique and aromatic spice in the spice section of your market, either already crushed or as whole pods, which you can grate as needed. I use the side of my little nutmeg grater to grate it fresh just before using it in a recipe.

If cookies lose their crispness during storage, recrisp them by heating on ungreased cookie sheets for 3 to 5 minutes in a 300°F oven.

College Care-Package Ginger Cookies

Makes about 4 dozen

The dough makes a nice soft cookie.

To make the cookies, using an electric mixer, cream together the shortening and sugar until light and fluffy. Beat in the eggs and molasses, keeping the mixture fluffy. Sift together 3½ cups of the flour, baking soda, cinnamon, salt, ginger, and cloves. Add one-third of the flour mixture to the creamed mixture, and beat well. Add half the buttermilk, and beat well, followed by half the remaining flour mixture, the remaining buttermilk, and the remaining flour mixture, mixing well after each addition. Transfer the dough to the freezer for 3 to 4 hours.

Preheat the oven to 400°F.

Working with small amounts at a time, place cold dough on a linen tea towel covered with the remaining ½ cup flour. With floured hands, pat out the dough about ½-inch thick, and cut with a 2-inch-round cookie cutter. Place on an ungreased cookie sheet, at least 1 inch apart.

Bake for 5 to 8 minutes, or until the centers of the cookies spring back when touched lightly. Do not overcook. If edges are brittle, they're overbaked.

Meanwhile, to make the frosting, combine all of the ingredients, and mix to a spreadable consistency for the soft cookies without damaging them. Frost while warm, then cool.

To Serve

Once cooled, store between sheets of waxed paper in an airtight tin.

For the Cookies:

1 cup vegetable shortening

1 cup granulated sugar

2 eggs

1 cup dark molasses

4 cups all-purpose flour, divided

2 teaspoons baking soda

2 teaspoons ground cinnamon

1 teaspoon salt

1 teaspoon ground ginger

¼ teaspoon ground cloves

1 cup buttermilk

For the Confectioners' Icing:

½ teaspoon butter, softened

1½ cups confectioners' sugar

⅛ teaspoon salt

½ teaspoon vanilla extract

2 to 3 tablespoons heavy cream, or as needed for a spreadable consistency

Breanne's Boiled Cookies
Makes 4 dozen

2 cups sugar

½ cup whole milk

¼ cup butter

3 tablespoons unsweetened cocoa powder

3 cups quick-cooking rolled oats

½ cup peanut butter

1 teaspoon vanilla extract

½ cup salted peanuts

All boil and no bake makes for a good cookie!

Combine the sugar, milk, butter, and cocoa in a saucepan, and bring to a boil. Cook for 1 minute. Remove from the heat. Quickly add the oats, peanut butter, vanilla, and peanuts. Stir well. Drop by teaspoons onto waxed paper. Let stand for about 30 minutes, or until dry.

To Serve
Place on a cookie platter, and serve.

Variation
You can substitute shredded coconut for the peanuts, if you like.

Pecan Pie Bars

Makes about 3 dozen

These tiny delicacies will please the smallest—and the largest—of appetites, so stock the cookie jar and don't be surprised if you have to make another batch!

Preheat the oven to 350°F.

Combine 1 cup flour, rolled oats, and ¼ cup brown sugar. Cut in the butter with a pastry blender or tines of two forks until the mixture resembles coarse crumbs. Press the mixture into a 9 x 9 x 2-inch baking pan. Bake for about 15 minutes.

Meanwhile, beat the eggs slightly, add the remaining ingredients, including the remaining brown sugar and flour, and blend well. Pour over the partially baked crust. Return to the oven, and continue baking about 25 minutes longer. Cool to room temperature.

To Serve

Cut into small bars. Place on a platter, and serve.

1 cup plus 1 tablespoon sifted all-purpose flour

½ cup rolled oats

¾ cup packed brown sugar, divided

½ cup firm butter

3 eggs

¾ cup light corn syrup

1 cup coarsely chopped pecans

1 teaspoon vanilla extract

¼ teaspoon salt

Angie's Shortbread Cookies

Makes 4 dozen

1 cup butter, softened

½ cup confectioners' sugar

2 cups sifted all-purpose flour

¼ teaspoon baking powder

¼ teaspoon salt

This is a favorite cookie at our house for special occasions. They melt in your mouth.

Preheat the oven to 350°F.

Cream the butter, adding the sugar gradually until the mixture is light and fluffy. Sift together the flour, baking powder, and salt, and blend into the creamed mixture. Flour a surface, and roll out the dough ¼-inch thick. Cut with a 2-inch-round cookie cutter, and place the cookies on cookie sheets.

Bake for about 15 minutes. Remove from the oven, and cool on wire racks.

To Serve

Place on a decorative cookie platter to serve.

Cranberry Apple Pie

Serves 6 to 8

This is a pie that tastes wonderful the next day, as the flavors set and meld. The tartness of the cranberries is a great foil against the sweetness of the apples. You can use premade frozen crusts, if you wish, cutting one into strips for the lattice top.

Preheat the oven to 425°F. Line a 9-inch pie plate with the bottom crust, draping it over the rim slightly.

Toss the remaining ingredients except the butter until well combined, and mound the filling into the piecrust. Dot the filling with bits of the butter. Cut the remaining piecrust into long strips, and weave a lattice top on the pie. Crimp around the edges to seal the top and bottom crusts together.

Bake the pie on the center rack for 50 minutes. You will know the pie is done when it smells wonderful and the glistening filling is bubbling up through the lattice-work of the pie. Remove from the oven, and cool on a wire rack.

To Serve

Serve as is, or à la mode; room temperature or warmed.

Variation

Add ½ cup raisins or currants in addition to the rest of the filling ingredients.

Although I am an excellent piecrust maker and pride myself on being so, I often use ready-to-bake piecrusts for their time-saving convenience. If you transfer the bottom piecrust into your own heavy-duty pie plate (instead of keeping it in the flimsy foil version they come in) and crimp on a second crust for the top, I guarantee no one will ever know. I won't tell if you won't.

Pastry for a double-crust, lattice-topped pie

1 cup sugar

¼ cup tapioca

1½ teaspoons grated orange zest

¼ teaspoon salt

4 to 5 cooking apples, peeled, cored, and sliced

1 cup fresh cranberries

1½ tablespoons butter, cut into little pieces

Gram's Southern Chess Pecan Pie

Makes 1 (9-inch) single crust pie or 2 (8-inch) single crust pies

Pastry for a large single-crust pie or 2 smaller single-crust pies

1 cup packed brown sugar

½ cup granulated sugar

1 tablespoon all-purpose flour

2 eggs

2 tablespoons whole milk

1 teaspoon vanilla extract

½ cup butter, melted

1 cup chopped pecans

Rich vanilla ice cream for serving

You'd better make two of these, because they won't last long. This pie is so densely sweet, I like to cut it with a little ice cream. It keeps well and tastes equally great the next day! I use ready-made piecrusts from the freezer section of my market.

Preheat the oven to 375°F.

To make the filling, mix together the brown sugar, granulated sugar, and flour. Beat in thoroughly, in order, the eggs, milk, vanilla, and melted butter. Fold in the pecans. Pour the filling into a 9-inch crust, or divide between 2 8-inch crusts.

Bake for 40 to 50 minutes, or until the filling is set and a knife inserted in the center comes out clean. Remove from the oven, and cool on a wire rack.

To Serve

This pie is very rich, so serve small pieces warm with rich vanilla ice cream. I like to use Edie's Homemade-style Custard Ice Cream.

Frank's Maple Nut Pie

Serves 8 to 10

This ultrarich pie makes the perfect autumn dessert.

Preheat the oven to 400°F.

Cream together the sugar and butter. Beat in the eggs, adding one at a time. Beat in the maple syrup and flavoring. Fold in the pecans. Pour the filling into the piecrust.

Bake on the center rack for 40 to 45 minutes, or until the filling is set. Remove from the oven, and cool on a wire rack.

To Serve

Serve warm or at room temperature, as is or à la mode. If serving with ice cream, for an extra touch use butter pecan!

½ cup sugar

¼ cup butter, softened

3 eggs

1 cup pure maple syrup

¼ teaspoon maple extract

1 cup coarsely chopped pecans

1 (9-inch) unbaked piecrust

Sweet Potato Pecan Pie

Makes 2 pies; each pie serves 8

For the Filling:

2 large sweet potatoes, boiled and mashed

⅓ cup brown sugar

1 egg

1 tablespoon heavy cream

1 tablespoon butter

1 tablespoon vanilla extract

¼ teaspoon salt

¼ teaspoon ground cinnamon

¼ teaspoon ground allspice

¼ teaspoon ground nutmeg

2 (9-inch) piecrusts for single-crust pies

For the Topping:

¾ cup granulated sugar

¾ cup dark corn syrup

2 eggs

2 tablespoons melted butter

2 teaspoons vanilla extract

Pinch ground cinnamon

Pinch of salt

1½ cups pecan pieces

Whipped cream or ice cream for serving (optional)

A very traditional pie, this makes a great Thanksgiving dessert.

Preheat the oven to 325°F.

To make the filling, mix together all the filling ingredients, and pour into the piecrusts; smooth the surfaces.

To make the topping, mix together all the topping ingredients, stirring in the pecans last. Pour on top of the filling.

Bake for 1 hour and 15 minutes. Remove from the oven, and cool on wire racks.

To Serve

Serve at room temperature as is, or topped with whipped cream or vanilla ice cream.

Perfectly Pumpkin Pumpkin Pie

Makes 1 large deep-dish single-crust pie or 2 smaller single-crust pies

The perfect pie for Thanksgiving! Note that baking times will vary, depending on the size of your pie.

Preheat the oven to 425°F.

Starting with the eggs, mix all the ingredients together in the order listed, stirring well. Pour into the piecrusts.

Bake on the center rack for 15 minutes; reduce the oven temperature to 350°F, and continue baking for 45 minutes more, or until a knife inserted in the center comes out clean.

To Serve

Serve at room temperature with a topping of whipped cream.

> Over the years I have customized my pumpkin pie recipe to this point. I believe one of the "funnest" (as my daughter would say) things a cook can do is to keep improving on her recipes. This pumpkin pie is a perfect example of that.

2 eggs, beaten

1 (16-ounce) can pumpkin puree

3/8 cup granulated sugar

3/8 cup brown sugar

1/2 teaspoon salt

1 teaspoon ground cinnamon

1/2 teaspoon ground cloves

1/2 teaspoon ground ginger

1/2 teaspoon vanilla extract

2 tablespoons brandy or amaretto

13 ounces canned evaporated milk or heavy cream

Pastry crust for a large single-crust pie or 2 8-inch single-crust pies

Whipped cream for serving

Jan's Carrot Pumpkin Cake with Cream Cheese Frosting

Serves many; recipe may be easily halved. The full recipe makes a 12 x 16-inch sheet cake, but it may be divided between smaller pans

For the Cake:

4 eggs

2 cups granulated sugar

1 cup vegetable oil

2 cups all-purpose flour

2 teaspoons baking soda

1 teaspoon salt

1 teaspoon ground cinnamon

13 ounces canned pumpkin purée

3 jars baby-food carrots or 2 jars junior carrots

For the Frosting:

2 cups confectioners' sugar

1 (3-ounce) package cream cheese, softened

2 tablespoons melted butter

½ teaspoon vanilla extract

The pumpkin and the baby carrots are a sublime match—and the cream cheese frosting just takes this cake over the top.

Preheat the oven to 350°F for a metal pan, or 325°F for a glass pan. Grease a 12 x 16-inch sheet pan or two equal-sized smaller pans. Beat the eggs until thick and pale. Add the sugar, and beat until fluffy and pale. Beat in the oil slowly, keeping the batter light. Mix together the flour, baking soda, salt, and cinnamon; fold into the sugar mixture, using a rubber spatula. Fold in the pumpkin and carrots. Pour into the prepared pan or divide between the two smaller pans.

Bake for 40 to 50 minutes, if using a single pan, 30 to 35 minutes, if using two pans, or until a toothpick inserted in the center comes out clean. Remove from the oven, and cool on rack or racks.

Meanwhile, to make the frosting, using an electric mixer, beat together the sugar, cream cheese, butter, and vanilla until smooth and creamy. Frost the cake when it is completely cool.

To Serve

Cut into serving-size squares, and serve.

Pumpkin Walnut Cake
Serves 12

Preheat the oven to 350°F.

To make the cake, sift together the flour, sugar, cinnamon, baking powder, baking soda, and salt in a large mixing bowl. Add and mix the remaining ingredients in the order listed, mixing well after each addition, until blended.

Bake in an ungreased 9 x 13-inch baking pan for 35 to 40 minutes. Remove from the oven, and cool completely.

Meanwhile, to make the frosting, blend together the butter and cream cheese. Add the confectioners' sugar and vanilla, mixing until it reaches a spreadable consistency. Spread the frosting on the cool cake.

To Serve
Slice into wedges, and serve. Cover and refrigerate leftovers.

For the Cake:

2 cups all-purpose flour

2 cups granulated sugar

2½ teaspoons ground cinnamon

2 teaspoons baking powder

2 teaspoons baking soda

2 teaspoons salt

4 eggs

2 cups pumpkin purée

1 cup olive oil

½ cup chopped walnuts

For the Frosting:

½ cup (1 stick) butter

1 (8-ounce) package cream cheese, softened

2 cups confectioners' sugar

1 teaspoon vanilla extract

Spice Cake with a Secret

Serves 12

2¼ cups all-purpose flour

1 cup granulated sugar

⅓ cup brown sugar, firmly packed

1 tablespoon baking powder

1 teaspoon baking soda

1 teaspoon ground cinnamon

1 teaspoon ground allspice

½ teaspoon ground cloves

½ teaspoon ground nutmeg

1 (10.75-ounce) can condensed tomato soup

½ cup vegetable shortening

2 eggs

⅔ cup raisins or currants (optional), tossed with flour to coat

Shhh…the secret ingredient is the tomato soup!

Preheat the oven to 350°F. Grease a 9 x 13-inch baking pan.

Sift together the dry ingredients. Add the soup and shortening; using an electric mixer, beat for 2 minutes, scraping the sides of the bowl. Add the eggs and ¼ cup water; beat 2 minutes more, scraping the sides of the bowl to mix all. Fold in the raisins or currants, if using. Pour the batter into the prepared pan.

Bake on the center rack for 40 to 45 minutes, or until a toothpick inserted in the center comes out clean. Remove from the oven, and cool the cake completely before frosting with Boiled Caramel Frosting.

1 cup firmly packed brown sugar

½ cup butter, softened

⅓ cup evaporated milk

2 cups confectioners' sugar

Boiled Caramel Frosting

Place the brown sugar, butter, and evaporated milk in a saucepan, and heat to boiling, stirring constantly. Boil for 2 minutes. Remove from the heat, and let cool for 10 minutes, stirring several times until the mixture thickens slightly. Gradually stir in the confectioners' sugar until incorporated. If needed, add 2 to 3 teaspoons water to make the frosting smooth and of a spreadable consistency.

To Serve

Cut the cake into squares, and serve. Let everyone guess the "secret ingredient."

June's Noodle Kugel
Serves 10 to 12 (unless I'm around)

This recipe is traditionally served as a side dish, but I love it so much, I've elevated it to entrée, side, and dessert!

Preheat the oven to 350° F. Melt ¼ cup of the butter, and pour it into a 9 x 13-inch baking dish to coat the bottom and sides; set aside.

Mix the noodles, cottage cheese, sour cream, sugar, and salt in a bowl; set aside. Add the eggs to the slightly warmed milk, and mix well. Add the egg/milk mixture to the noodle mixture, and stir to combine; the mixture will be slightly loose. Pour it into the prepared baking dish, distributing evenly. Melt the remaining ¼ cup butter, and drizzle over the top of the casserole.

Bake for 1 hour and 15 minutes.

To Serve
Cut into squares and serve warm, topped with sour cream.

Variation
For a sweeter kugel, add a handful of plumped raisins before baking. Sprinkle warm servings with a little sugar to taste, and pour on half-and-half to your liking.

½ cup butter, divided

16 ounces medium or wide flat egg noodles, cooked and drained

1 (16-ounce) container small-curd cottage cheese

1 (16-ounce) container sour cream plus more for serving

1 tablespoon sugar

1 teaspoon salt

4 eggs, lightly beaten

2 cups whole milk, lightly warmed

Wild Rice Harvest Cake

Serves 16

For the Cake:

2½ cups all-purpose flour

1 teaspoon baking powder

1 teaspoon baking soda

½ teaspoon salt

½ teaspoon ground nutmeg

¼ teaspoon ground cinnamon

¼ teaspoon ground allspice

2 cups packed brown sugar

¾ cup (1½ sticks) butter, softened

3 eggs

1 cup soured milk (page 157) or buttermilk

1 teaspoon vanilla

2 cups cooked wild rice, steamed dry (directions follow)

1 cup chopped pecans, toasted, if desired

For the Maple Whipped Cream:

2 cups heavy cream

2 tablespoons brown sugar

¼ teaspoon maple flavoring

For Garnish:

Caramel sauce, to taste

Toasted pecans, to taste

Truly a taste of autumn harvest in the north woods, this wild rice cake has a nutty, rustic, hearty flavor reminiscent of times gone by. Use commercial caramel sauce.

Preheat the oven to 350°F. Grease a 10-inch tube pan or a Bundt pan.

Sift together the flour, baking powder, baking soda, salt, and spices; set aside. Cream together the brown sugar and butter. Add the eggs, one at a time, beating after each addition. Add the sour milk and vanilla. Add in the flour mixture. Beat the batter until well blended. Fold in the wild rice and pecans. Pour into the prepared pan. Bake for 1 hour. Cool for 20 to 30 minutes before removing from the pan. Continue to cool completely on a wire rack. To make the Maple Whipped Cream, whip together the cream, brown sugar, and maple flavoring until stiff.

To Serve

Drizzle caramel sauce on each dessert plate. Place a slice of cake on each plate, and top with Maple Whipped Cream. Drizzle with more caramel sauce and chopped toasted pecans. Alternatively, you may frost the cooled cake with a Caramel Frosting (page 199) or a white frosting to which you have added maple flavoring.

To Prepare Wild Rice

Buy the best wild rice you can find, with a nice, long grain. Choose rice that is dark in color and doesn't look dried out. (For the Wild Rice Harvest Cake you will need ½ cup uncooked rice, which will yield 2 cups cooked rice.)

Rinse and sort, if need be, in cold water. Boil in a deep pot (wild rice has a tendency to foam up) in 4 parts water to 1 part rice, for 45 minutes, or just until the rice has puffed and popped open, becoming plump and tender. Remove from the heat, and drain; wrap the rice in a clean towel. Transfer the wrapped rice to a steamer basket or colander, and set in a deep pot with 1 to 2 inches of boiling water in the bottom. Cover with foil, and cover loosely with the pot lid. Steam the rice for at least 20 minutes; this will make it wonderfully puffy and dry, not soggy, tough, or chewy. Your rice is now ready for this cake recipe. Or the rice is ready for any other dish you might be serving that requires wild rice—such as a vegetable casserole or stuffing, or baked or sautéed dishes. And, I might add, this is the absolutely best way that I have found to successfully cook wild rice. I often make extra at this point, and bag, freeze, and date it to use in future dishes.

Years ago a friend and I were privileged to attend a late-summer Wild Rice Festival in a small Northern Wisconsin Chippewa community. We were the only non–Native Americans in attendance—the costumes and dancing were authentic and incredible. The celebration was to honor their yearly harvest of wild rice—an age-old staple of the American Indians of the Upper Midwest. Much like cranberries, wild rice is now cultivated on marshland farms (some Indian-owned) and is commonly available in grocery stores today in its raw state. Some of your better grocery stores may offer hard-to-find canned cooked wild rice—which may be substituted in place of cooking your own from scratch—a nice convenience if you can find it.

Mocha Flan with Coffee Sauce

Serves 10

5 eggs

½ cup sugar

1½ teaspoons instant powdered coffee or instant espresso powder

4 teaspoons unsweetened cocoa powder

1⅔ cups half-and-half, scalded and slightly cooled

1 teaspoon vanilla extract

This flan is a coffee-lover's dream.

Preheat the oven to 350°F. Butter an 8-inch round cake pan.

Beat together well the eggs, sugar, instant coffee, and cocoa. Slowly beat in the slightly cooled half-and-half. Add the vanilla. Pour the flan mixture into the prepared pan. Place in a larger pan filled with ½-inch warm water.

Bake in the water bath for 30 minutes, or until set and a knife inserted in the center comes out clean. Cool to room temperature. Turn out onto a serving platter. Refrigerate until serving time.

To Serve

Cut in wedges as if you were cutting a pie. Top the chilled flan with warm Coffee Sauce (recipe follows) and toasted pecans, if desired.

½ cup sugar

¾ cup hot, very strong decaf coffee

1 tablespoon cornstarch dissolved in 2 tablespoons water

1 tablespoon butter

Coffee Sauce

Melt the sugar in your heaviest saucepan over low heat, stirring constantly. Add the remaining ingredients, and heat, stirring, until thickened and blended. Use warm, as a dessert sauce.

Alvina's Brandied Fruit Sauce (Rumtopf)

This is a delicious fruit sauce that makes a wonderful gift-from-the-kitchen for the holidays. Put in sterilized canning jars (see page 201 for sterilizing directions), attach a recipe card and serving suggestions, and give as a special holiday treat. Start your sauce in November and it will be ready for gift-giving by Christmas.

Gently combine all the fruits with the sugar and brandy. Store in a large bowl, crock, restaurant jar, or Rumtopf crock made specifically for this purpose. Do not use a metal container. Cover and let stand at room temperature to proof for three weeks. Gently stir once or twice a week. At the end of three weeks, the sauce will be ready to serve. The fruit will have absorbed the sugar and brandy, and the sauce will have thickened to a syrupy consistency.

To Serve

Serve over ice cream, pound cake, spice cake, or crêpes as a dessert sauce.

> Always save 1 cup of the sauce to use as a "starter" for renewing the next batch. When you get down to 1 or 2 cups of remaining sauce, renew the batch with new fruits, sugar, and brandy. Mixing some of the "old" with the "new" will help to proof and flavor the next batch.

1 (20-ounce) can pineapple chunks, drained

1 (16-ounce) can sliced peaches, drained

1 (16-ounce) can pear halves, drained

1 (17-ounce) can apricot halves, drained

1 (10-ounce) jar maraschino cherries, drained

1½ cups sugar

1½ cups brandy

Neil's Popcorn Cake

Serves 12

4 quarts popped popcorn

2 cups dry roasted peanuts

2 cups plain M&M's

1 pound marshmallows

1 cup butter

¼ teaspoon vanilla extract

This is a fun treat for kids to help make on a bad-weather day, to share with their friends. It also makes a great snack for sleepovers. The next time your kids say they don't know what to do, put them to work making this unique treat.

Lightly grease an angel food cake pan; set aside. Combine the popcorn, peanuts, and M&M's in a large bowl, and mix well. Melt together the marshmallows, butter and vanilla over low heat. Pour the marshmallow mixture over the popcorn mixture, and mix until totally combined. Press into the prepared pan. Refrigerate for at least 1 hour or until set.

To Serve

Unmold from the pan. Using a sharp knife (and cleaning it between slices), slice like a cake.

Caleb's Cherry Clafouti

Serves 8

A *favorite of my son, this makes a heavenly dessert any time of the year. If fresh cherries aren't available, use canned pitted dark cherries, drained very well, or frozen pitted cherries, thawed and drained.*

Preheat the oven to 350°F. Butter a 9- or 10-inch deep-dish glass pie plate, tart dish, or similar shallow casserole.

Arrange the cherries evenly over the bottom of the dish; set aside. Using a blender, wire whisk, or electric mixer, combine the milk, flour, sugar, salt, eggs, butter, and almond extract until very smooth. (The mixture will be similar to pancake batter). Pour evenly over the fruit in the baking dish.

Bake on the center rack for 30 to 40 minutes, or until the top is puffed and golden. Cool slightly before serving; the puffed center will drop a bit as the dessert cools.

To Serve

Serve warm or at room temperature, dusted with confectioners' sugar sifted through a sieve. Top with whipped cream, if desired.

Variations

Blueberries; fresh plums, pitted and halved; sliced peaches; and soft pitted prunes also work well for this French farmhouse dessert, as does crème fraîche for a garnish. When fruits other than cherries are used, the dessert is called a *flaugnarde.*

2 to 2½ cups fresh Bing cherries, pitted

1 cup whole milk

½ cup all-purpose flour

⅓ cup sugar

Pinch of salt

4 eggs

3 tablespoons butter, melted and cooled

½ teaspoon almond extract

Confectioners' sugar for garnish, to taste

Whipped cream for garnish (optional)

June Wallace's Almond Biscotti

Makes 2 dozen

1¾ cups all-purpose flour

½ teaspoon baking soda

½ teaspoon baking powder

⅛ teaspoon salt

½ teaspoon freshly ground black pepper

1 cup sugar

½ cup (1 stick) unsalted butter, slightly softened

2 eggs

Zest of 1 orange

Zest of 1 lemon

1 teaspoon vanilla extract

½ teaspoon lemon extract

¼ teaspoon almond extract

1½ cups chopped almonds, toasted

Just perfect when you want something sweet, but not too sweet.

Preheat the oven to 350°F. Lightly grease a cookie sheet.

Sift together the flour, baking soda, baking powder, salt, and pepper; set aside. In a large bowl, beat together the sugar and butter until light and fluffy. Add the eggs, one at a time, beating after each addition. Add the zests and extracts. Fold in the sifted dry ingredients and the nuts, and mix. Do not overwork the dough! Divide the dough into half, and using your hands, shape the halves into two logs about 13 inches long by 3 inches wide. Place on the prepared pan, spacing well apart.

Bake for 20 minutes. Remove the logs from the oven, and let cool for 10 minutes on the cookie sheet. Using a serrated knife, cut the logs cross-wise into ¾-inch thick slices. Lay the slices cut-side down on the cookie sheet. Reduce the oven temperature to 325°F, and bake for 15 minutes more. Cool completely, and store in tins.

To Serve

Serve with your favorite cup of coffee or tea for dunking.

Twelve

December

"At Christmas play and make good cheer,
For Christmas comes but once a year."
—Thomas Tusser, "The Farmer's Daily Diet"

Recipes
Our kitchens are brimming with holiday fare.

Barbara's Bourbon Pound Cake

Andy's Favorite Eggnog Pie

Toffee Squares

Toffee Bars

Walnut Slices

Crispy Date Bars

German Caramel Bars

Danish Sugar Cookies

Mother's Almond Crescents

Darlene's Five-Minute Fudge

Peanut Butter Fudge

Butter Fudge

Breanne's Fudge Nougats

• Peanut Butter Nougats

Pecan Creams

Auntie Joan's French Chocolate Truffles

MAK's Chocolate-Coated Chocolate Truffles

Dawn's Chocolate Mints

Gram's Festive Mint Patties

Yum Candy

Mincemeat Pie with Hard Sauce

• Hard Sauce

Auntie Joan's Old-Fashioned Plum Pudding with Warm Custard Sauce

• Warm Custard Sauce

Nutcracker Sweets

Date Nut Fondant

The Lady Ione's German Chocolate Ladyfinger Torte

Old-Fashioned Taffy Pull

Barbara's Bourbon Pound Cake

Makes one 10-inch tube pan cake, or two 9 x 5 loaves; the recipe may be cut in half and baked in a single loaf pan.

1 pound butter

3 cups sugar, divided

8 eggs, separated

3 cups all-purpose flour

1/3 cup bourbon

2 teaspoons vanilla extract

2 teaspoons almond extract

This pound cake is so rich and delicious it may be served totally as is—no embellishment needed here!

Preheat the oven to 350°F. Grease generously one 10-inch tube pan or two 9 x 5 loaf pans.

Cream the butter and 2 cups of the sugar until fluffy, using an electric mixer. Add the egg yolks one at a time, beating thoroughly after each addition. Add the flour and the bourbon alternately, one-third of each at a time, mixing after each addition. Add the vanilla and almond extracts.

In a separate large bowl, beat the egg whites until stiff but not dry. Beat in the remaining 1 cup sugar gradually, forming a meringue. Gently fold the bourbon-flour-batter mixture into the meringue mixture. Gently fold the final mixture into the prepared pan or pans.

Bake for 1½ hours. Remove from the oven, and cool on a wire rack before removing from the pan.

To Serve

Cut into 1-inch-thick slices.

> Did you know that pound cake originally got its name from an old recipe that consisted of one pound butter, one pound eggs, one pound sugar, and one pound flour? Since each ingredient was a pound, the recipe was easy to remember.

Andy's Favorite Eggnog Pie
Serves 8

A great holiday pie!

Soften the gelatin in 3 tablespoons cold water in a small bowl. In a saucepan over low heat, warm the eggnog; stir in the gelatin mixture. Continue heating until the gelatin is completely dissolved. Remove from the heat, and chill until partially set.

Meanwhile, using an electric mixer, beat the heavy cream, sugar, rum flavoring, and almond extract until stiff. Fold the eggnog mixture into the whipped cream mixture; pour into the piecrust. Refrigerate at least 2 hours, or until serving time.

To Serve
Serve chilled, sprinkled with a dusting of nutmeg and a dollop of sweetened whipped cream. Return any leftovers to the refrigerator.

1 (0.25-ounce) envelope unflavored gelatin

2 cups commercial eggnog

1 cup heavy cream

¼ cup sugar

1 teaspoon rum flavoring

½ teaspoon almond extract

1 (9-inch) piecrust, baked and cooled

Dusting of ground nutmeg

Sweetened whipped cream for serving

Toffee Squares

Makes about 3 dozen

1 cup (2 sticks) butter

1 cup packed brown sugar

1 egg yolk

1 teaspoon vanilla extract

2 cups all-purpose flour

¼ teaspoon salt

6 standard-size Hershey bars, broken into pieces

½ cup walnuts, finely chopped in a blender

This is one of my favorite Christmas recipes, simply because these squares are so easy and so delicious. Make sure to cut them into small squares because they are very rich! I like to stretch out all my Christmas cookies by making them small—that way we can always go back for a second or third!

Preheat the oven to 350°F.

Cream together the butter, sugar, egg yolk, and vanilla. Sift together the flour and salt; blend into the creamed mixture. Pat the dough evenly into a nonstick jelly-roll pan.

Bake for 20 to 25 minutes. Remove from the oven, and immediately cover with the chocolate pieces, which will start to melt. Working quickly, spread the melting chocolate with a spatula to form an even frosting. Do this while the dough is warm. After frosting, sprinkle the cake with the walnuts. Cut into small squares with a sharp knife while still warm.

To Serve

Once cooled, store between layers of waxed paper in an airtight tin.

Toffee Bars

Makes 16+

These toffee bars are very rich, so when cutting them into squares, keep them small.

Preheat the oven to 350°F. Grease a 9 x 13-inch baking pan.

Cream together the butter and brown sugar. Using an electric mixer, beat in the egg and vanilla. Stir in the flour and salt, and blend well. Spread into the prepared pan.

Bake for 20 minutes. Meanwhile, melt and blend the chocolate and shortening in a saucepan over very low heat. Spread over the bars immediately after removing them from the oven. Sprinkle with the pecans. Cool the bars completely before cutting.

To Serve

Cut into small squares, and serve.

1 cup (2 sticks) butter, softened

1 cup brown sugar, packed

1 egg

1 teaspoon vanilla extract

2 cups all-purpose flour

½ teaspoon salt

½ pound semisweet chocolate

1 tablespoon vegetable shortening

½ cup pecans, chopped

Walnut Slices

Makes 12+

1 cup cake flour, sifted

½ cup (1 stick) butter

1½ cups brown sugar

1 cup walnuts, chopped

½ cup shredded coconut

¼ teaspoon baking powder

¼ teaspoon salt

2 eggs, well beaten

1 teaspoon vanilla extract

2 tablespoons all-purpose flour

I remember my Mom baking walnut slices at Christmas time. Because of their rich taste we always felt really special.

Preheat the oven to 350°F. Put the cake flour into a bowl, and work in the butter until well blended. Pat evenly into the bottom of a 9 x 13-inch baking pan. Bake for 15 minutes. Mix the remaining ingredients together, and pour over the crust. Return to the oven, and bake for another 25 minutes. Remove from the oven, and cool.

To Serve

You can frost these with your favorite frosting or just serve them plain. Slice in small pieces; they're very rich.

Crispy Date Bars
Makes 24

Stirring constantly is the key to this recipe.

Preheat the oven to 375°F. To make the crust, combine the flour, brown sugar, and butter; mix until crumbly. Press into an ungreased 7 x 11-inch or 9-inch square baking pan. Bake for 10 to 12 minutes, or until golden brown.

Meanwhile, to make the filling, combine the dates, sugar, and butter in a saucepan. Cook over medium heat until the mixture comes to a boil. Cook for 3 minutes, stirring constantly. Blend about ¼ cup of the date mixture into the beaten egg to temper it, and return this mixture to the saucepan, stirring to blend. Continue cooking just until the mixture bubbles, stirring constantly. Remove from the heat; stir in the cereal, walnuts, and vanilla. Spread over the baked crust; cool completely before frosting.

To make the frosting, combine all of the ingredients, and beat with an electric mixer on low speed until smooth. Spread over the filling. Cool the filling completely before cutting.

To Serve

Cut into bars. Serve with an extra date on each plate.

For the Crust:

1 cup all-purpose flour

½ cup firmly packed brown sugar

½ cup (1 stick) butter, softened

For the Filling:

1 cup dates, chopped

½ cup granulated sugar

½ cup (1 stick) butter

1 egg, well beaten

2 cups puffed rice cereal

1 cup walnuts, chopped

1 teaspoon vanilla extract

For the Frosting:

2 cups confectioners' sugar

2 to 3 teaspoons whole milk

½ teaspoon vanilla extract

1 (3-ounce) package cream cheese, softened

Extra dates for serving

German Caramel Bars
Makes 16

50 caramels (14-ounce package)

1/3 cup evaporated milk

1 (18-ounce) box German chocolate cake mix

1/2 cup (1 stick) butter, melted

1 cup walnuts or pecans, chopped

6 ounces chocolate chips

Caramel. Chocolate. Need I say more?

Preheat the oven to 350°F. Grease and flour a 9 x 13-inch baking pan.

Combine the caramels and the evaporated milk in the top of a double boiler over simmering water, and cook until melted; set aside. In a large bowl, hand-mix the German chocolate cake mix, melted butter, nuts, and 1 tablespoon water. Mix together until crumbly. Press three-fourths of this mixture into the prepared pan.

Bake for 8 to 10 minutes, or until the crust looks dry. Sprinkle the chocolate chips over the hot baked crust, pour the caramel mixture over the chips, and sprinkle the remaining crumbly mixture over the top. Bake 15 minutes more. Remove from the oven, and cool until firm.

To Serve
Cool and cut into squares.

> When buying the caramels, look at the back of the package to see how many caramels there are. If you are off by one or two don't worry—the recipe will still turn out okay; it's not necessary to buy an extra package.

Danish Sugar Cookies

Makes 4 dozen

These cookies will melt in your mouth and you'll beg for more. In fact, they will probably disappear faster than you can bake them!

Preheat the oven to 350°F.

Sift together the flour, baking soda, cream of tartar, salt, and confectioners' sugar into a large bowl. Add the butter and vegetable shortening. Using an electric mixer, beat on low speed until the mixture resembles coarse crumbs. Blend the egg and vanilla. Add to the dry ingredients, mixing only until blended. The dough will be fairly soft. Shape into 1-inch balls, and roll in the granulated sugar. Place the balls 2 inches apart on ungreased cookie sheets. Flatten to ¼-inch thick with the bottom of a glass dipped in sugar.

Bake for about 10 minutes, or until the edges brown. Remove from the oven, and cool.

To Serve

Place on a cookie plate, and serve.

2 cups sifted all-purpose flour

¾ teaspoon baking soda

1 teaspoon cream of tartar

¼ teaspoon salt

1 cup confectioners' sugar

½ (1 stick) cup firm butter

½ cup vegetable shortening

1 egg

1 teaspoon vanilla extract

1 cup granulated sugar

Mother's Almond Crescents

Makes 3 dozen

1 cup (2 sticks) butter

2 tablespoons confectioners' sugar plus more for rolling the cookies

2 cups all-purpose flour

1 teaspoon vanilla extract

½ teaspoon salt

¼ pound blanched almonds, grated

My mother made these every Christmas. I don't know who ate more of them, my dad or me.

Preheat the oven to 350°F.

Cream together the butter and sugar. Mix in the remaining ingredients until a soft dough is formed. If the dough remains too crumbly or dry, add one egg yolk and mix well to bind the dough. Divide the dough in half, and form into two logs about 2½ inches in diameter. Wrap the logs in wax paper, and refrigerate for 1 hour. When ready to bake, remove the dough from the refrigerator, and cut the logs cross-wise into half-inch-thick slices; cut the slices cross-wise in half. With your fingers, shape each piece into a half-moon (or crescent) shape, and place on cookie sheets..

Bake for 10 to 15 minutes. Roll in confectioners' sugar while still warm.

To Serve

Place the cookies on a platter.

Darlene's Five-Minute Fudge

Makes an 8-inch square pan full

Rich and delicious—five minutes and you have a wonderful treat for fudge lovers.

Butter an 8-inch-square baking pan; set aside.

Combine the sugar, milk, and salt in a saucepan, and bring to a boil over medium heat. Cook 5 minutes, stirring constantly. Remove from the heat. Add in the marshmallows, chocolate chips, and vanilla. Stir until the marshmallows melt, about 1 minute. Pour into the prepared pan to cool and set.

To Serve

Cut into bite-size squares, dipping your knife into hot water between slices.

1 $2/3$ cups sugar

$2/3$ cup evaporated milk

$1/2$ teaspoon salt

$1 1/2$ cups mini marshmallows

$1 1/2$ cups semisweet chocolate chips

1 teaspoon vanilla extract

Peanut Butter Fudge
Makes 18

2 cups sugar

2 tablespoons light corn syrup

¾ cup whole milk

⅛ teaspoon salt

1 ounce semisweet chocolate, grated

1 teaspoon butter

3 tablespoons peanut butter

1 teaspoon vanilla extract, divided

Homemade candy is always better than most store-bought candies.

Butter a 5 x 8-inch pan; set aside.

Combine the sugar, corn syrup, milk, and salt in a saucepan. Heat over medium heat, stirring constantly, until the sugar dissolves and the mixture comes to a boil. Cook to the soft-ball stage, 234°F to 236°F on a candy thermometer. Remove from the heat, and set aside.

Meanwhile, melt the chocolate and butter in a second saucepan. Pour half of the corn syrup mixture over this chocolate/butter mixture. Without stirring, let it cool to lukewarm, or 110°F.

Meanwhile, add the peanut butter and ½ teaspoon of the vanilla to the remaining corn syrup mixture; mix well. Pour at once into the prepared pan to form the bottom layer. Add the remaining ½ teaspoon vanilla to the cooling chocolate mixture; beat until thick. Spread over the first layer. Refrigerate for several hours until firm.

To Serve
Cut into 18 small squares.

Butter Fudge
Makes 18

This recipe makes a rich and creamy fudge.

Butter a 5 x 8-inch pan. Combine the sugar, milk, chocolate, and cream of tartar in a saucepan. Heat over medium heat, stirring constantly, until the sugar dissolves and the mixture boils. Cook to a soft-ball stage, 234° to 236°F on a candy thermometer. Add the butter, and cool to lukewarm. Add the vanilla. Beat until thick, and add the walnuts. Pour into the prepared pan. Cool completely for several hours

To Serve
Cut into 18 small squares.

As with any of the candy recipes in this book, work very carefully—hot sugar, marshmallows, and the like can cause burns.

2 cups sugar

1 cup whole milk

2 ounces semisweet chocolate, grated

$1/8$ teaspoon cream of tartar

½ (1 stick) cup butter

1 teaspoon vanilla extract

1 cup walnuts, chopped

Breanne's Fudge Nougats
Makes 12+

1 cup sugar

¾ cup all-purpose flour

½ cup butter

1 (15-ounce) can sweetened condensed milk

1 cup semisweet chocolate chips

1 cup graham cracker crumbs

¾ cup walnuts, chopped

1 teaspoon vanilla extract

1 cup mini marshmallows

Miniature marshmallows are the secret ingredient in this holiday candy.

Butter an 8 x 12-inch pan. Combine the sugar, flour, butter, and condensed milk in a saucepan. Heat over medium heat, stirring constantly, until it boils; boil for 1 minute. Remove from the heat.

Add the chocolate chips, graham cracker crumbs, walnuts, and vanilla, mixing well. Stir in the marshmallows. Spread in the prepared pan. Cool before cutting.

To Serve
Cut into pieces, and serve.

Peanut Butter Nougats
Substitute 1 cup chopped peanuts for the walnuts, and add ¼ cup peanut butter with the chocolate chips.

Pecan Creams
Makes 1 pound

A great candy for the pecan lover.

Butter a cookie sheet. Stir together the first five ingredients in a saucepan, and heat over medium heat, stirring constantly, until the mixture reaches the soft-ball stage, 234°F to 236°F on a candy thermometer.

Remove from the heat, and cool without stirring until lukewarm, or 110°F. Add the vanilla, and beat until creamy. Stir in the pecans. Drop by teaspoonfuls onto the prepared cookie sheet. Cool completely until firm, or for several hours.

To Serve
Arrange in a candy dish.

Variation
This recipe can be made with any nuts you desire.

2 cups sugar

1 cup whole milk

¾ cup heavy cream

1 tablespoon light corn syrup

⅛ teaspoon salt

1 teaspoon vanilla extract

1 cup pecans, finely chopped

Auntie Joan's French Chocolate Truffles

2 cups heavy cream

1½ pounds of the finest semisweet chocolate you can find, melted

½ cup (1 stick) unsalted butter, softened

2 teaspoons Grand Marnier or rum (optional)

Cocoa powder or chocolate sprinkles to decorate

This recipe requires overnight chilling for the first step. Although the recipe might seem a bit complicated, it's more a matter of keeping the buttery-creamy-chocolate mixture chilled but malleable and not so soft that it begins to melt while forming into balls with your hands. The truffle mixture must be kept cool at all times, and the finished candy should be stored in the refrigerator.

Bring the cream just to a boil, remove from the heat, and stir in the melted chocolate until blended. Refrigerate the mixture overnight.

The next day, let the chocolate warm up to room temperature, just enough to beat in the butter and the Grand Marnier or rum, if desired. Refrigerate again, if necessary. Once the mixture is workable, form into small ½- to ¾-inch balls. Roll in cocoa or sprinkles to coat. Return to the refrigerator for storage.

To Serve

Remove from the refrigerator, and place on a doily-lined serving plate. Return any leftovers to the refrigerator.

MAK's Chocolate-Coated Chocolate Truffles
Makes 12 or more

This takes the concept of "double-dipping" off the charts.

Break one of the chocolate bars into pieces, and melt it in the top of a double boiler over simmering water, stirring occasionally. Remove from the heat, and stir in the butter. Add the cream and liqueur, combining well. Chill the mixture, stirring occasionally, until thick enough to hold its shape, for 15 to 20 minutes. Line a plate with aluminum foil, and drop the chilled chocolate mixture onto it by the teaspoonful to form 12 truffles. Shape into balls by rolling with your hands. Place in the freezer for 30 minutes.

Meanwhile, break the remaining chocolate bar into pieces, and melt it in the top of a double boiler over simmering water. When it's melted, remove from the heat, and stir in the cooking oil; this will be your dipping mixture.

Remove the truffles from the freezer, and, while well-chilled, dip one at a time, using a fork, into the dipping mixture, spooning chocolate over all sides to coat. Remove the dipped truffles to a plate, and sprinkle generously with the chopped, toasted almonds and crystal sugar to coat again. Refrigerate for several hours before serving.

To Serve
Serve cool, and always return any that are leftover to the refrigerator.

> An easy and decorative way to store and serve truffles is to place them in individual mini-sized paper or foil baking cups. These little cups may be found in the baking section of your market or at specialty cooking supply stores.

2 (3.5-ounce) bars fine-quality bittersweet chocolate

1 tablespoon unsalted butter

3 tablespoons heavy cream

1 tablespoon almond liqueur

1 tablespoon cooking oil

1 cup finely chopped toasted almonds

1 cup crystal sugar

Dawn's Chocolate Mints

Makes about 80

1½ cups dark brown sugar

¾ cup (1½ sticks) butter

2 cups semisweet chocolate chips

2 eggs

2½ cups all-purpose flour

1¼ teaspoons baking soda

¼ teaspoon salt

1 pound Andes chocolate-mint candies

A cookie/candy combo—these are as pretty as they are delicious. I use Andes brand chocolate mints.

Heat the sugar, butter, and 2 tablespoons of water in a saucepan over low heat until the butter is melted. Add the chocolate chips, and stir until partially melted. Pour into a large mixing bowl, and let stand for 10 minutes. Using an electric mixer on high speed, beat in the eggs one at a time. Reduce the speed to low, and add the dry ingredients, beating just until blended. Refrigerate for 1 hour.

Preheat the oven to 350°F.

Roll single teaspoons of dough into balls and place 2 inches apart on ungreased cookie sheets. Bake for 12 to 13 minutes. Remove from the oven, and immediately place a chocolate-mint candy on top of each cookie. As soon as the candy begins to melt, swirl it with the back of a spoon. Cool on a wire rack.

To Serve

Serve on a cookie plate with extra candies sprinkled on the plate.

Gram's Festive Mint Patties

Makes about 80

Delicate and pretty, these melt-in-your-mouth candies are perfect to pass with an after-dinner cup of coffee or to set out on a buffet table.

Stir or beat together the corn syrup, butter, peppermint extract, salt, and confectioners' sugar, adding the sugar 1 cup at a time and blending until smooth after each addition. Divide the mixture into three parts, leaving one part white. Add the red food coloring to a second part and the green food coloring to the third part, making three different colors of dough. With your hands, shape the dough into ¾-inch balls, and place on waxed paper. Flatten the balls with a fork. Let dry, uncovered, at room temperature, for at least 2 hours on the waxed paper. Store in an airtight tin.

To Serve

Place on a fancy doily-lined glass serving plate or footed glass cake plate, or stack in a crystal candy dish to serve.

⅓ cup light corn syrup

¼ cup soft butter

1 teaspoon peppermint extract

¼ teaspoon salt

1 pound confectioners' sugar

2 drops red food coloring

2 drops green food coloring

Yum Candy

Makes 24

2 cups brown sugar

2 cups granulated sugar

1½ cups whole milk

½ cup light corn syrup

2 tablespoons butter

1⅛ teaspoons vanilla extract

1 cup walnuts, chopped

1 cup coconut flakes plus extra for garnish

Butter a 9 x 13-inch pan. Combine the first six ingredients in a saucepan. Heat over medium heat, stirring constantly, until the mixture boils; cook to soft-ball stage, 234°F to 236°F on a candy thermometer. Cool; add the vanilla, and beat until stiff. Add the walnuts and coconut. Pour into the prepared pan. Cool completely until set.

To Serve

Cut and place in a candy dish with additional coconut flakes sprinkled around the candy for garnish.

Mincemeat Pie with Hard Sauce

Makes enough filling for 6 (9-inch) pies

This is a labor-intensive project, so you will want to make a full batch and store it, or give it as gifts. Look for the candied fruit in the baking section of your market.

Cook the stew meat in a large pot of water to cover over medium-low heat, for 1½ hours, or until tender. Cool and grind in a food processor or blender; set aside. Grind the suet, or see if your butcher will grind it for you; set aside.

In the largest stockpot, dissolve the sugar in the cider, and bring to a boil. Add all the ingredients, including the stew meat and suet (except the brandy). Bring the mixture to a boil and boil for 5 minutes. Stir in the brandy, remove from the heat, and ladle the hot mincemeat into 6 sterilized quart-size wide-mouth canning jars. Immediately put the tops on the jars to create a vacuum seal. Let the jars settle and cool undisturbed. Then refrigerate them for up to 1 month or freeze for up to 1 year. Each jar contains enough filling for one double-crust pie.

To bake a pie, fill one 9-inch pastry shell with 1 quart (1 jar's worth) mincemeat. Put on the top crust, crimp around the edges to seal, and vent by piercing the crust with tines of a fork. Bake at 375° for 1 hour. Cool on a wire rack.

To Serve

Serve this very rich pie in small wedges at room temperature or warmed, topped with vanilla ice cream or the very rich Hard Sauce (recipe follows).

2 pounds well-trimmed, boneless beef stew meat

1 pound fresh beef suet

2 pounds brown sugar

4 cups apple cider

3 pounds apples, peeled, cored, and finely chopped

1 pound chopped candied fruit

1 tablespoon salt

1 tablespoon ground nutmeg

1 tablespoon ground allspice

1 tablespoon ground cloves

2 tablespoons ground cinnamon

1½ cups corn syrup

1 pound golden raisins

1 pound dark raisins

3 (10-ounce) boxes currants

2 cups brandy

Vanilla ice cream or Hard Sauce for serving

1½ cups confectioners' sugar

½ cup (1 stick) butter, softened

3 tablespoons brandy

Hard Sauce

Makes about 1½ cups

Beat together all three ingredients to mix into a stiff sauce. Store in the refrigerator until serving time. Serve at room temperature.

To Serve

Remove the sauce from the refrigerator when you sit down for dinner, so the sauce will come up to room temperature by dessert time. Serve as an accompaniment to Mincemeat Pie.

Auntie Joan's Old-Fashioned Plum Pudding with Warm Custard Sauce

Makes 2 puddings; each serves 8 to 10

This make-ahead Christmas Pudding is labor intensive; give one pudding as a special gift (along with directions for resteaming) if you don't need them both. The puddings' flavor improves with time, so try making them at least one week in advance and storing them, wrapped in foil, in the refrigerator.

Grease two 2-quart pudding molds or two 2-pound clean coffee cans. Mix together all ingredients in the order listed. Divide the mixture equally, and pack into the prepared molds or cans. Cover tightly with aluminum foil. Place the containers into two very deep pots. Add water to fill about two-thirds of the way up the containers, and steam the containers, one per pot, over low heat for 8 hours. Add more water as needed to keep the level constant.

Remove the puddings from the water, remove the foil, and let stand for 24 hours to cool and dry. Wrap in foil and store in the refrigerator, where they can stay for up to one month.

To Serve

Reheat the puddings by steaming them for 30 minutes to 1 hour. Let the puddings cool for 10 minutes before carefully unmolding. Place the pudding on a pedestal cake plate to show it off. You may ladle ¼ cup warm brandy ignited and poured over the pudding, if desired. Let the flame go out before serving. Serve warm slices topped with Warm Custard Sauce (recipe follows).

3 cups packed fresh white bread crumbs (about ½ pound)

2 cups ground beef suet

2 cups peeled, cored, and chopped tart apples

2 cups raisins

2 cups brown sugar

½ cup candied fruit peel, chopped

¾ cup chopped walnuts

½ teaspoon ground ginger

½ teaspoon ground nutmeg

½ teaspoon ground allspice

1 teaspoon salt

Juice and grated zest of 1 lemon

8 eggs, beaten

½ cup brandy

1 cup heavy cream

1 cup sugar

½ cup (1 stick) unsalted butter

4 egg yolks

2 tablespoons brandy

1 teaspoon vanilla extract

Warm Custard Sauce

Combine the cream, sugar, butter, and egg yolks, and mix well. Transfer to the top of a double boiler, and heat over simmering water. Whisk until the mixture thickens and coats the back of a spoon. Fold in the brandy and vanilla. Serve the sauce warm. You can make this ahead and store in the refrigerator, but reheat it to serve as a dessert sauce.

To Serve

Use as a dessert sauce with plum pudding.

This recipe is a true labor of love and I include it only because it is a very special Christmas dessert for those of you who are traditionalists at heart. My sister always served an English Christmas dinner with prime rib, Yorkshire pudding (popovers), and all the fixings—followed by Plum Pudding (page 271) or Mincemeat Pie (page 269). If you are not as adventurous, try a commercially made plum pudding, steamed according to the package directions, but still make and use homemade custard sauce.

Folklore has it that it is traditional to make a wish before eating your plum pudding. And the "plums" in the plum pudding are not really plums, but "raisins." In some countries, it has been a tradition to bake a silver good-luck charm or a coin in the middle of the pudding, for some lucky diner to find!

Nutcracker Sweets

Makes 36

Mmmmm, it's so good.

Preheat the oven to 350°F. Grease a 10 x 15 x 1-inch pan.

To make the cookie base, cream together the peanut butter and shortening in a large bowl using an electric mixer at medium speed. Blend in the brown sugar. Beat in the eggs, one at a time, and continue beating until creamy; set aside. In a separate bowl, combine the flour, baking powder, and salt; set aside. In another bowl, combine the milk and vanilla. Add the dry ingredients and the milk mixture alternately to the peanut butter mixture, mixing at low speed and scraping the sides of the bowl frequently. Beat until blended. Spread the batter into the prepared pan.

Bake for 18 to 20 minutes. Remove from the oven, and cool before frosting.

To make the frosting, cream together the peanut butter and shortening in a large bowl, using an electric mixer at medium speed. Gradually add the sugar and milk, and beat until fluffy. Spread on the cooled cookie base; set aside.

Meanwhile, to make the drizzle, melt the chocolate chips over low heat, stirring until melted. Drizzle the melted chocolate from the end of the spoon back and forth over the frosted cookies. Refrigerate until firm.

To Serve

Cut into 2-inch squares.

For the Cookie Base:

½ cup creamy peanut butter

1/3 cup butter-flavor vegetable shortening

1½ cups brown sugar

2 eggs

1½ cups all-purpose flour

1½ teaspoons baking powder

½ teaspoon salt

¼ cup whole milk

1 teaspoon vanilla extract

For the Frosting and Drizzle:

2/3 cup creamy peanut butter

¼ cup butter-flavor vegetable shortening

4 cups confectioners' sugar

½ cup whole milk

½ cup semisweet chocolate chips

Date Nut Fondant

Makes about 1½ pounds. Cut into 64 1-inch squares or 36 1¼-inch squares

⅔ cup sweetened condensed milk

1⅛ teaspoons vanilla extract

4 cups confectioners' sugar

1 cup walnuts, chopped

½ cup pitted dried dates, finely chopped

Pecan halves for garnish

People of all ages like this never-fail, smooth, flavorful fondant.

Blend together the sweetened condensed milk and vanilla in a large mixing bowl. Gradually stir in the sugar. Blend in the walnuts and dates. Turn into 8 x 8 x 2-inch pan, and press evenly onto the bottom. Refrigerate until firm.

To Serve

With a sharp knife, cut into 1- or 1¼-inch squares. Top each piece with a pecan half. Arrange in a candy dish.

The Lady Ione's German Chocolate Ladyfinger Torte

Serves 12+

Note: The final recipe contains partially cooked egg yolks and raw egg whites.

For this recipe you will need soft, whole lady fingers to split in half. Most often you will find them already split in the package, so that has already been done for you. Be sure to purchase your ladyfingers well in advance, as they can be in short supply during the busy holiday season! I remember one year traipsing all over town with my son-in-law trying to find the needed ladyfingers. In a pinch, you can substitute slices of pound cake or angel food cake, although your torte won't be quite the same as if you were using the real thing. Look for the German sweet chocolate bars in the baking section of your market.

Butter the bottom and sides of a spring-form pan; set aside. Break the chocolate bars into pieces. In the top of a double boiler over simmering water or a saucepan set in a water bath, mix together and cook the chocolate pieces, sugar, ¾ cup water, and egg yolks over medium heat until melted, thickened, and smooth; remove from the heat, and set aside to cool.

Meanwhile, beat the egg whites until stiff. When the chocolate mixture is cool, fold in the beaten whites until the filling is smooth and well-incorporated. Line the sides and bottom of the prepared pan with an attractive arrangement of ladyfingers, standing ladyfingers on end, side by side around the side of the pan, and completely covering the bottom of the pan with a single layer. Spoon one-third of the chocolate filling over the bottom layer of ladyfingers. Arrange another layer of ladyfingers on the chocolate layer, and repeat, ending with the last one-third of the chocolate filling on the top. Refrigerate until serving time.

For the topping, beat the heavy cream, confectioners' sugar, and vanilla until stiff, and refrigerate.

To Serve

Remove the sides of the springform pan so the torte is free standing. Cut slices 1 to 2 ladyfingers in width. Store any leftovers in the refrigerator.

32 whole soft ladyfingers, split in half

6 (4-ounce) bars German sweet chocolate

¾ cup granulated sugar

12 eggs, separated

2 cups heavy cream

¼ cup confectioners' sugar

½ teaspoon vanilla extract

Old-Fashioned Taffy Pull

Novelty recipe, makes about 80 pieces

For Lemon Taffy:

2 cups sugar

¾ cup water

¼ cup lemon juice

2 tablespoons butter

½ teaspoon grated lemon zest

For Traditional Southern Taffy:

2 cups dark molasses

1 cup sugar

2 tablespoons butter

1 tablespoon vinegar

Fun for everybody and fun to eat, an old-fashioned taffy pull can be a great treat for adults and a memory-maker for the young.

Butter a large platter or cookie sheet. Carefully cook all the ingredients for either recipe in a saucepan over medium heat, stirring constantly, until a candy thermometer reads 270°F. Pour onto the prepared platter to cool. When cool enough to handle, oil your fingers, and pull and stretch, pull and stretch, and pull some more, until the candy becomes creamy looking and lighter in color. Finally pull into long strips. Cut into small bite-sized pieces with oiled scissors, and wrap in small squares of waxed paper, twisting the ends of the paper closed.

To Serve

Serve wrapped candy in a fancy candy dish, along with all your other favorite confections of the season.

Glossary of Ingredients and Cooking Terms Used in This Book

All-purpose flour—As the name suggests, all-purpose flour is a type of wheat flour that is suitable for all kinds of recipes. Also known as "plain," "general purpose," or "family" flour, it is the most commonly used flour in household baking and cooking.

Allspice—A spice that tastes like a blend of cinnamon, cloves, and nutmeg.

Bain marie—French for "water bath"—usually used for cooking custards or egg-based dishes. The smaller food pan is placed in a larger pan, which is filled with hot water to a level about half way up the side of the smaller pan. This technique can be used on the stove top or in the oven, and as the food cooks, it is surrounded by the gentle heat of the water.

Bake—To cook in the oven, using dry heat.

Baking powder—A leavening agent containing sodium bicarbonate, cream of tartar, and also a drying agent (usually starch), used to make batters rise.

Baking soda—Also a leavening agent, baking soda is pure sodium bicarbonate. Baking powder can be substituted for baking soda BUT baking soda cannot be used solely in place of baking powder, when baking powder is called for.

Bar cookies—Soft cookies baked as a single dough in a pan and then when cooled, cut into individual cookies in the form of bars or squares—such as brownies.

Beat—To stir a mixture rapidly. One minute with an electric mixer equals about 100 brisk strokes by hand.

Blend—To mix ingredients together to acquire a uniform texture.

Box grater—A four-sided, stainless-steel, free-standing utensil used for hand slicing, shredding and grating. Each side has different perforations to accommodate slicing, shredding, coarse grating, and fine grating.

Bundt pan—A brand name for a fluted tube pan, with curved sides. Often used for pound cakes.

Butter—To spread a fat such as oil, shortening, butter, or a non-stick spray in a pan to prevent food from sticking—also called "greasing" a pan.

Butter-flavored shortening—A solid vegetable shortening that has been flavored to taste like butter. Can be used in baking in place of regular shortening.

Buttermilk—Although rich in flavor, contrary to popular belief buttermilk does not contain butter and is not high in fat. Basically buttermilk is the liquid left behind after milk has been churned and all the fat has been extracted from it as butter. If you don't have buttermilk available you can do one of two things: 1) substitute a mixture made of half sour cream (or plain yogurt) and half whole milk; or 2) you can make what is known as "sour milk"—a mixture made with a ratio of ⅞ cup whole milk with 1 tablespoon lemon juice or white vinegar and left to stand for 10 minutes to thicken. Buttermilk adds wonderful richness to baked goods, such as muffins and chocolate cake, and also makes great pancakes.

Butter-vanilla flavoring—An artificial flavoring used to add extra depth and flavor to cakes, icings, and pastries.

Cake flour—A highly specialized type of wheat flour, intended for use in making cakes, cookies, and other delicate baked goods. Many grocery stores carry cake flour, but if you can't find it a substitute can be made by mixing a ratio of ⅞ cup all-purpose flour with two tablespoons of cornstarch and sifting 5 times.

Caramelize—To cook sugar until it melts and turns a caramel color.

Cardamom—A spice that has a sweet, lemony, ginger flavor—particularly favored in Scandinavian cooking. Comes whole or ground.

Chill—To refrigerate food until it is cold throughout, or as in a gelatin mold, until set.

Chop—To cut food into small pieces, using a knife, food processor, blender, or food chopper—such as chopping nuts.

Coarse chopped—When a food is chopped into uneven pieces—such as 1 cup nuts, coarsely chopped

"Coat a spoon"—A test to determine doneness of a soft custard or sauce—the mixture adheres to the back of a spoon when it's dipped into the sauce.

Combine—To blend ingredients into a uniform mixture.

Condensed milk (also known as Sweetened condensed milk)—Evaporated milk that has had sugar added to it, to make a very sweet, thick, syrupy milk product. The sugar acts as a preservative and an unopened can of condensed milk will have a shelf life of up to two years. Condensed milk and evaporated milk cannot be substituted for one another to get the same results in a recipe. Condensed milk and sweetened condensed milk are one and the same—sometimes older cookbooks specified the word "sweetened" just because it was so easy to confuse condensed milk and evaporated milk.

Cookie tins—Airtight, lidded tins in which to store cookies. If you haven't inherited a few of your grandmother's holiday-decorated tins, you can find new ones at hardware stores and dollar stores. It is also fun to look for old-fashioned tins at antiques and collectables stores—because the winter scenes are so pretty and the old-time graphics so interesting on the lids. (Just be sure the interiors are still clean and suitable for storing cookies.) The collectable tins themselves make great decorations during the holidays.

Cool—To let a food stand at room temperature until it is no longer warm to the touch—as to cool completely before storing in the refrigerator or placing in an airtight container.

Cream—To mix ingredients together until light and fluffy, smooth and creamy, such as cream together the butter and sugar.

Cream of tartar—A white powder used to stabilize egg whites when beating them stiff and increasing their volume. It is used for making meringues.

Crème fraîche—A thick cream mixture similar to sour cream, it is used to garnish desserts.

Crêpe—A thin French pancake.

Crimp—To join and seal a top and bottom piecrust together by pinching a high scalloped edge around the pie. This raised edge can help contain fruit fillings and prevent spillovers.

Crush—To mash food into small pieces (such as making graham cracker crumbs).

Curdling—The undesirable separation of eggs or dairy products in a custard or smooth sauce. The coagulation looks like small curds.

Custard cups—Small individual-size glass dishes (or ceramic bowls) in which to bake custard.

Cut—Mix together, with a wire pastry blender or two knives, shortening or butter with dry ingredients until crumbly, or the size of small peas.

Dab—About 1/8 teaspoon.

Dash—About 1/8 teaspoon, or 2 to 3 drops.

Dice—To chop fine in uniform cubes, about 1/8- to 1/4-inch in size.

Dollop—A spoonful of soft food, such as whipped cream added as a garnish.

Dot—To place small bits on the surface of a food, such as dots of butter.

Double boiler—A "double-decker" saucepan used to cook foods, such as custards, cream sauces, and chocolate, when the food needs to be protected from direct heat. The food cooks in the upper part over simmering water, not touching the water underneath in the larger pot.

> **How to make one:** Place a bowl, a little larger than the saucepan itself, over the saucepan containing an inch or two of simmering water. The bottom of the bowl should not touch the water. The steam will gently heat or melt the ingredients in the bowl—such as melting chocolate.

Drizzle—To pour a liquid over a food in a very fine stream, such as garnishing a cake with a drizzle of chocolate sauce.

Drop cookies—The dough is dropped from a teaspoon or tablespoon onto the cookie sheet to form individual cookies, then baked, such as sugar cookies.

Dust—To coat a food lightly with a dry ingredient, such as confectioners' sugar or cocoa powder, tapped through a sieve to garnish a cake.

Egg wash—A mixture of beaten egg and water, which is brushed onto piecrust before baking, to give the pie a golden finish.

Evaporated milk—Whole milk from which 60 percent of the water has been removed, making a thicker and more concentrated milk product. Once the can is opened, it needs to be refrigerated. The main difference between evaporated milk and condensed milk in the United States is that no sugar is added to the evaporated milk, which isn't the case in foreign countries, where you might find many brands that contain sugar. Evaporated milk and condensed milk cannot be substituted for one another to get the same results in a recipe, so make sure you use the correct ingredient called for.

Extract—A concentrated flavoring extracted from a food—such as vanilla or almond extract. (Can also be called essence.)

Flaked—Grated into flat shavings as opposed to shreds or slivers, as in flaked coconut.

Flambé—To pour a warm alcoholic liquid into a ladle, ignite, and then pour over a food.

Flan—A caramel-and-egg custard dessert.

Flan pan—A shallow round pan in which to make flan.

Flour—To cover a surface with a light coating of flour, to prevent dough from sticking when being handled, such as rolling out the piecrust on a floured surface, or grease and flour a cake pan.

Flute—To make a scalloped edge around a piecrust, by pressing and pinching with your fingers.

Fold—To incorporate a lighter mixture, such as beaten egg whites, into a heavier mixture, such as a batter, using a spatula or a spoon to gently mix one mixture over and into the other.

Fondant—A type of candy cooked to the "soft-ball" stage.

Fork-tender—When a food reaches the desired tenderness when pierced with the tines of a fork.

Freestone peaches—When buying canned peach halves look for "freestone" on the label. Freestones are a large, succulent variety of peach with wonderful flavor and a pretty red center where the stone (or pit) was. If it's not the season for fresh peaches, canned freestones are the way to go. They got their name from the fact that the stone is "free" and can easily be removed, leaving all the sweet flesh behind—as opposed to "clingstone" or "cling" peaches, which are smaller, harder to pit, have a little less flavor, and are less decorative for presentation.

Frothy—When an ingredient has been vigorously beaten until light and foamy.

Foam—A bubbly or frothy mixture that can form on the surface of a liquid (such as the foam on top of jams or jellies), or can spill up over the edge of a boiling pot when cooking.

Gel—To set or congeal.

Gelatin, unflavored—Unflavored gelatin comes in small packets called "envelopes." One envelope equals .25 ounce. Usually comes 32 envelopes to an 8 ounce box. Directions are on the package for how to soften and use in a recipe. Used to make gelatin desserts and molds.

Glaze—A thin type of frosting. To cover with a glossy finish.

Granulated tapioca—Starch grains extracted from the cassava plant, used to thicken sauces and make pudding. The pellet form known as small pearl tapioca, or seed pearl tapioca, can be used in place of granulated.

Grease; grease and flour—To spread oil, butter, shortening, or nonstick cooking spray on the surface of a baking pan to form a coating so food doesn't stick. When baking cakes, "dust" the greased surface with flour and shake off any excess. "Greasing" a pan can also be called "buttering" a pan.

Grated—When food has been cut into very fine shreds on a grater.

Grind—To pulverize to a very fine texture.

Half-and-half—A mixture of half milk and half cream, with a fat content of about 10 to 12 percent.

Heavy cream, also known as whipping cream—Cream that has a fat content of about 30 to 36 percent, and can be beaten stiff.

Head space—The amount of room left at the top of a container allowing for expansion in the container as the food cools.

Ice—To cover with frosting.

Icing—Another name for frosting.

Ice bath—A bowl of ice cubes and water, in which to set a second bowl containing warm ingredients, to chill quickly.

Ice water—Very cold water added a tablespoon at a time to make flaky piecrust.

Incorporate—When items are mixed thoroughly (as in blend all ingredients until incorporated).

Jell—To congeal or set up.

Jelly-roll pan—A flat baking pan (similar to a cookie sheet) with 1-inch sides (traditionally used to bake cake for a jelly-roll). Most commonly used size is a pan of about 10½ x 15½ x 1-inches.

"Jimmies"—Small baking sprinkles used to decorate cookies and candy, or sprinkle on frosting, such as roll the chocolate truffles in chocolate jimmies to coat.

Ladyfingers—Long, delicate, finger-like cookies made from a sponge-cake batter, typically used in fancy desserts such as trifles and tortes.

Lard—Clarified fat from a pig (can be used in place of shortening)—particularly good for making tender, flaky piecrust.

Lattice top (for a pie)—A woven top crust, used for fruit pies. Strips of piecrust are woven in a basket-weave pattern.

Lemon-colored—When an ingredient is beaten to a light yellow color.

Loaf pan—A rectangular pan used for baking bread—the most common size being 9 x 5 x 3-inches.

Macaroons—A type of crispy cookie made with sugar, egg whites, and coconut or ground nuts.

Macerate—To soften and flavor a food (such as raisins in rum, or strawberries with sugar and their own juices) by letting the food "marinate" and exchange flavors.

Maraschino cherries—A type of very sweet preserved cherries with or without stems—usually placed as a garnish on top of whipped cream or chopped and included in a batter.

Melt—To heat a solid food over low to medium heat until it becomes liquefied, such as melting chocolate.

Meringue—A light and airy, very sweet concoction of egg whites beaten stiff with sugar and cream of tartar. The egg whites can be baked on top of meringue pies or baked into dessert shells or little cookies. Meringue shells are baked at a low temperature in the oven and left to cool and dry. Meringue on top of pies is baked quickly just until golden; the pie should be stored in the refrigerator.

Microplane—A small, hand-held grater for fine grating and scraping, such as making lemon zest or grating whole nutmeg.

Mince—To chop food very, very fine

Mix—To blend ingredients together until incorporated.

Mousse—A light, airy dessert, either baked or chilled, usually containing beaten egg whites or whipped cream.

Overwork—Mixing a dough too long, resulting in a tough, dense, or less flaky baked item.

Parchment paper—A heavy paper used to line baking pans. Do not confuse with wax paper that is used for wrapping and storage.

Parfait—A chilled dessert, similar to a sundae, made by layering various fruits, purées, custards, gelatins, whipped cream, or ice cream and topping with assorted nuts, syrups, or whipped cream. A parfait is normally made in a tall clear glass so all layers are visible.

Parfait glasses—A type of glassware in which to serve parfaits, so all the layers can be seen.

Partially set—A term describing gelatin when it has chilled and has started to thicken.

Pastry blender—A U-shaped wire utensil, used to "cut" shortening or butter into flour; particularly when making piecrust.

Pat—To form a crust or dough to desired thickness or shape with your hands.

Pinch—A small amount that can be held between the pointer finger and thumb, about 1/8 teaspoon.

Pipe—To squeeze frosting or a whipped topping through a pastry bag to make a decorative design. Usually the pastry bag has different tips, to make different designs. A plastic baggie, with a bottom corner cut off works well in place of a pastry bag. Just fill the baggie, squeeze, and "pipe."

Pith—The bitter white membrane just under the peel (or zest) of citrus fruit.

Plump—To soften and increase the volume of a food (such as raisins or dried fruits) by soaking in a liquid.

Plum pudding—(Also called Christmas pudding) a steamed, bread-like pudding; the plums refer to the raisins used in the pudding.

Potato peeler—A small handheld metal-bladed tool used for more than just peeling potatoes—great for peeling apples or running down the side of a square of chocolate to make shaved chocolate pieces for garnish.

Preheating the oven—Bringing the oven up to temperature desired, before inserting the food to be cooked. This usually takes about 10 minutes.

Proof—To set a mixture aside, undisturbed to arrive at the consistency or flavor desired.

Pulse—To chop or mix in short spurts with a food processor.

Purée—To blend, process, or force a food through a sieve to arrive at a smooth consistency like baby food.

Ramekins—Small, individual-size baking dishes used to make soufflés, custards, and flan.

Raw eggs—Uncooked eggs. See special note about pasteurized-in-the-shell eggs on page xvi, when uncooked eggs are called for in a recipe.

Roll—To move something around to coat all sides, such as roll the chocolate candy in chopped nuts to coat.

Roll out—To form piecrust or dough into desired thickness with a rolling pin, such as roll out the dough to ¹/₈-inch thickness.

Rolling boil—When a mixture comes to a full boil and cannot be stirred down.

Sauté—To fry food quickly in butter or oil until browned or softened.

Scald—To heat a liquid, such as milk, in a saucepan on the stovetop to just under boiling. Small bubbles will form around the sides of the pan when the liquid is ready. Scalding can also mean rinsing a food with boiling water, such as scalding peaches to remove their skin.

Seizing—A term used to describe melted chocolate that becomes hard and lumpy, rather than silky and smooth. This can occur when even a droplet of water or condensation drops or spatters into the chocolate. Chocolate should always be melted carefully and uncovered.

Set—When something has congealed, jelled, or firmed up, as in chill the gelatin mold until set.

Sheet cake—A simple, single layer cake frosted on the top, as opposed to a layered cake that is frosted between layers and the layers stacked. Usually cut and served directly from the pan and used for large parties and celebrations.

Sheet cake pan—A large cake baking pan, typically about 12 x 16 or 12 x 18-inches, used to bake a single layer cake.

Sift—To pass dry ingredients through a fine meshed sieve or sifter, to become more uniform in texture—such as sift together the flour, baking powder, and salt; or shake powdered sugar through a sieve to dust top of cake.

Shortening—A solid vegetable fat used like butter or margarine in baked goods.

Shredded—Food that has been cut into small long slivers (as opposed to chopped or diced) usually using a grater.

"Size of a walnut"—About 2 tablespoons

Skim—To remove with a spoon, the top layer of fat, foam, or scum from a liquid, such as skimming the foam off of homemade jam.

Soft-ball stage—A term used in making candy or boiled frosting when a sugar-syrup mixture reaches 234° to 236°F on a candy thermometer. This stage can be determined by dropping a spoonful of the hot syrup into a bowl of very cold water. In the water, use your fingers to gather the cooled syrup into a ball. If it has reached soft-ball stage, the syrup easily forms a ball while in the cold water, but flattens once removed from the water.

Soft peaks—When a mixture, such as egg whites or heavy cream, is whipped stiff, but only until it forms peaks that curl over when the beater is removed.

Soufflé—A light, airy dessert usually containing beaten egg whites or whipped cream.

Sour milk—A mixture of 7/8 cup whole milk with 1 tablespoon lemon juice or white vinegar, left to stand for 10 minutes to thicken before using. Sour milk is the most commonly used substitute for buttermilk. Sour milk makes a great addition to chocolate cakes and many other baked goods.

Spring-form pan—A round pan with sides higher than a cake pan held on by a clamp that can be released to unmold the finished cake, such as used for cheesecakes and tortes.

Square (as in baking chocolate)—1 square equals 1 ounce.

Steam—To cook covered over simmering water.

Stick of butter—A pound of butter is made up of 4 sticks, sometimes called quarters. 1 stick equals ¼ pound, ½ cup, or 8 tablespoons. Usually there is a measuring guide printed right on the wrapper of each stick for our convenience.

Stiff peaks—When a mixture such as egg whites or heavy cream is whipped to a stiff state, where the peaks remain upright and do not curl over when the beater is pulled out.

Stiff but not dry—When an ingredient is beaten stiff but remains glossy.

Stir—To combine ingredients with the circular motion of a spoon.

Sugar—See pages xvii–xviii for the different types of sugar used in this book.

Suet—Animal fat, usually beef—used for mincemeat and plum pudding.

Tablespoon—1 tablespoon equals ½ fluid ounce and 3 teaspoons equal a tablespoon.

Tapioca—The starch from the cassava plant that is used to make a creamy pudding by the same name, or to thicken sauces. And for that perfect pie; a tablespoon of instant (or quick-cooking) tapioca sprinkled on the bottom crust of a fruit pie helps thicken the filling's juices. Tapioca comes in granulated, small pearl, large pearl, and an instant (quick-cooking) form—all having their particular uses.

Tart—A filled pastry without a top crust.

Tart pan—A shallow round pan with fluted sides and a removable bottom.

Temper—To heat beaten raw eggs gradually so they don't curdle. Usually a small amount of a hot mixture is mixed into the eggs, then the egg mixture is added back into the main hot mixture, stirring all the while.

Thread stage—Thread stage refers to a specific temperature range when cooking sugar syrups, that occurs at 223° to 235°F. This stage can be determined by dropping a spoonful of hot syrup into a bowl of very cold water. If the syrup drips from a spoon and forms thin threads in the cold water, thread stage has been reached.

Torte—A fancy decorated cake or dessert with several layers.

Toss—To lightly mix together ingredients with a gentle lift-and-drop motion, rather than stirring or beating.

Tube pan—A round, high-sided pan with a center tube, used for baking angel food cakes. Standard size is 10 inches in diameter. This may also be referred to as an "angel-cake pan."

Wax paper (also called waxed paper)—A kind of paper that is made moisture proof through the application of wax. Use it to wrap cooled baked goods or to layer between cookies and candies in tins. Do not confuse it with parchment paper, which is used for baking, as waxed paper cannot take the heat of cooking.

Water bath—Usually used for cooking custards or egg-based dishes. The smaller food pan is placed in a larger pan, filled with hot or simmering water to a level about half-way up the side of the smaller pan, thus surrounding the smaller pan with gentle heat as it cooks. This technique can be used on the stove top or in the oven. Also a good way to melt chocolate, if you don't have a double-boiler.

Whip—To incorporate air into a mixture to increase its volume, using an electric mixer or wire whisk.

Whip—An old fashioned airy dessert made of sugar and stiffly beaten egg whites or whipped cream and flavored with fruit. Serve chilled.

Whisk—To whip or stir ingredients with a wire whisk.

Wire whisk (or whip)—Indispensable in the kitchen, a wire whisk is used to stir sauces, whip egg whites, blend ingredients, and even take the place of an electric mixer, if need be.

Zest—The outer skin of citrus fruits, rich in aromatic oils and essence. When grating zest, be careful not to include the white pith underneath, as it is bitter.

Zwieback—The German word for "twice baked"—is a toast, in the form of a hard dry biscuit, made from specially baked bread.

Recipe and Tip Index

About the Authors

About Wendy Louise

A Wisconsin resident, Wendy Louise currently lives near her daughter, son-in-law, and granddaughter. When she is not busy pursuing life-long interests in the fine arts, quilting, crafting, and gardening, she turns her interest to cooking and sharing in the family dinner hour. She believes that enjoying good food is one of the finer pleasures in life and that eating well is an important element toward attaining family comfort and well-being.

About MaryAnn Koopmann

Born and raised in Wisconsin, MaryAnn Koopmann has lived with her husband Glenn in the Milwaukee area for many years and is currently anticipating a move to her favorite place in northern Wisconsin. When not in her kitchen cooking up a favorite recipe, she enjoys crafting, beading, and visiting with her grandchildren. A true Wisconsinite, she can be found on Sunday afternoons watching the latest Green Bay Packers football game.